CW01085276

BYE BYE

STUDIO

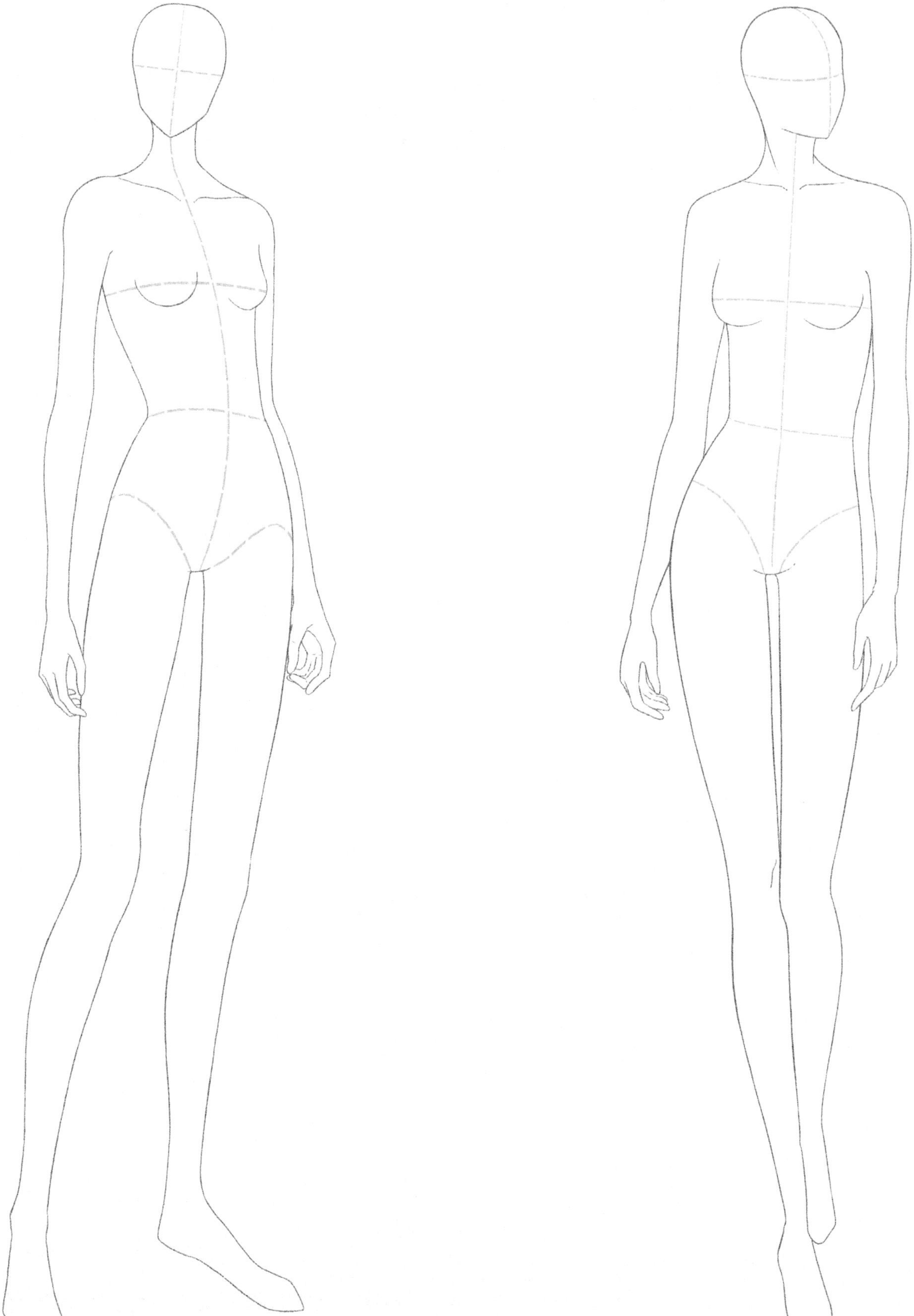

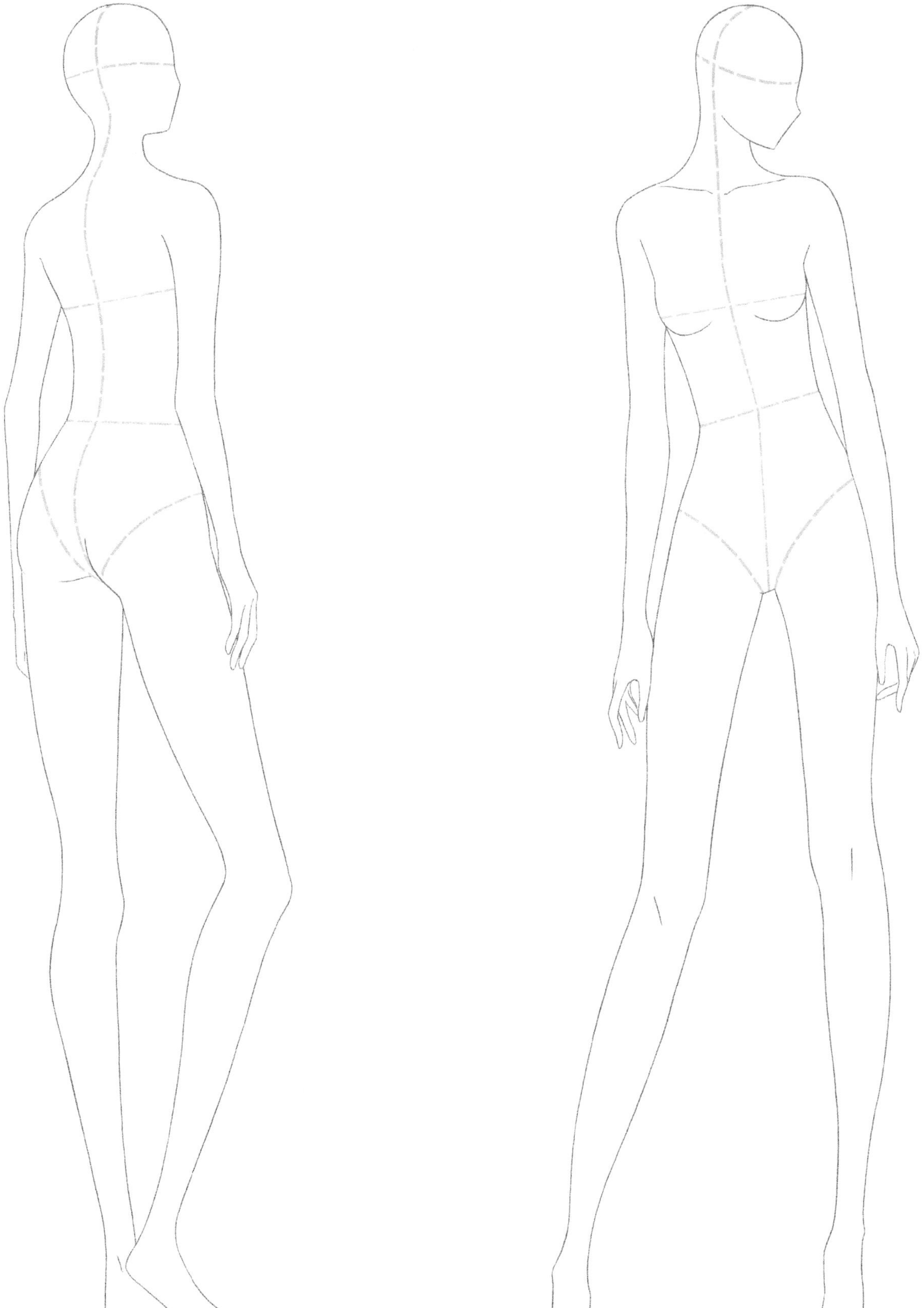

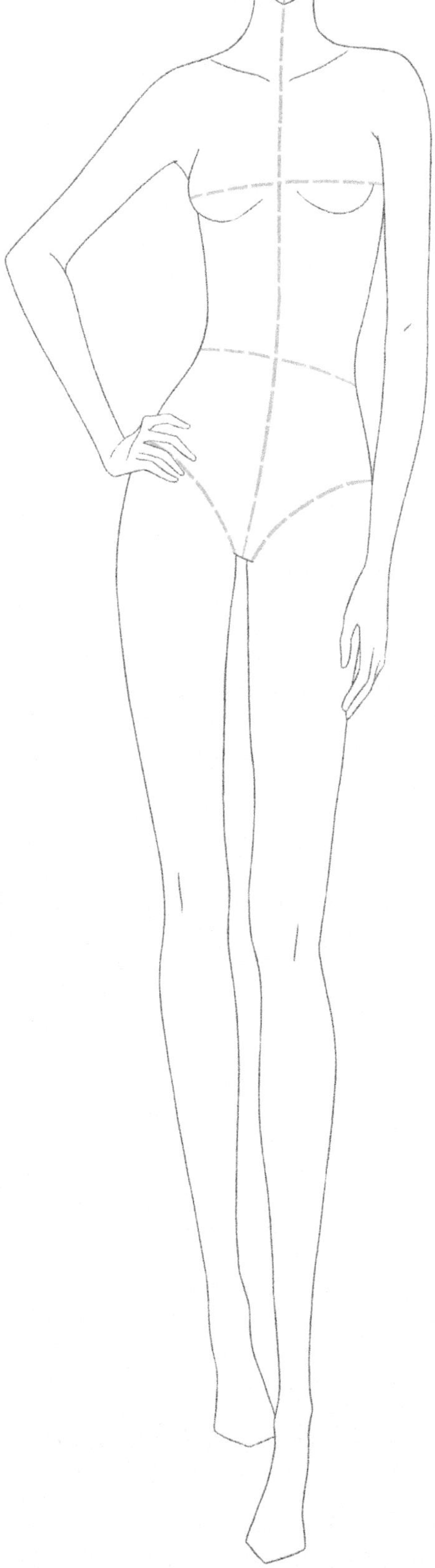
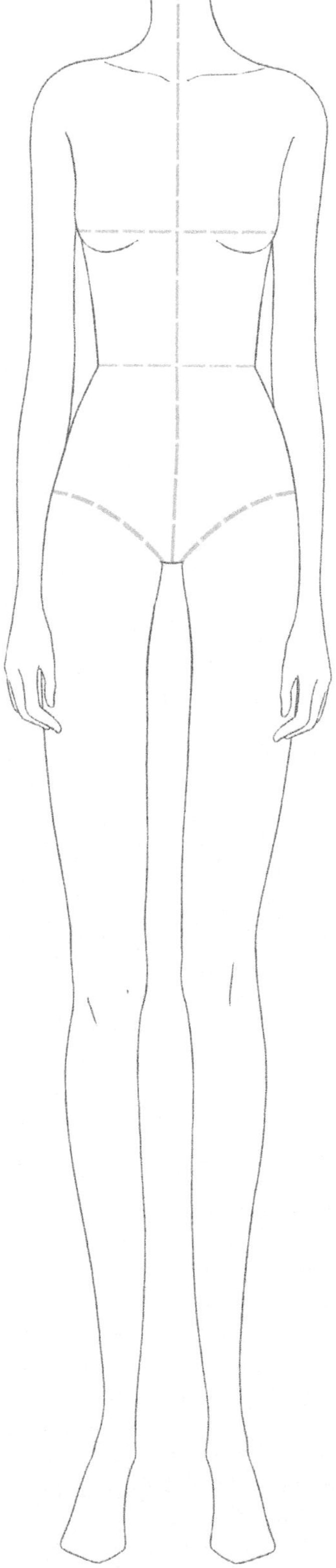

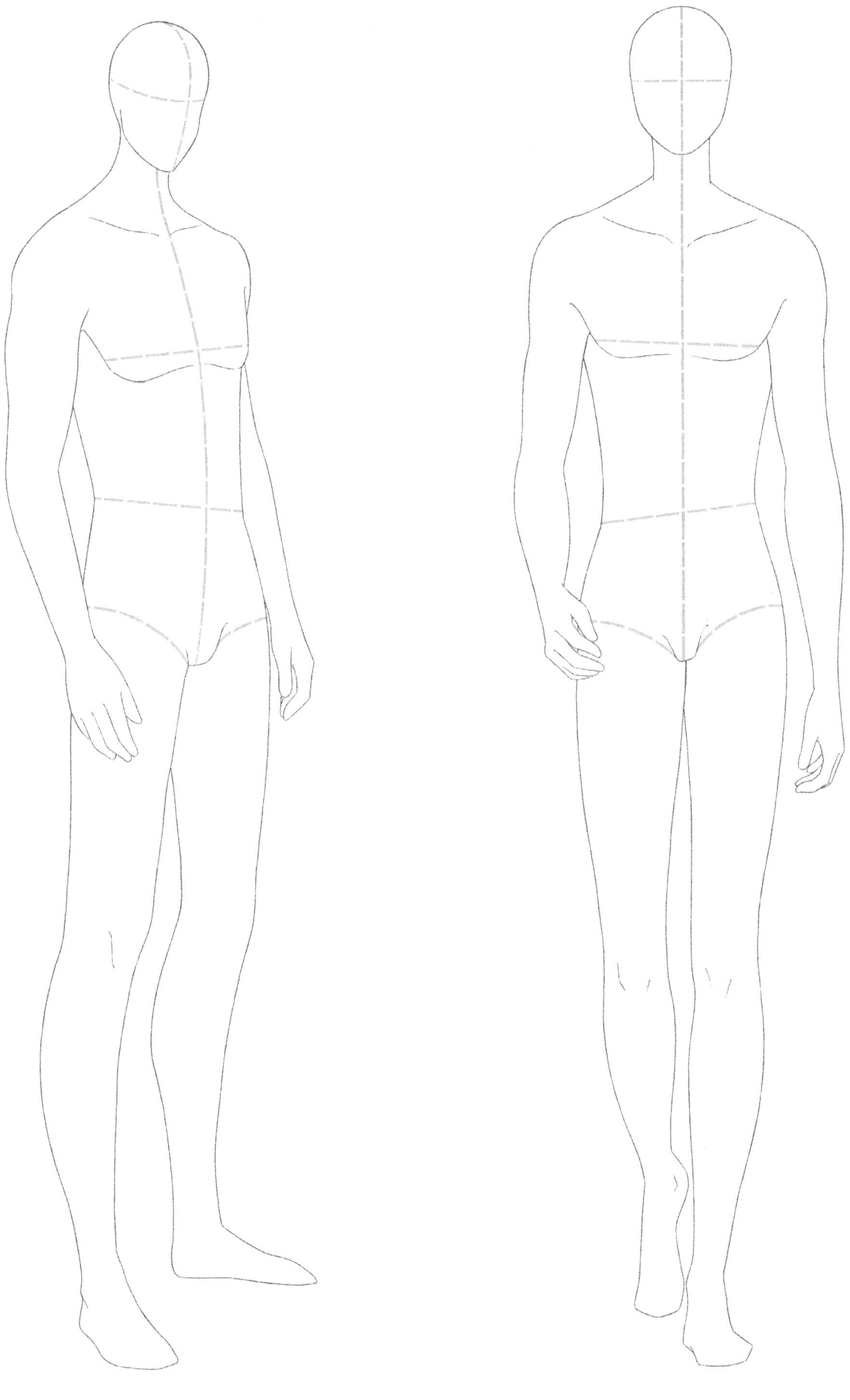

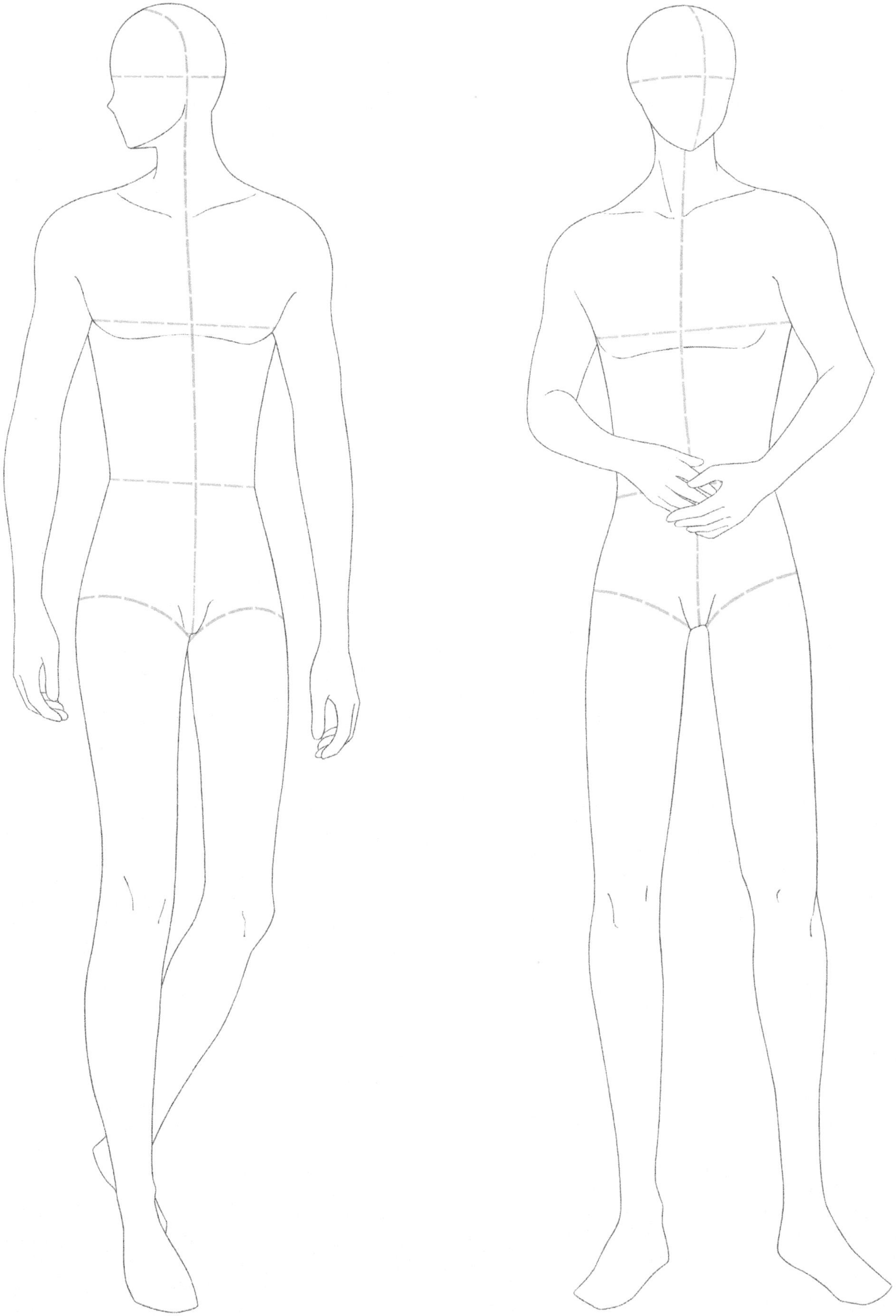

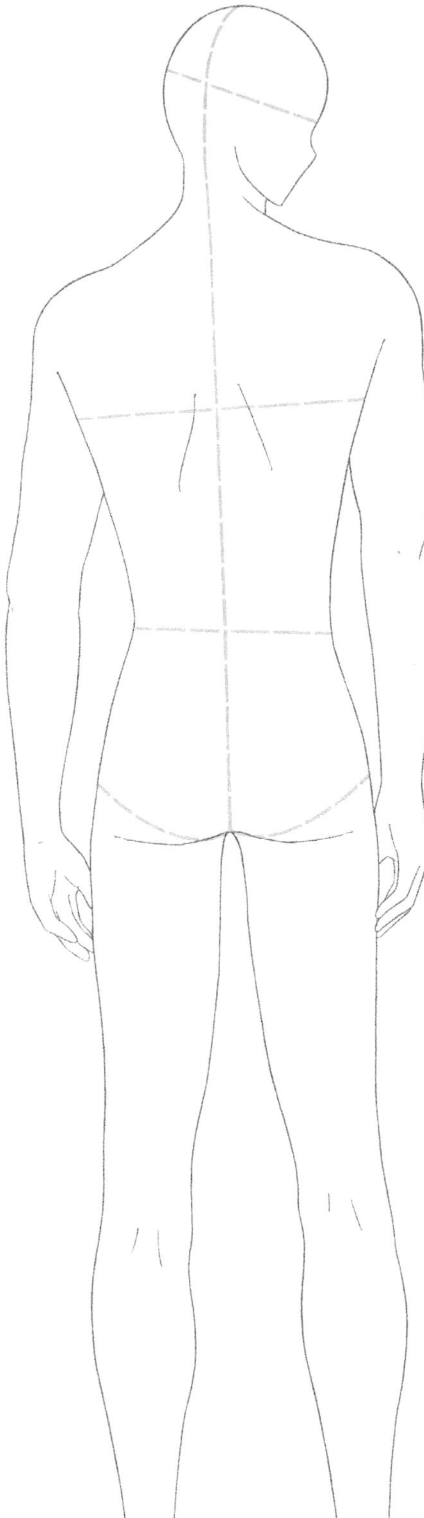

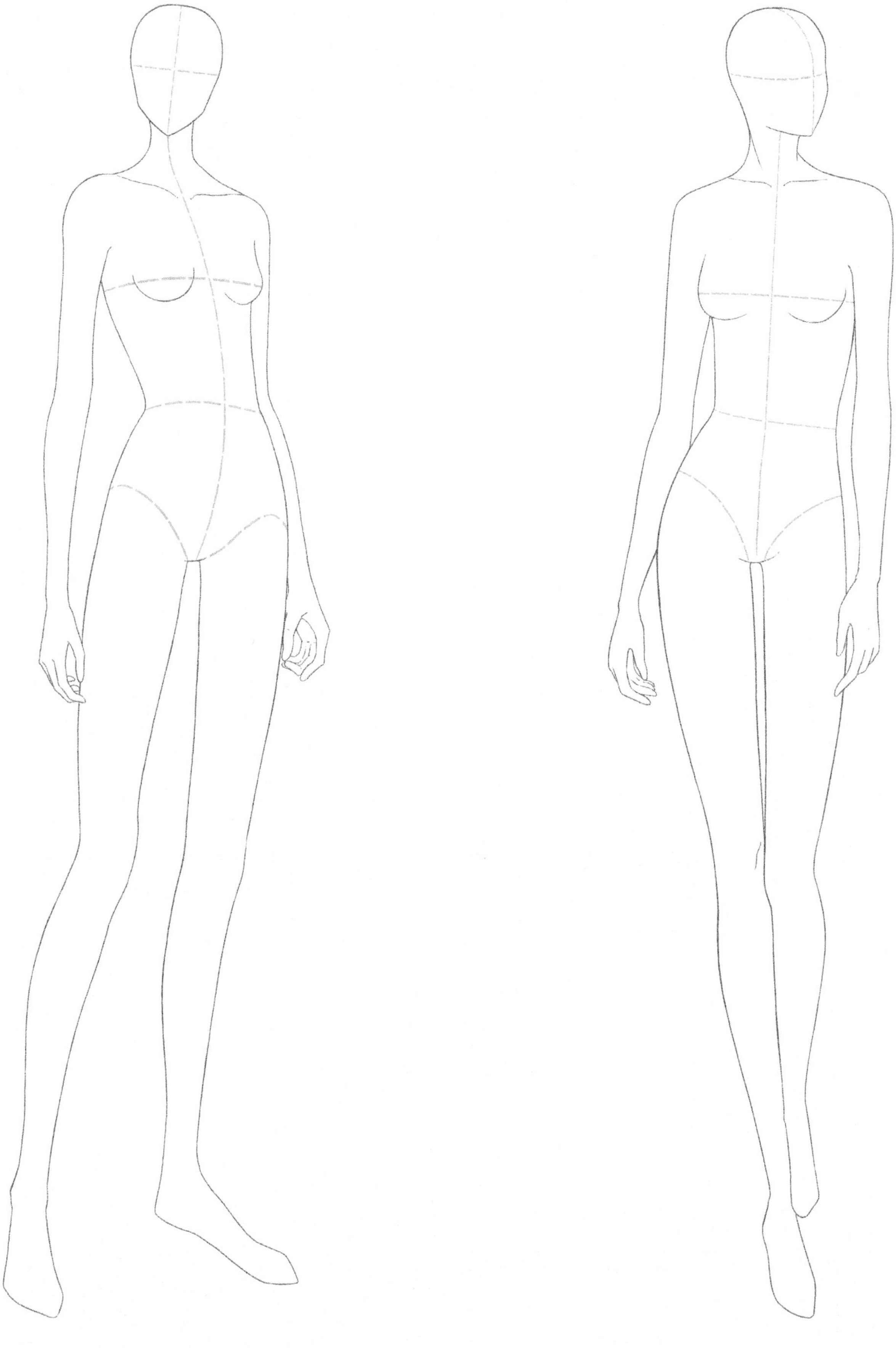

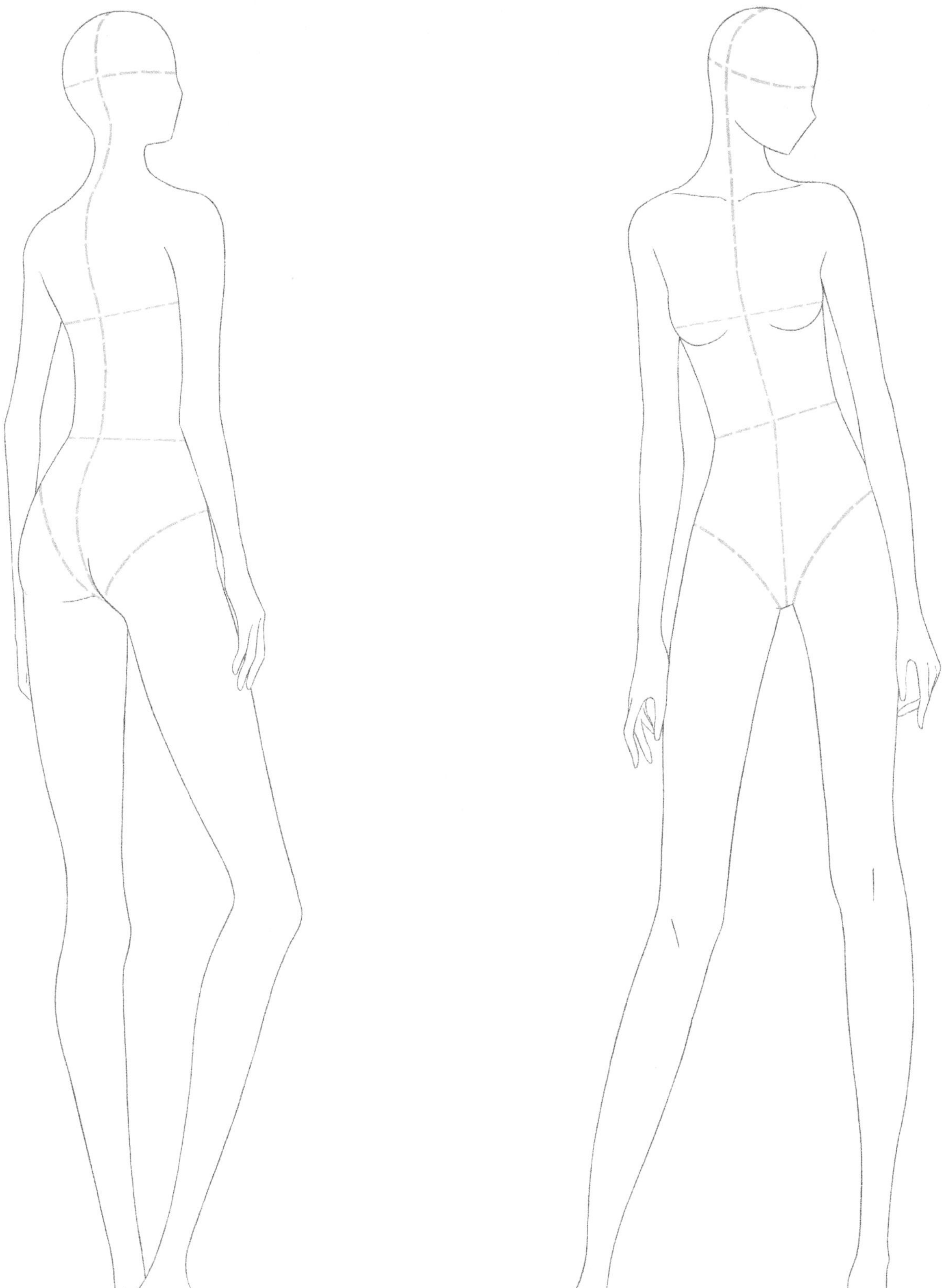

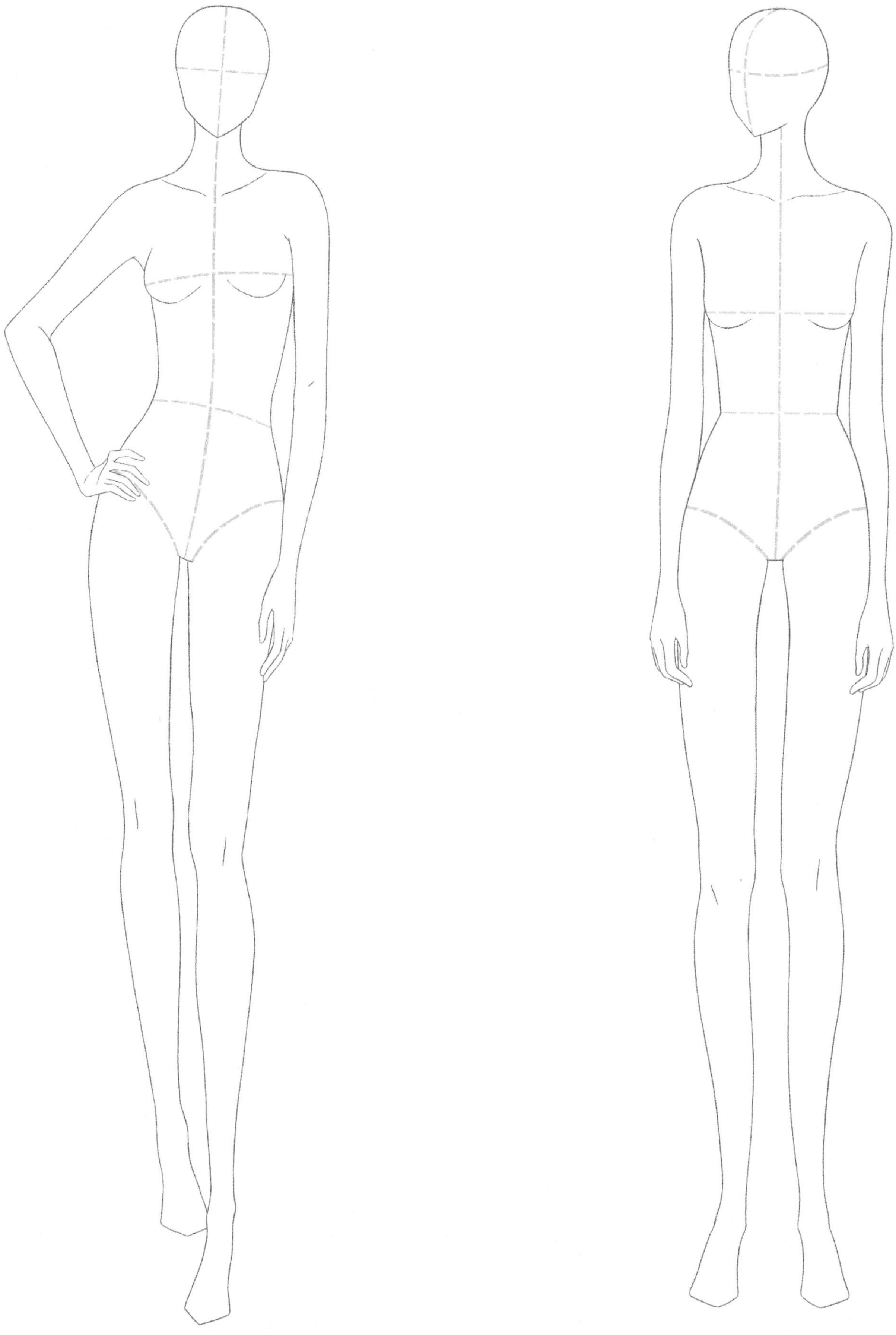

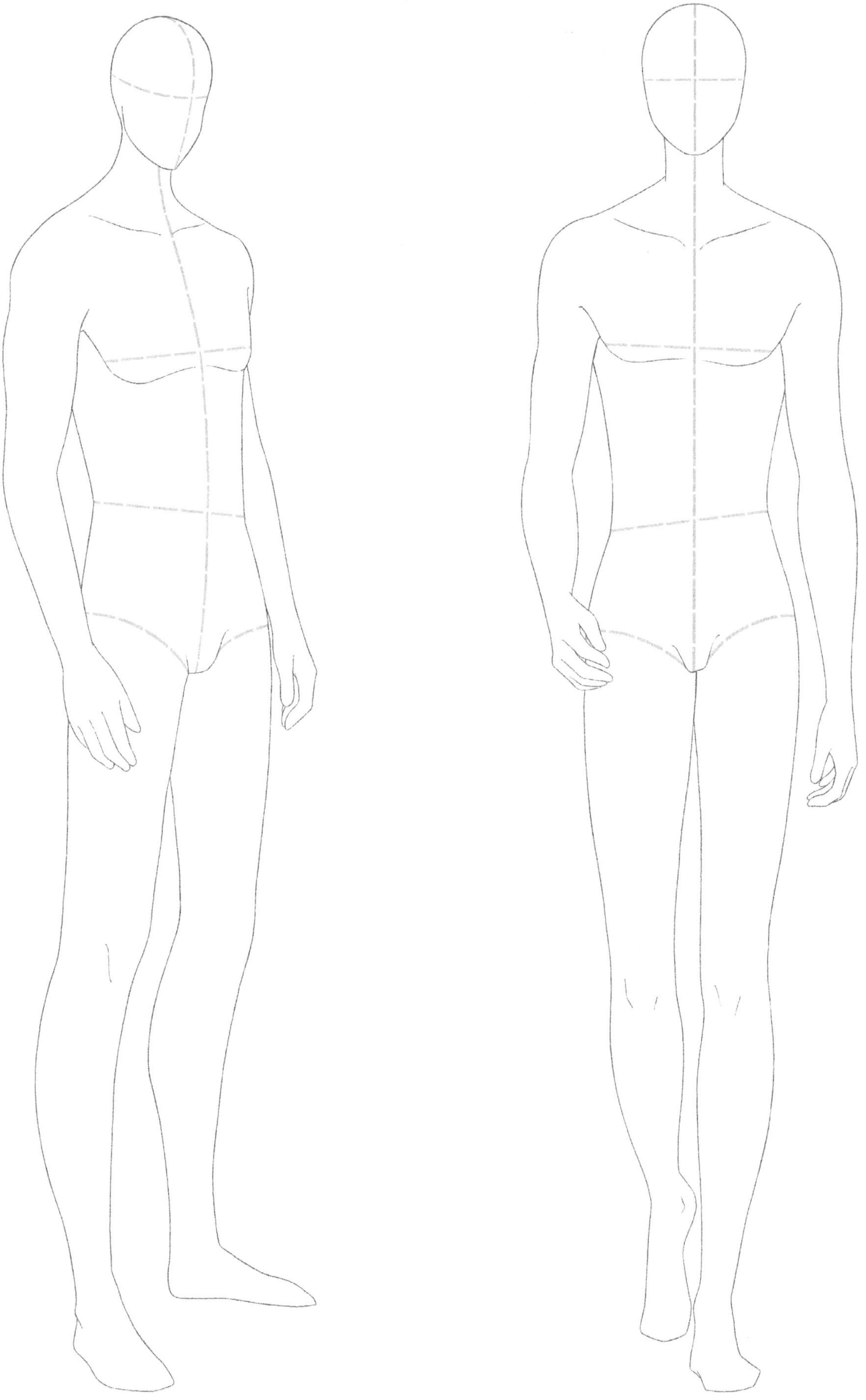

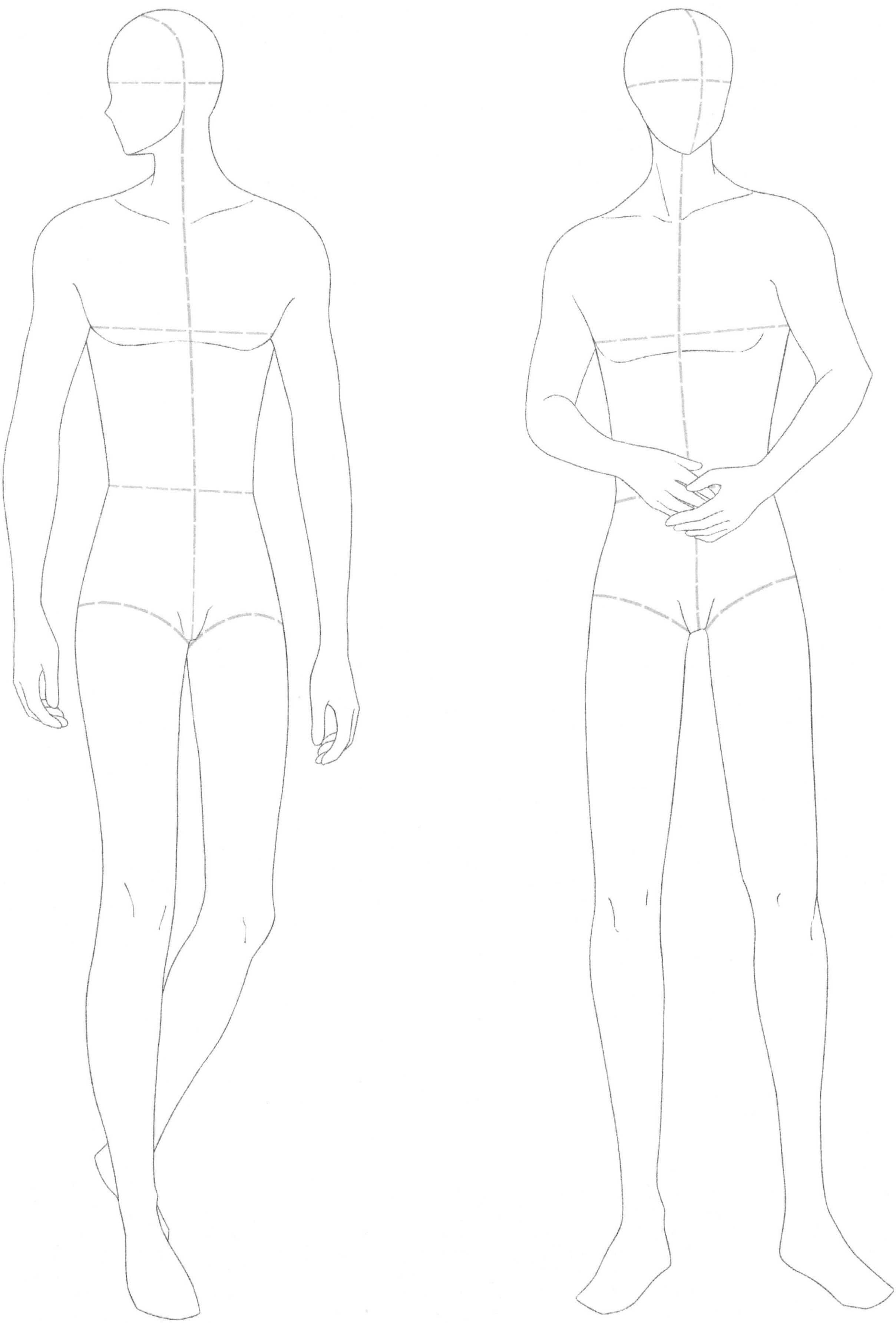

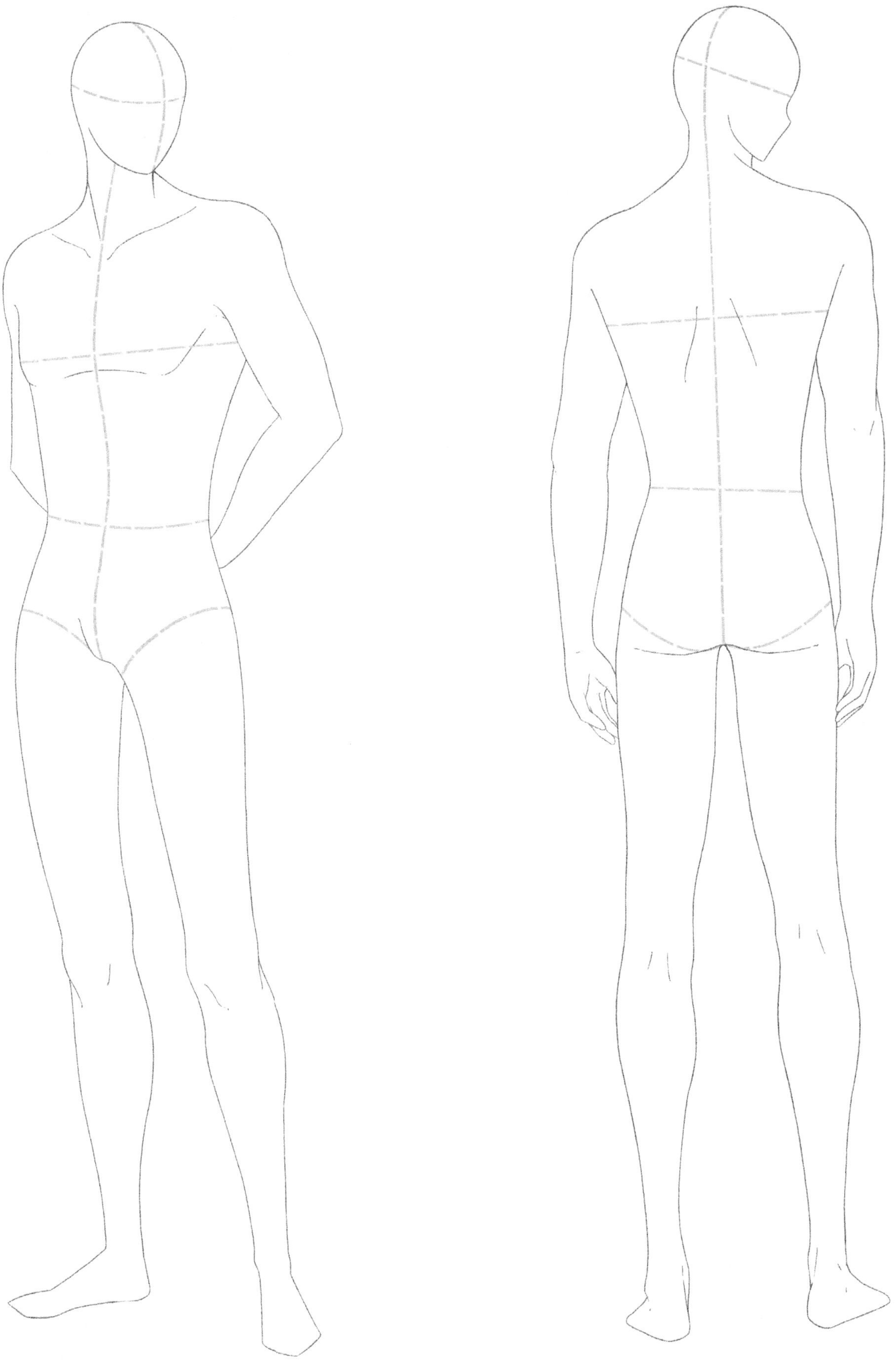

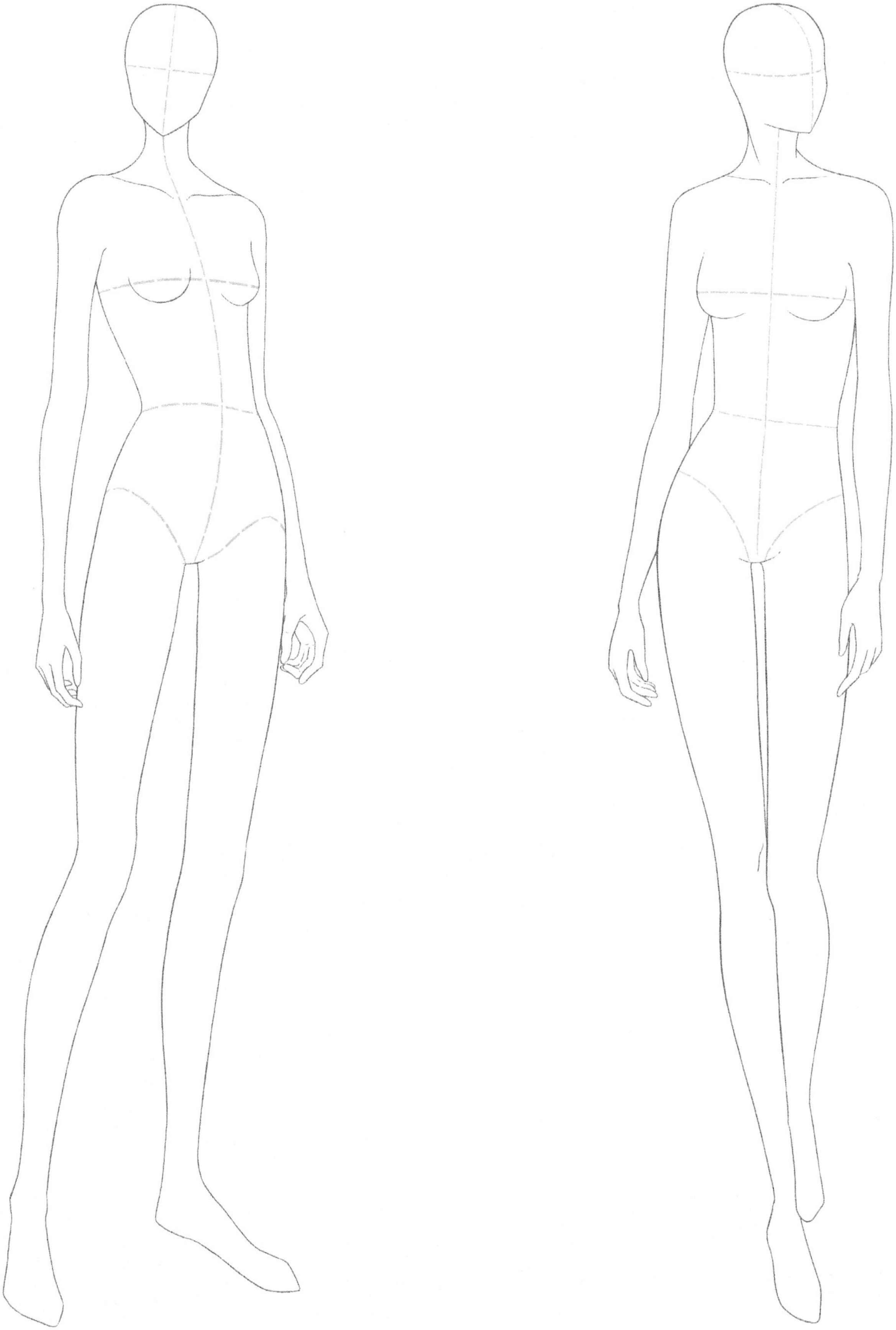

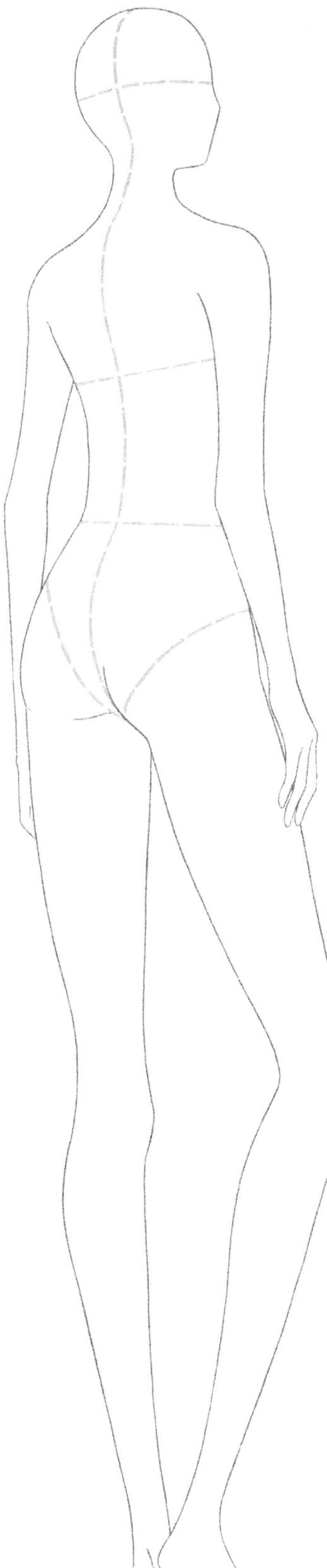

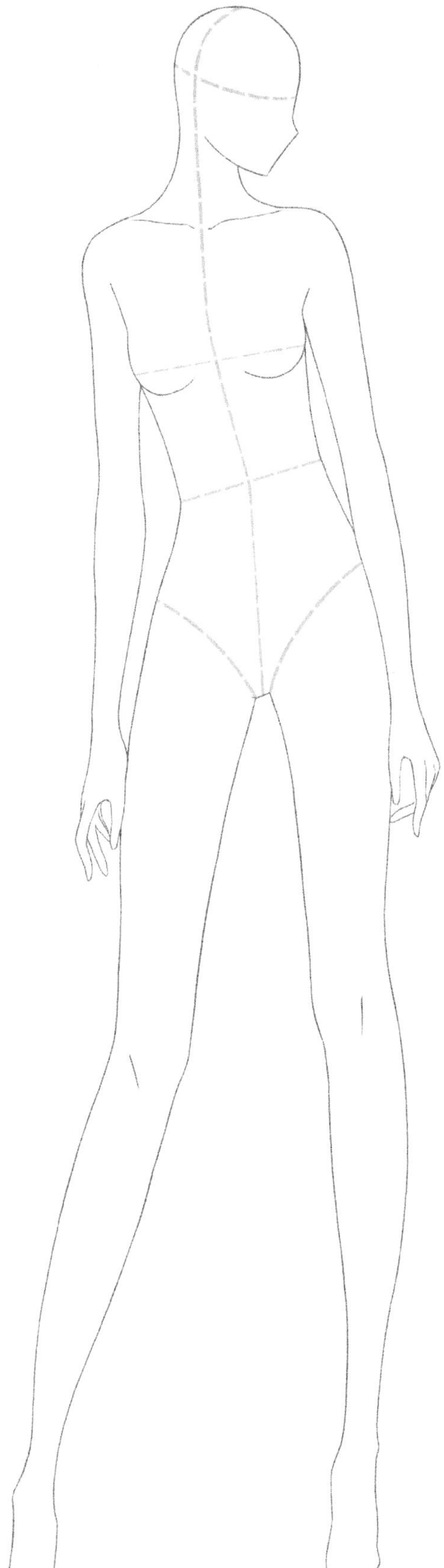

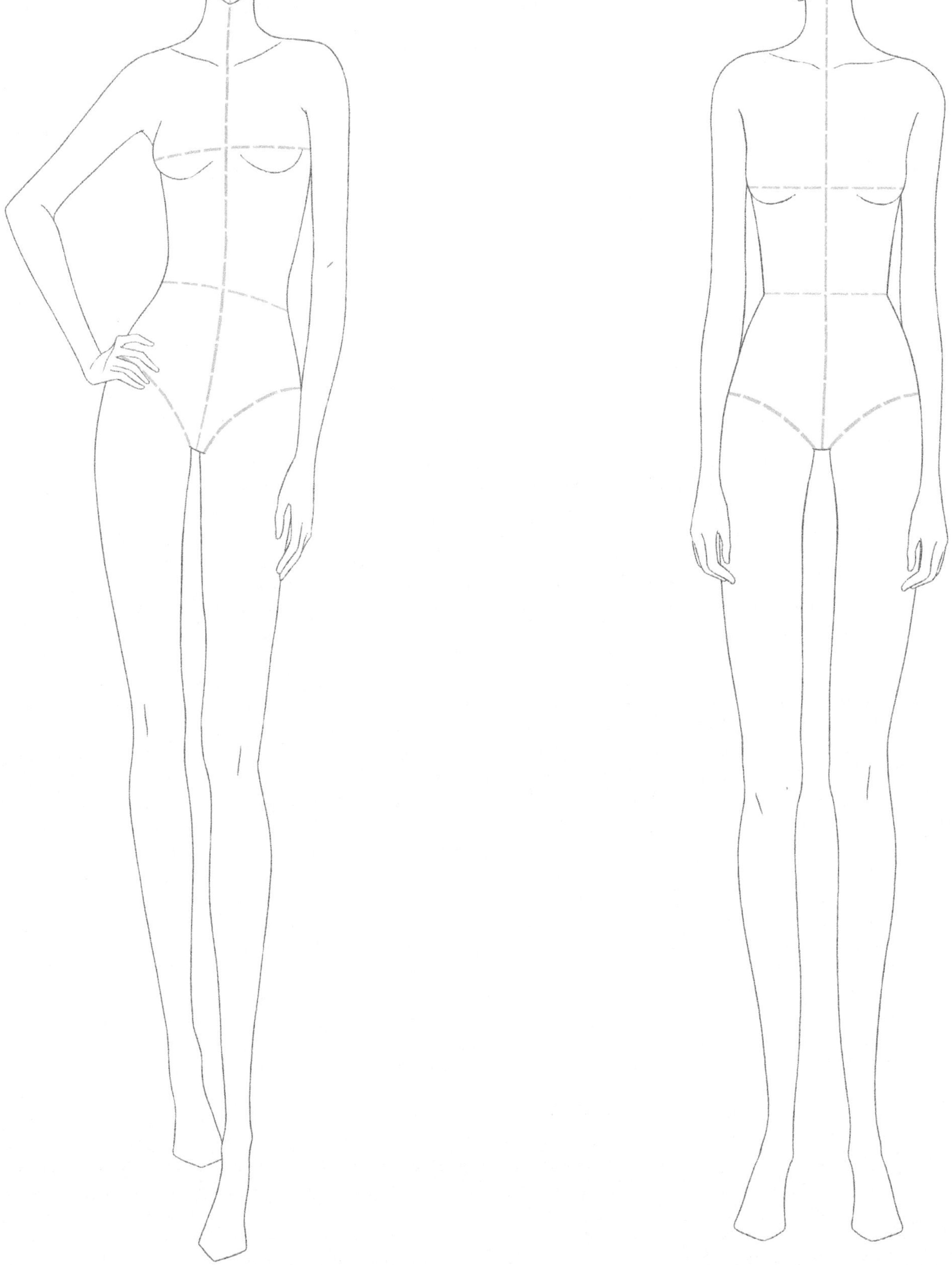

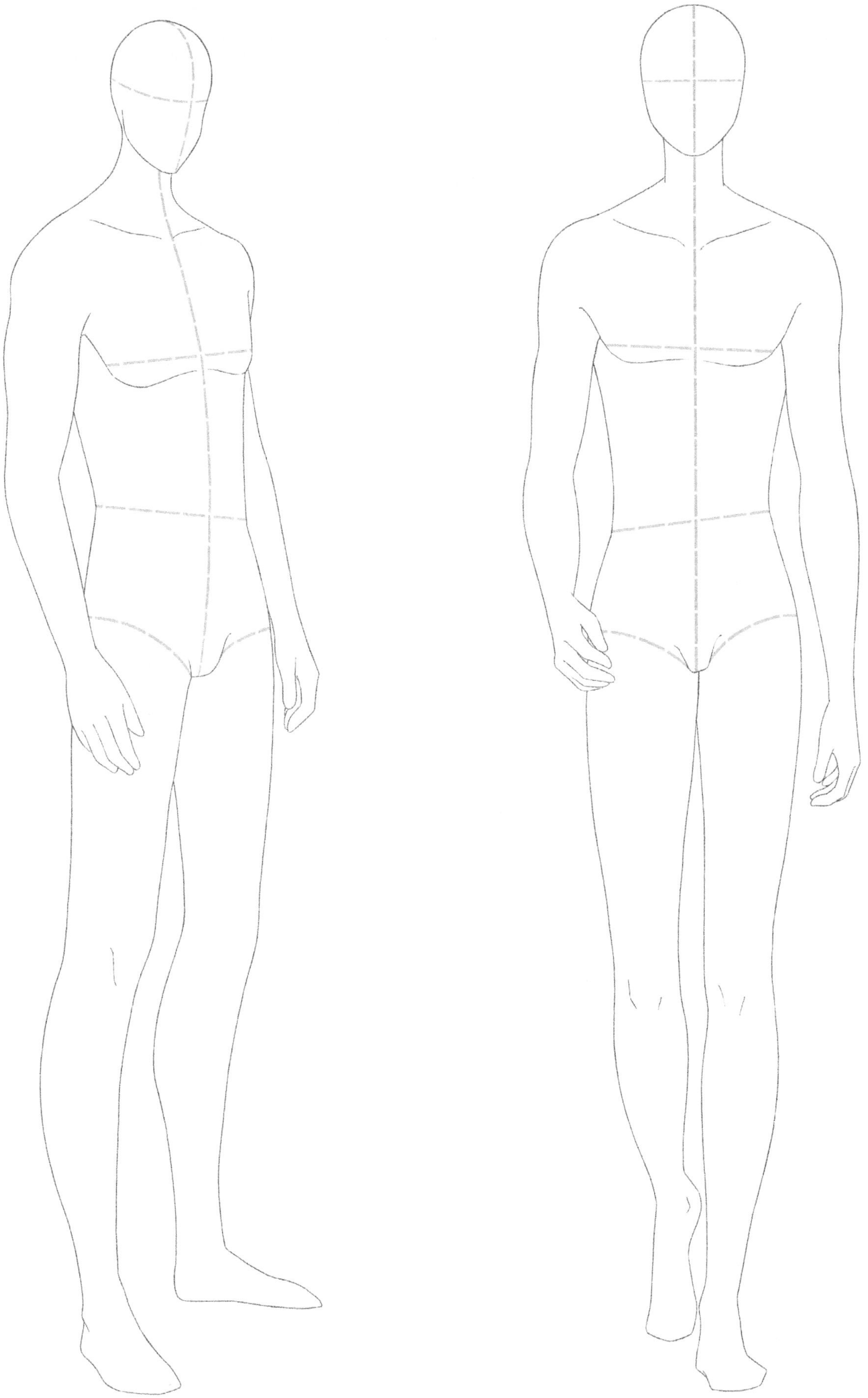

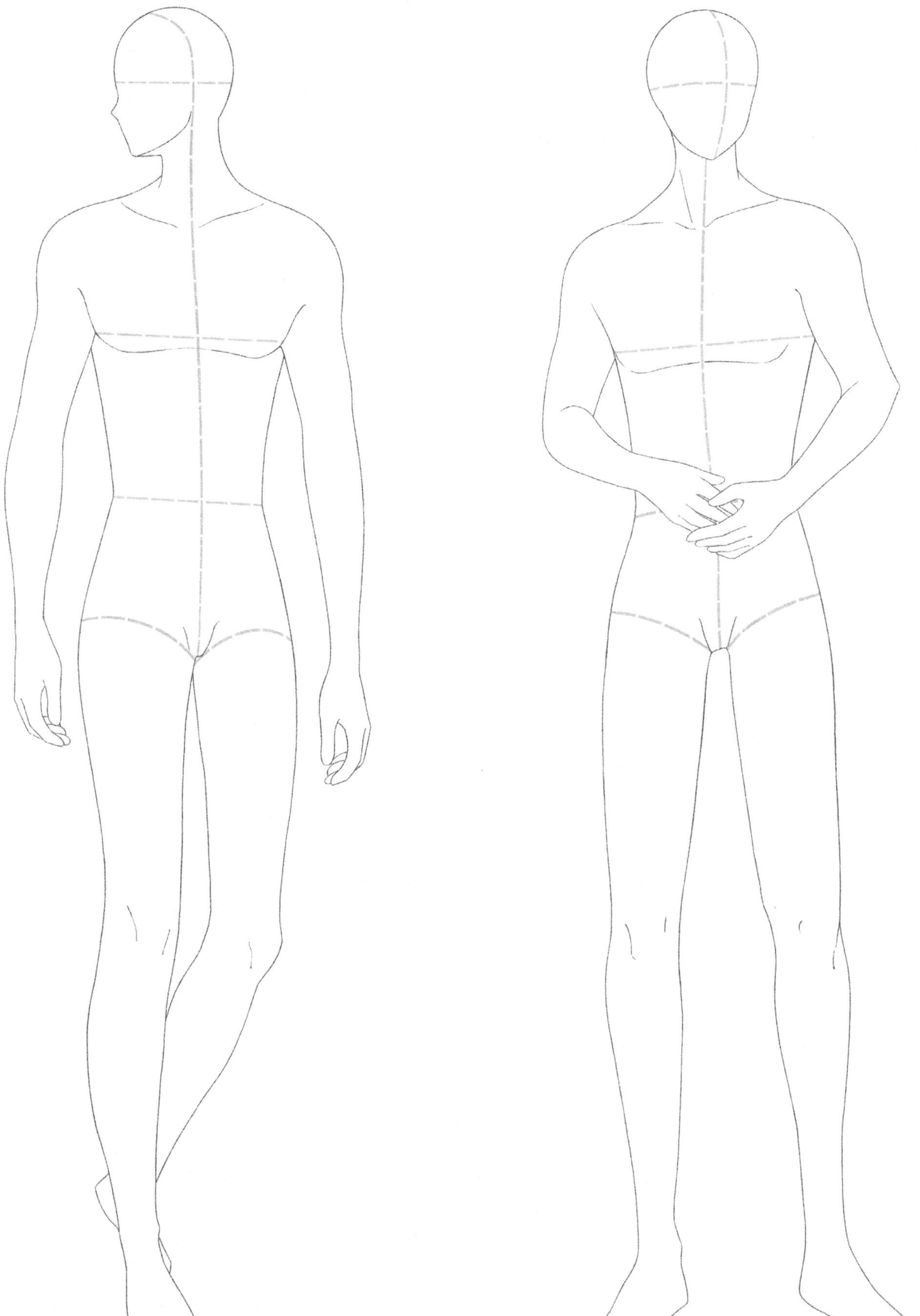

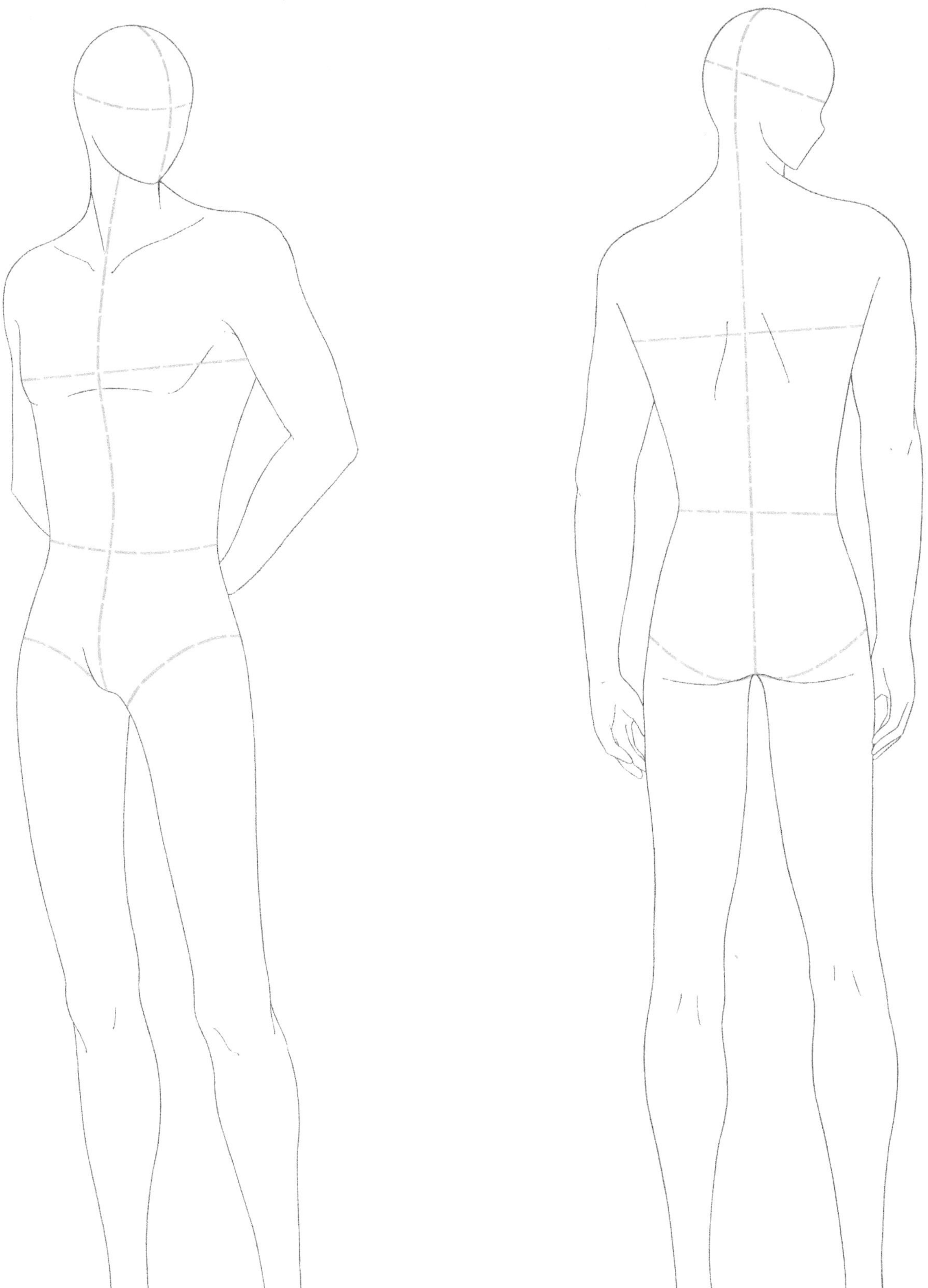

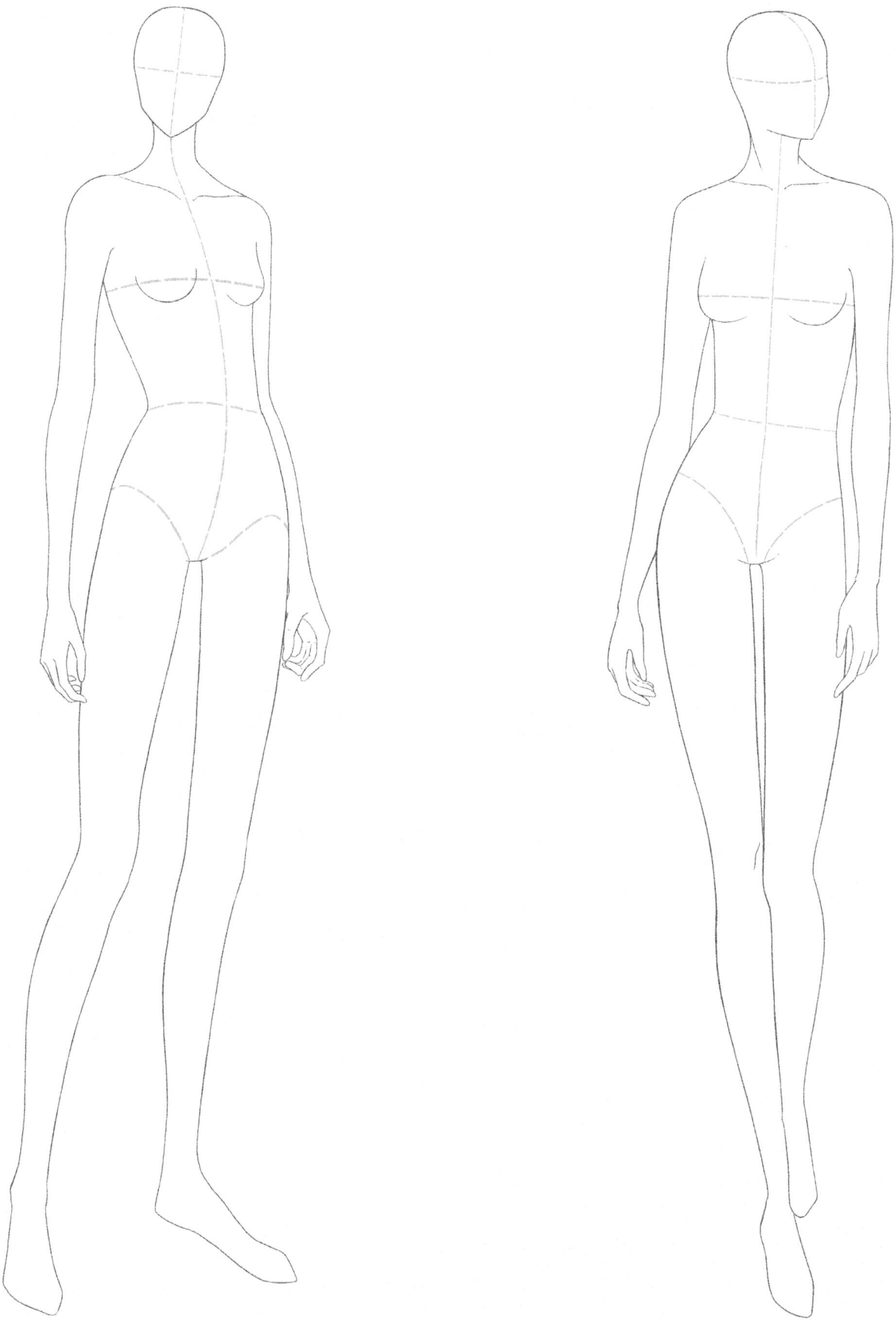

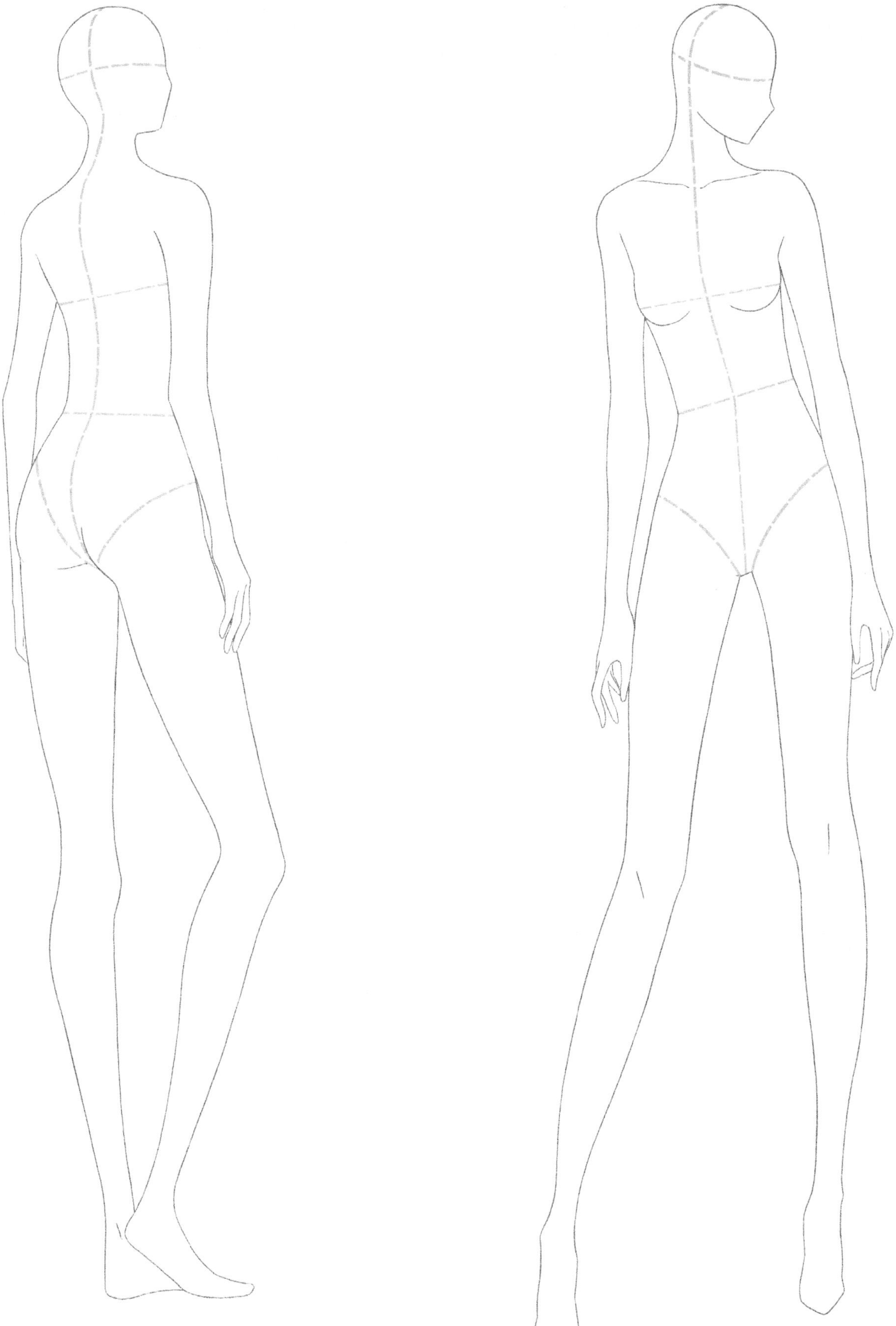

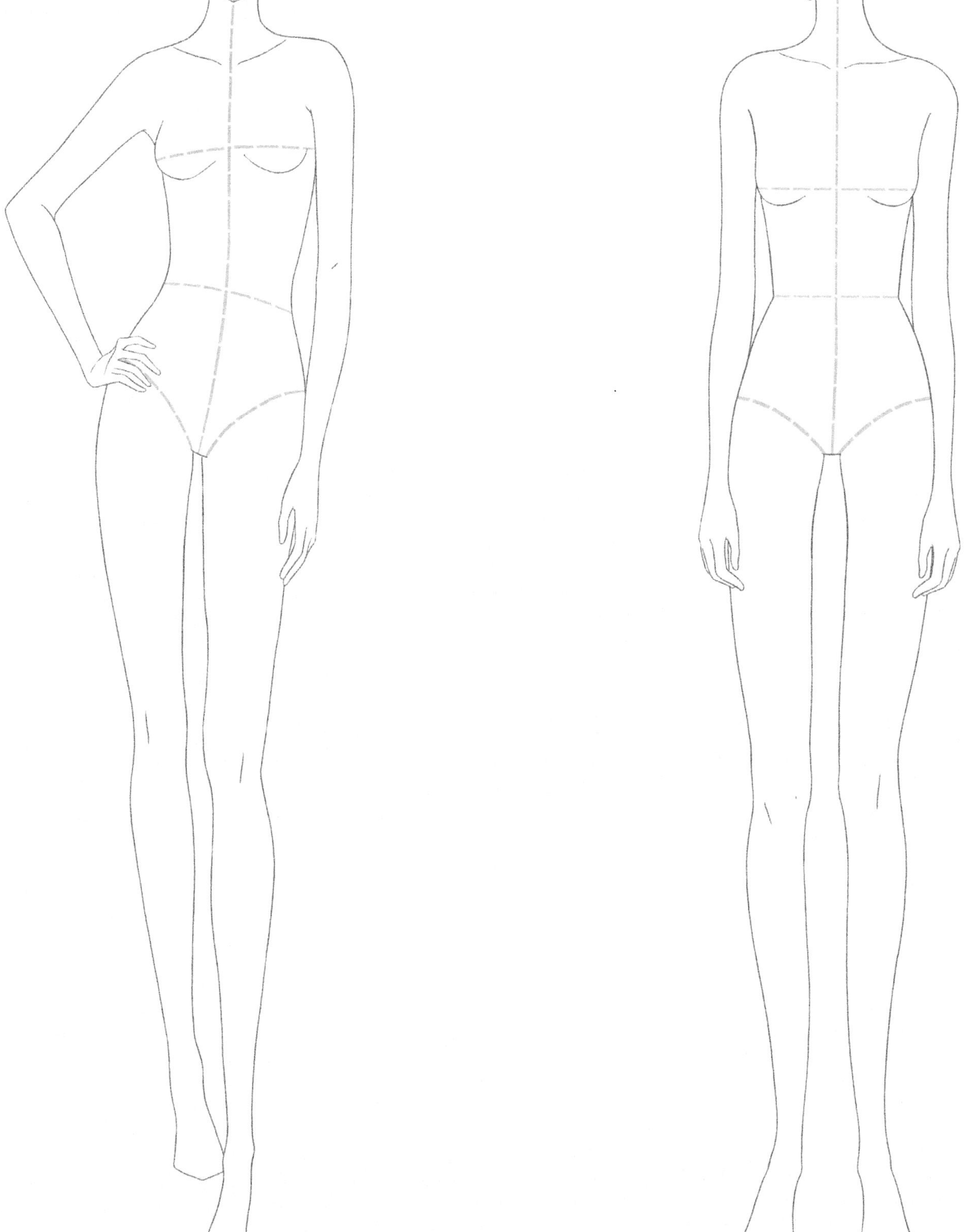

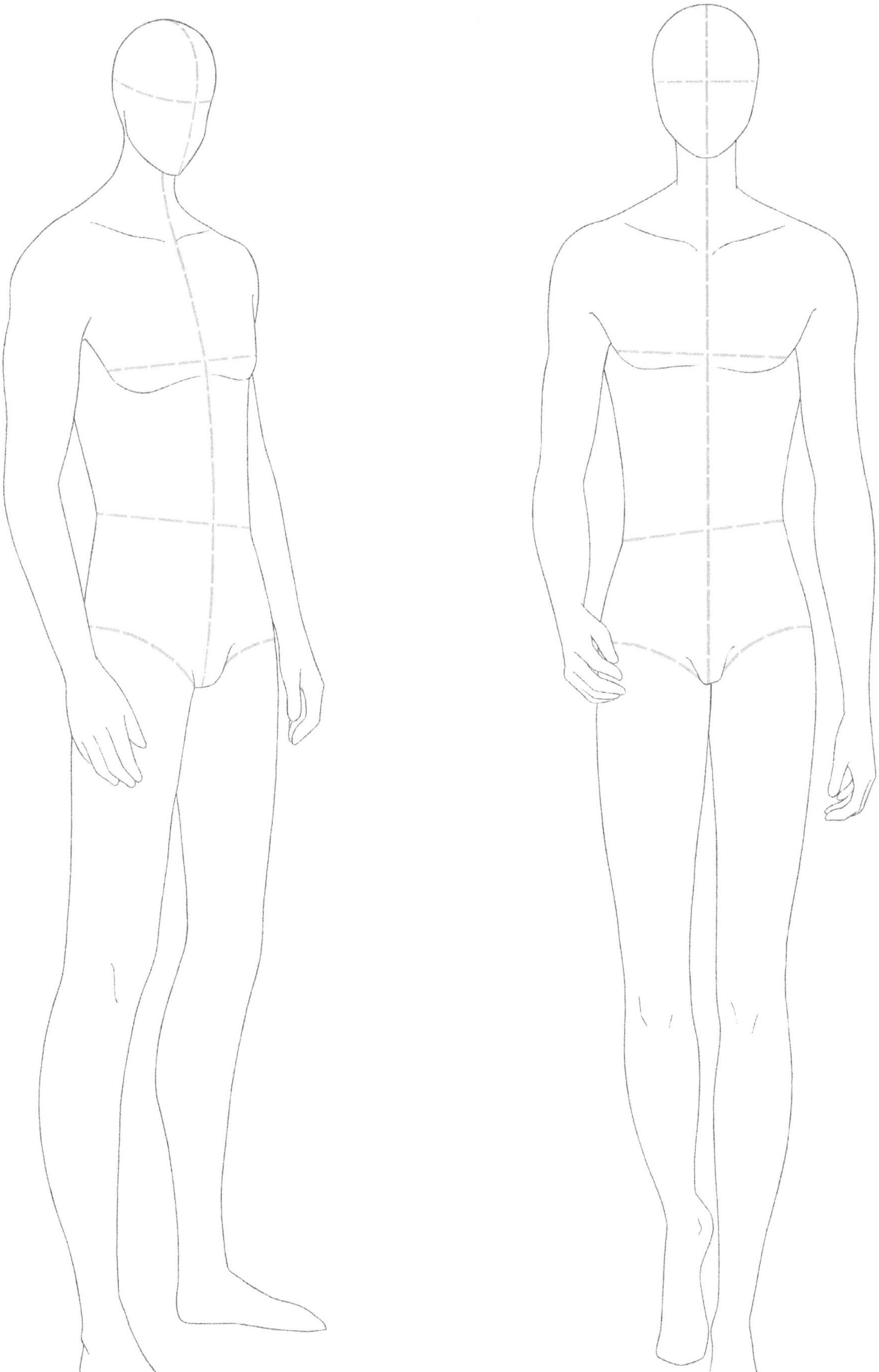

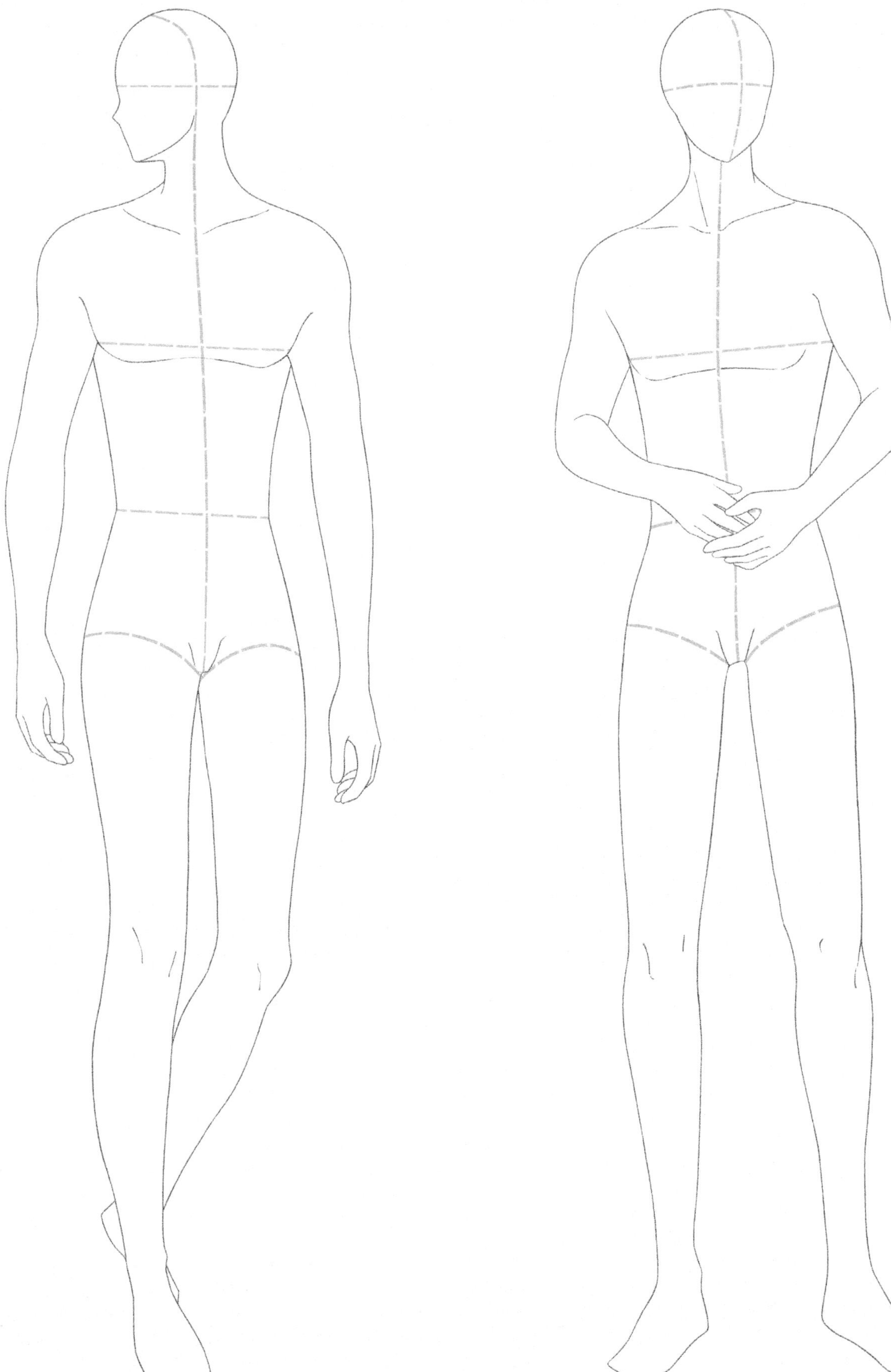

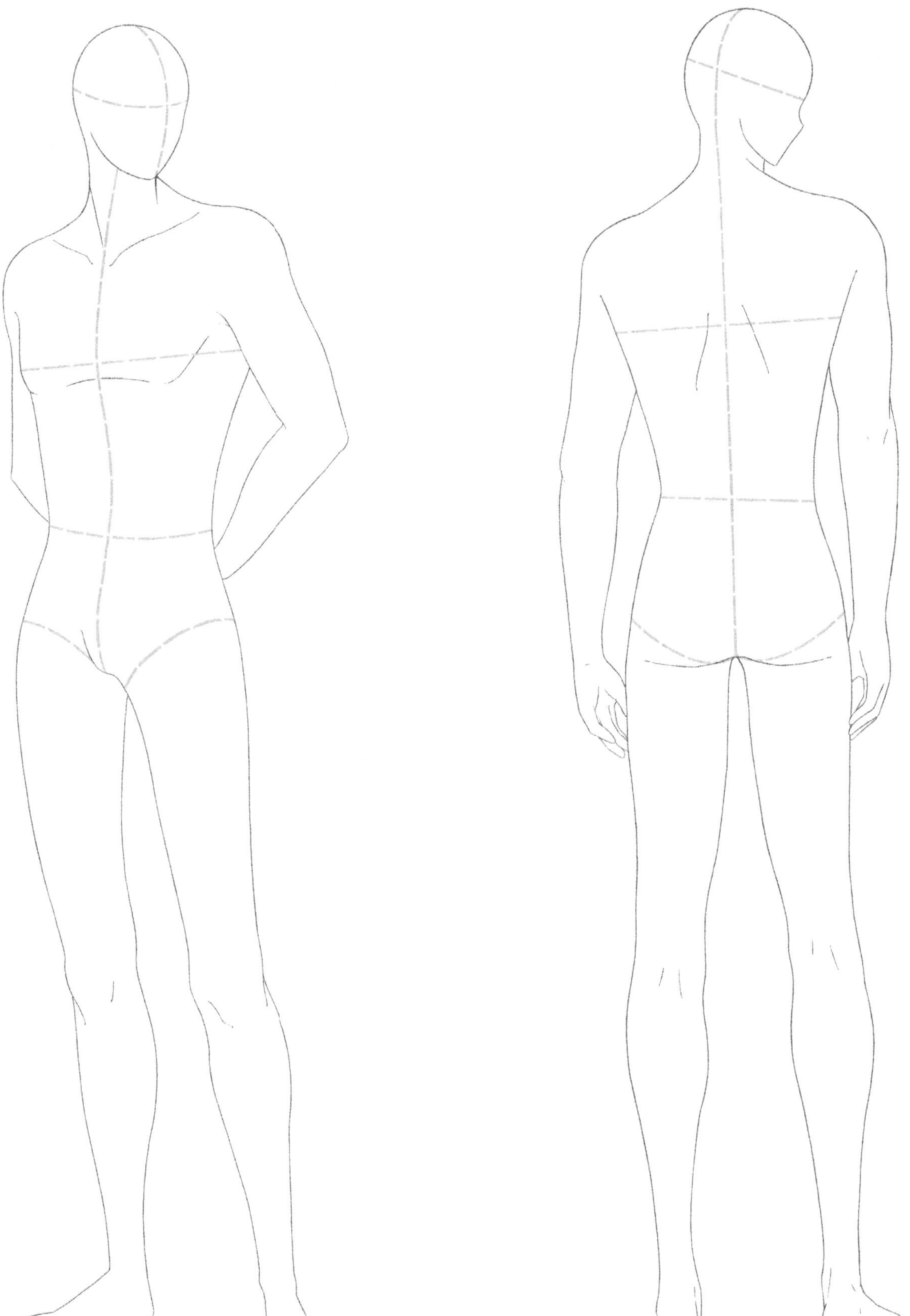

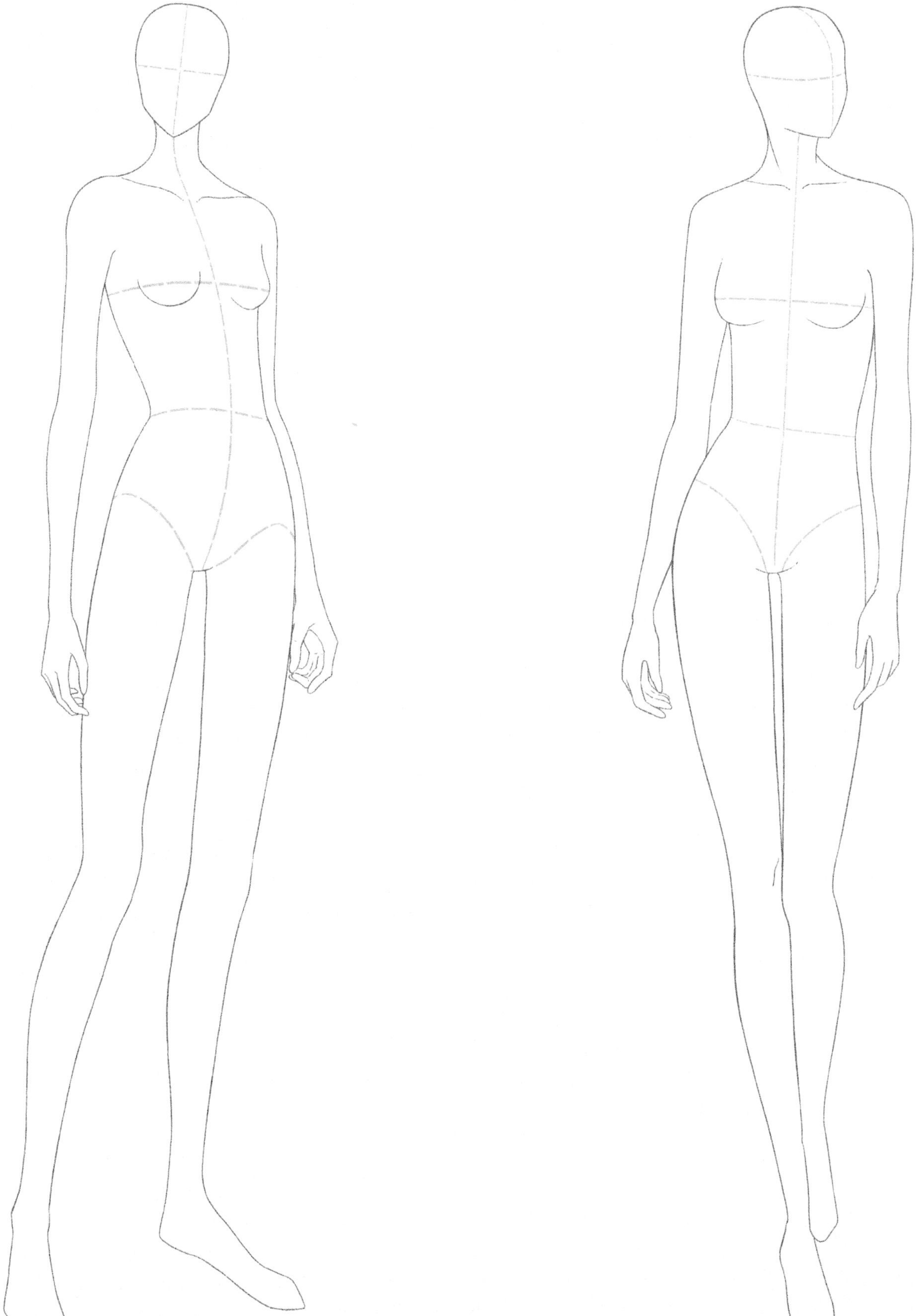

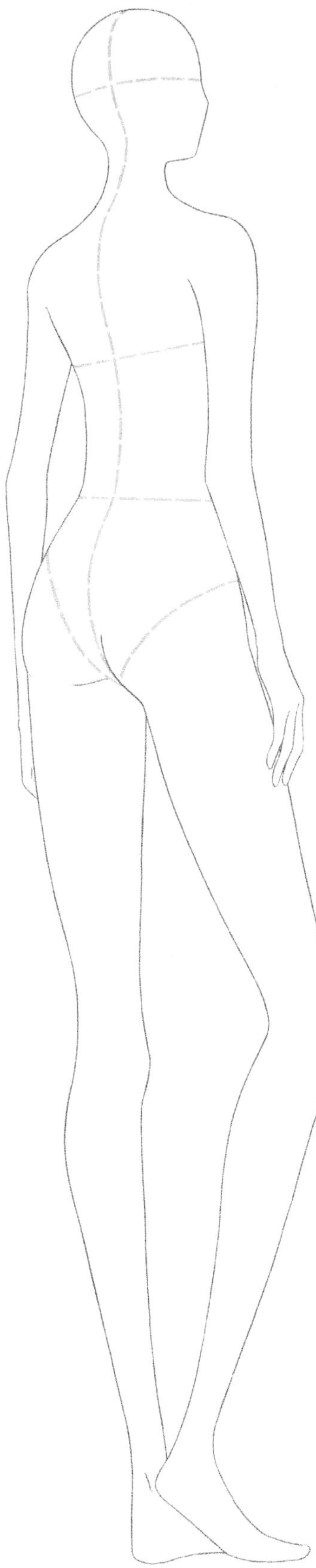
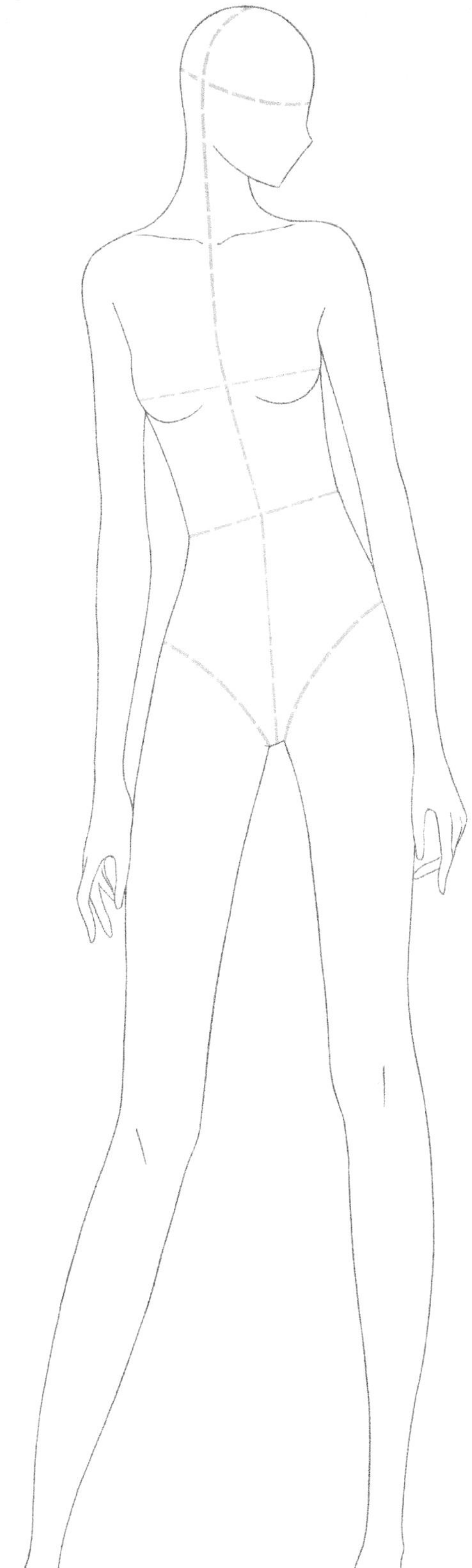

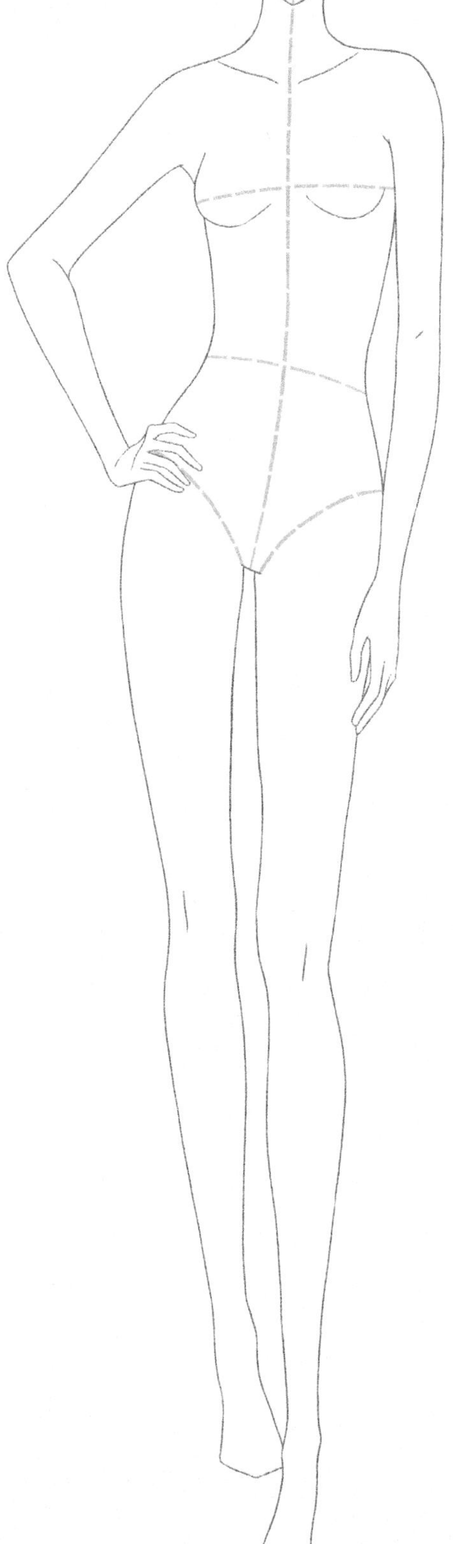
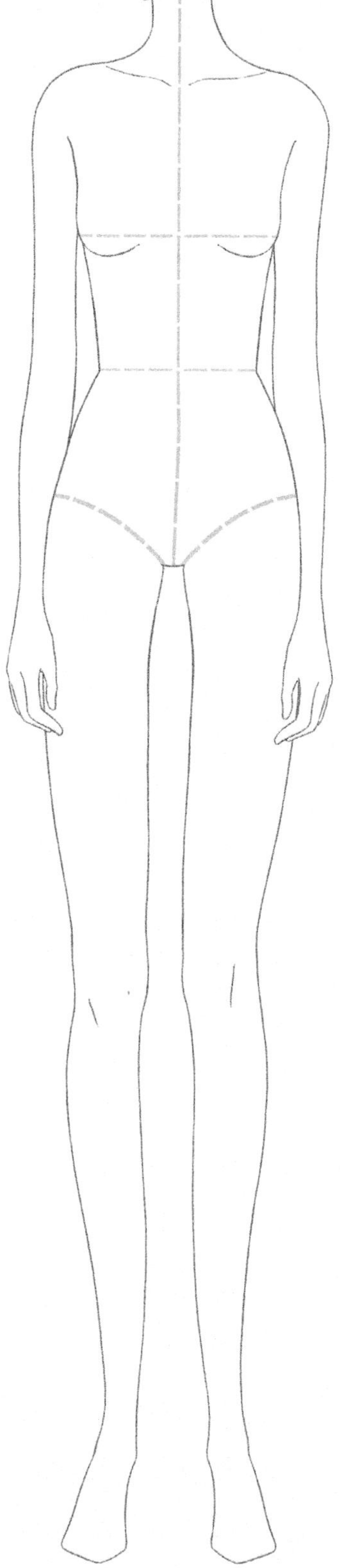

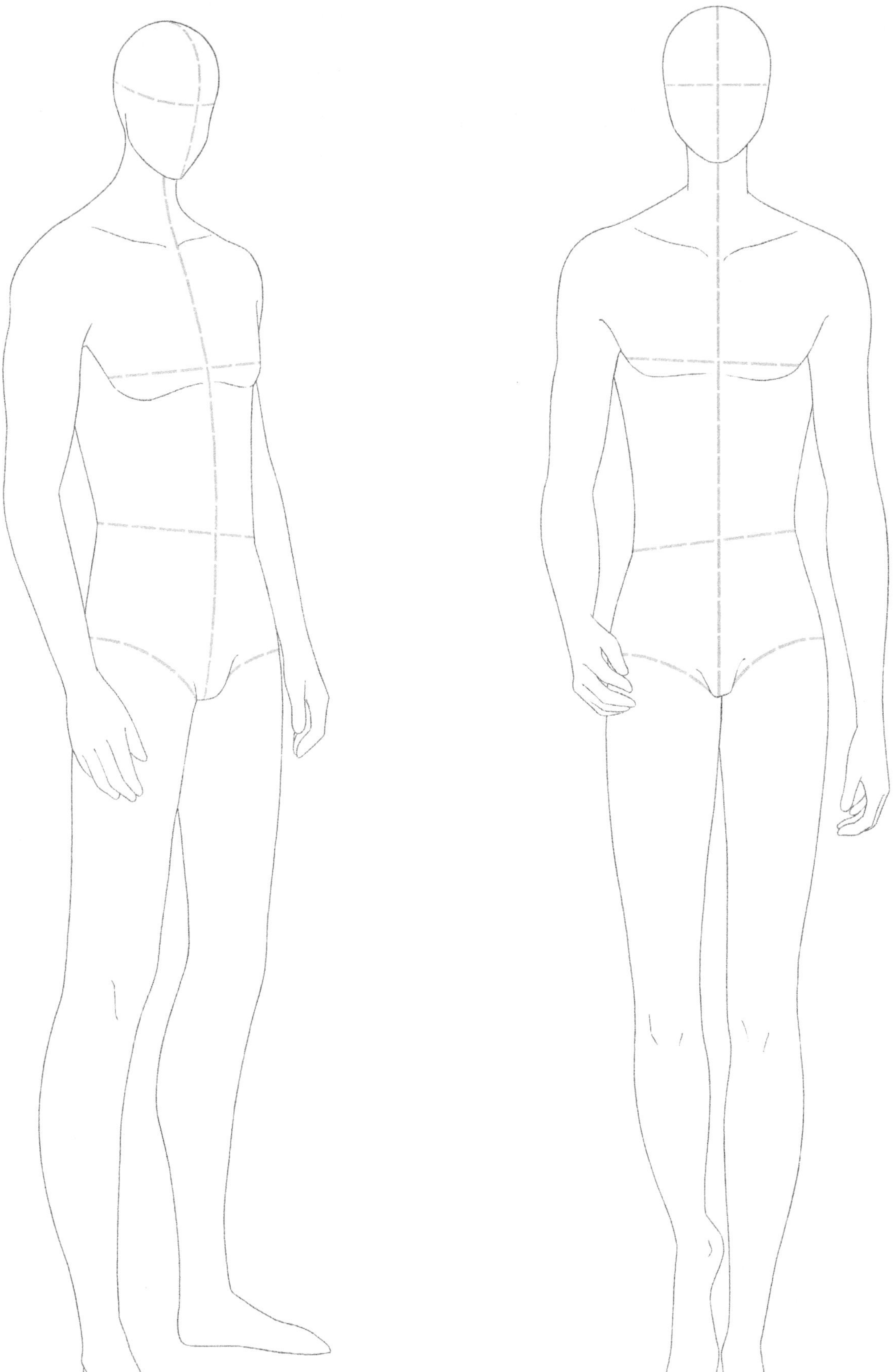

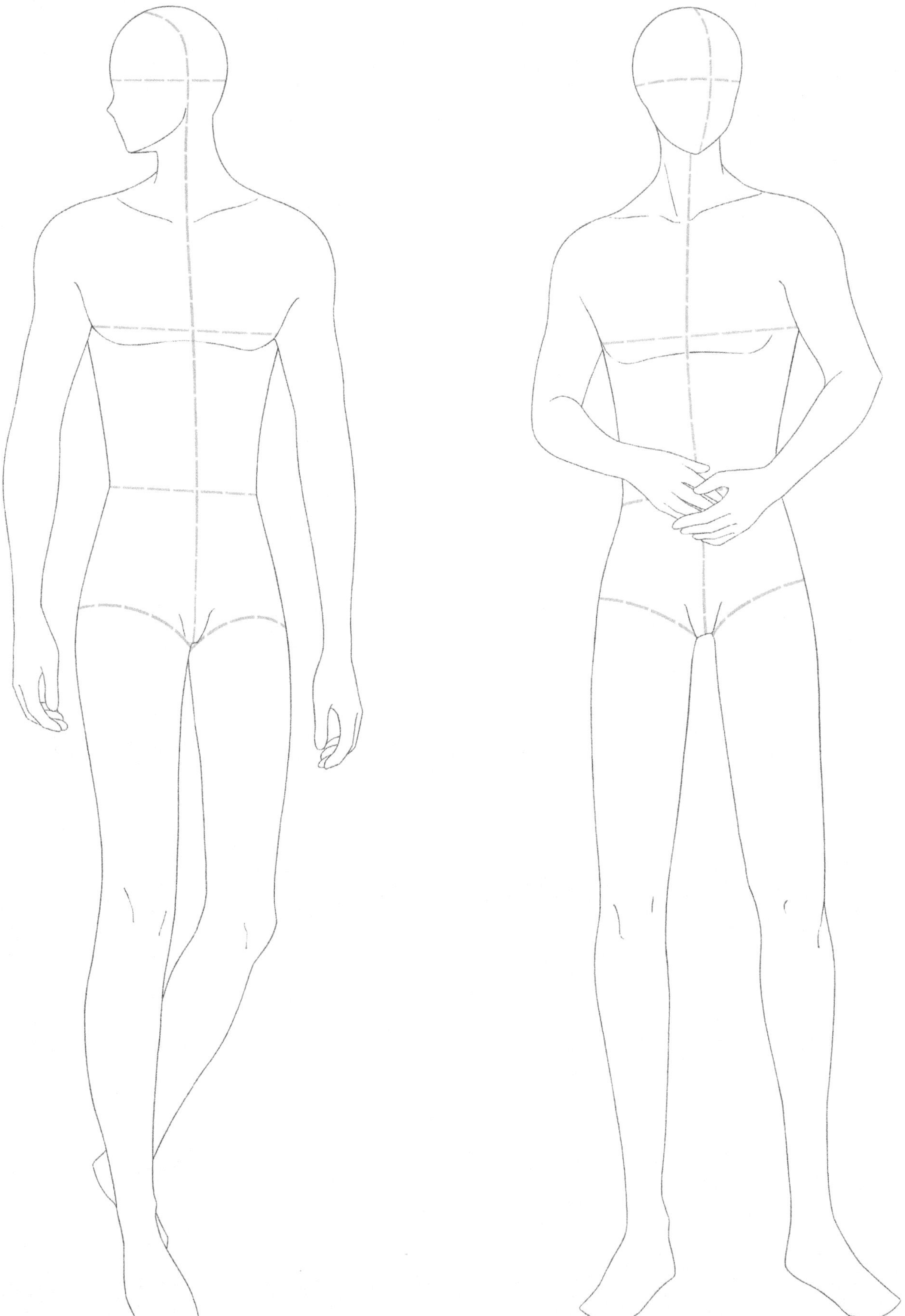

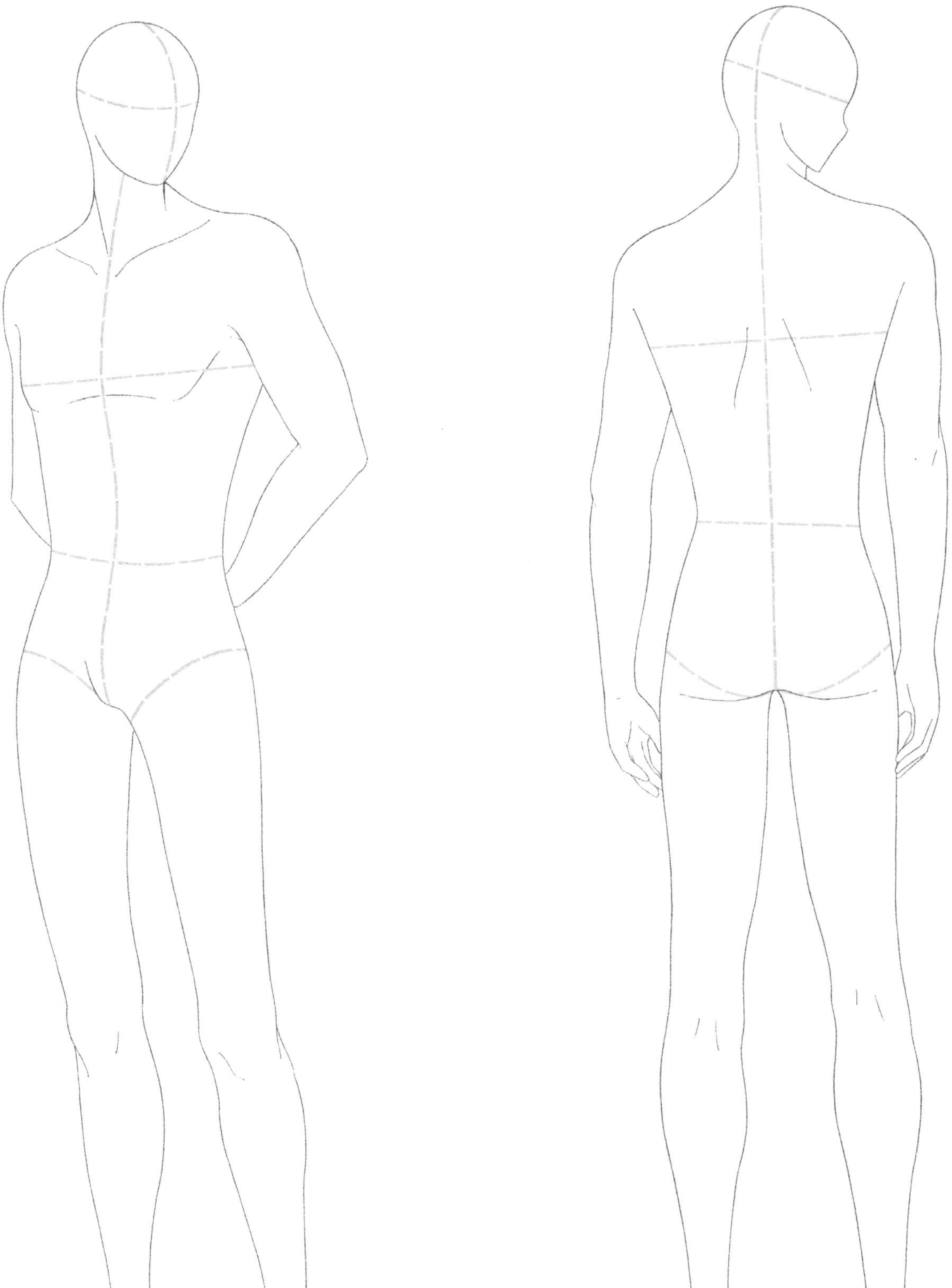

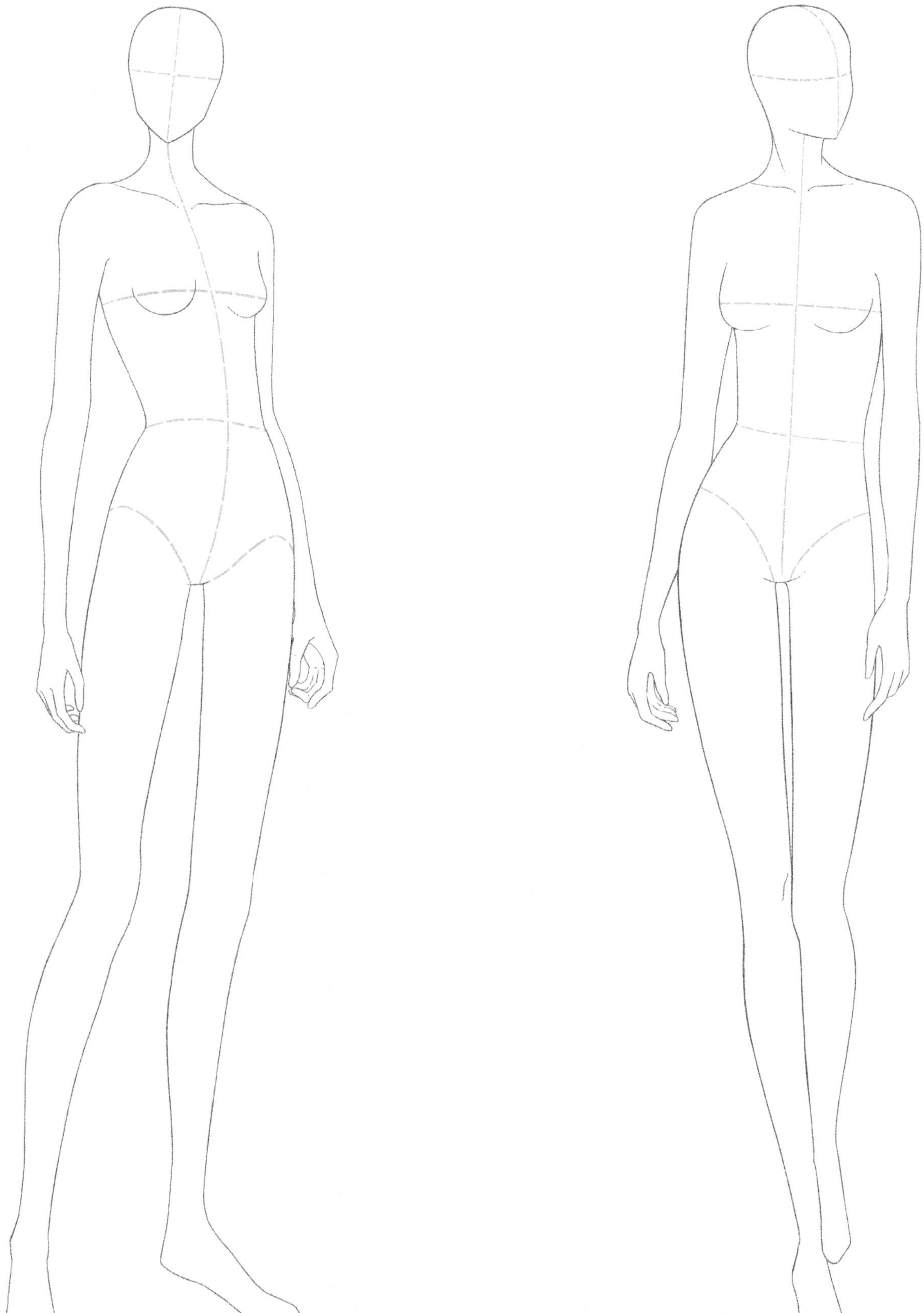

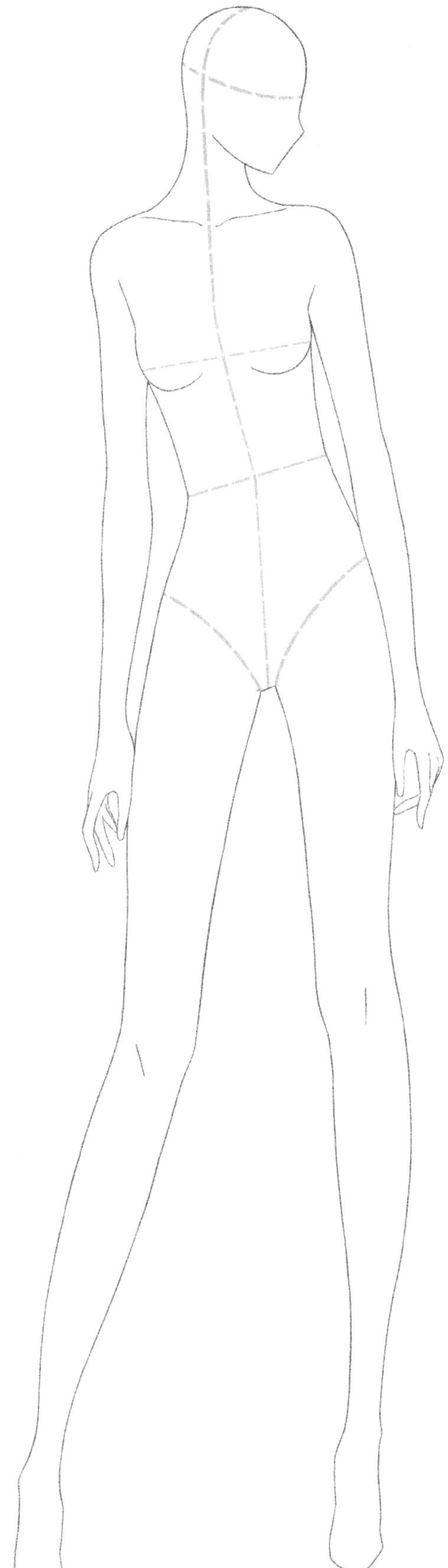

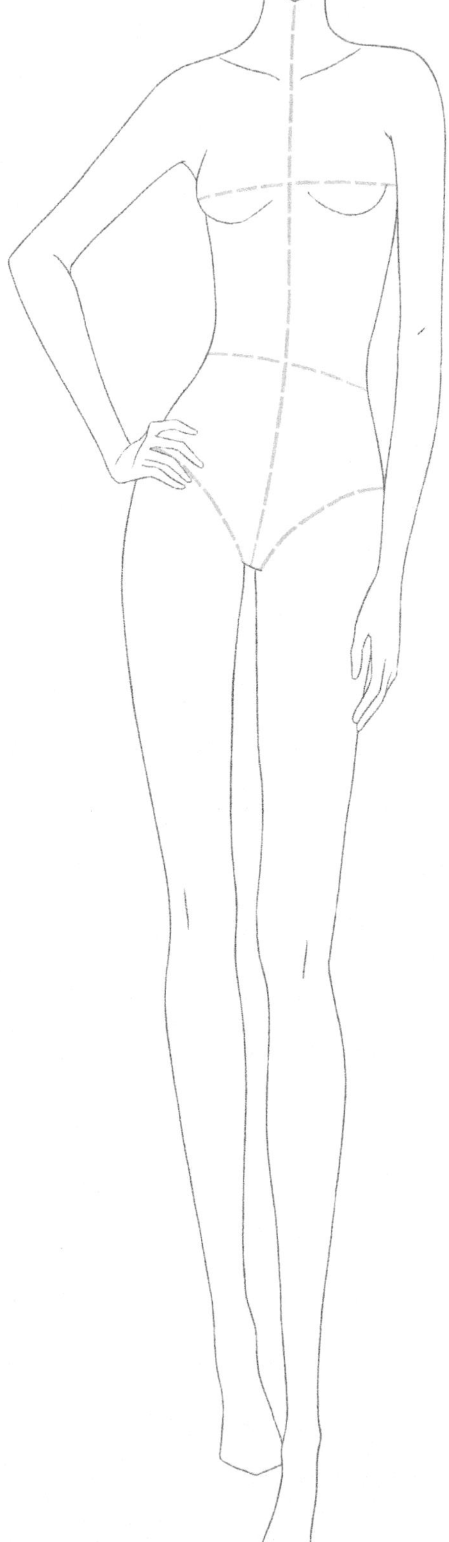
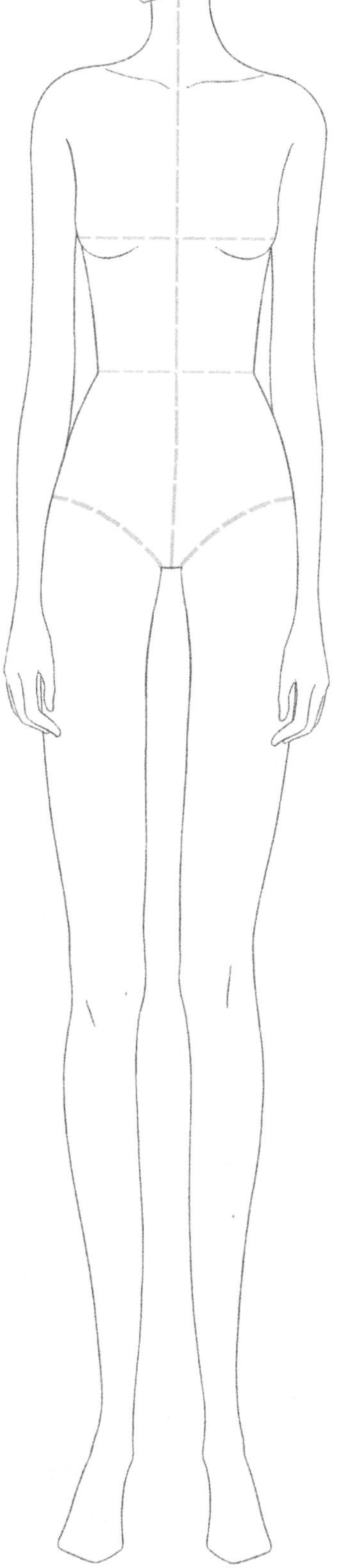

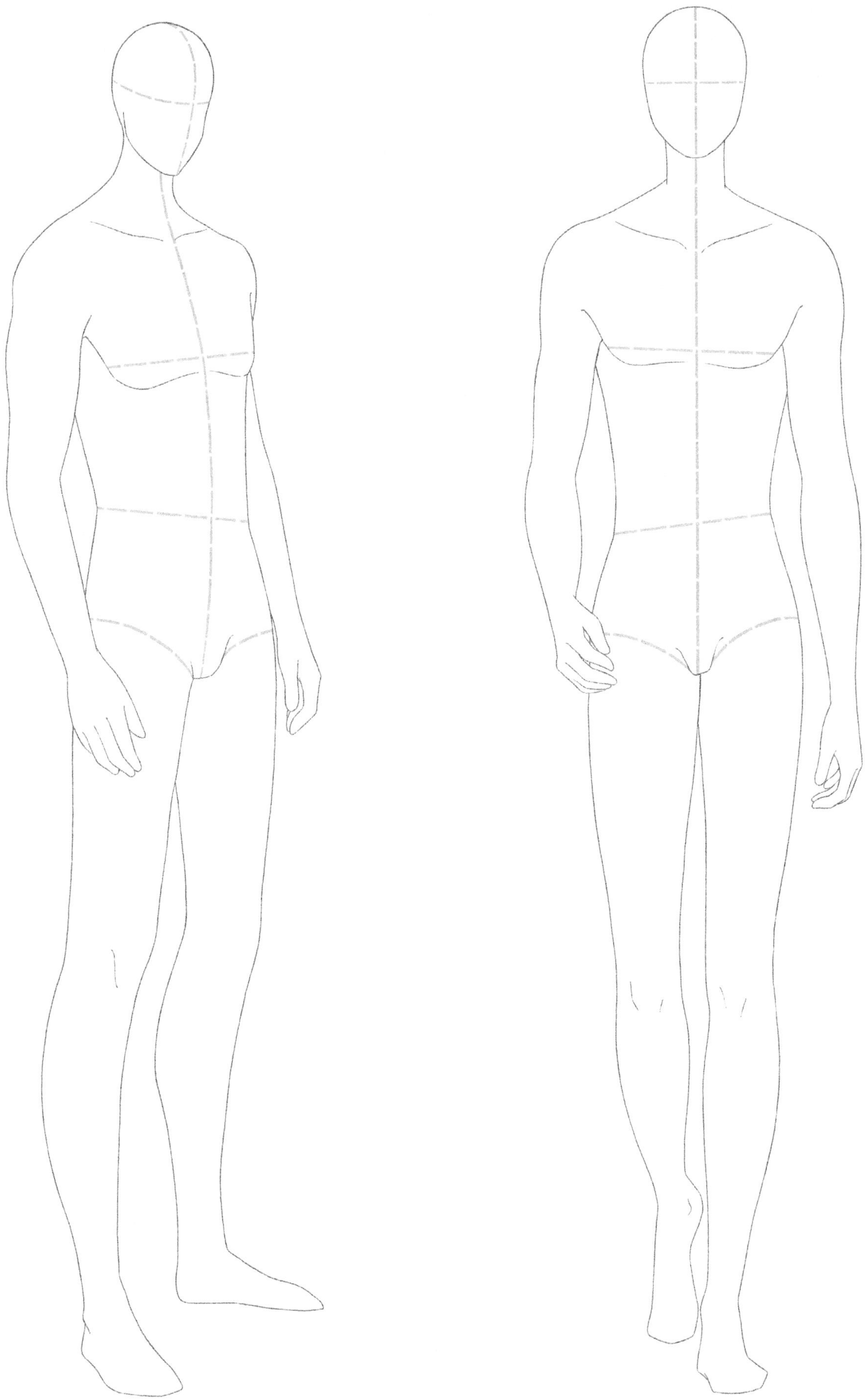

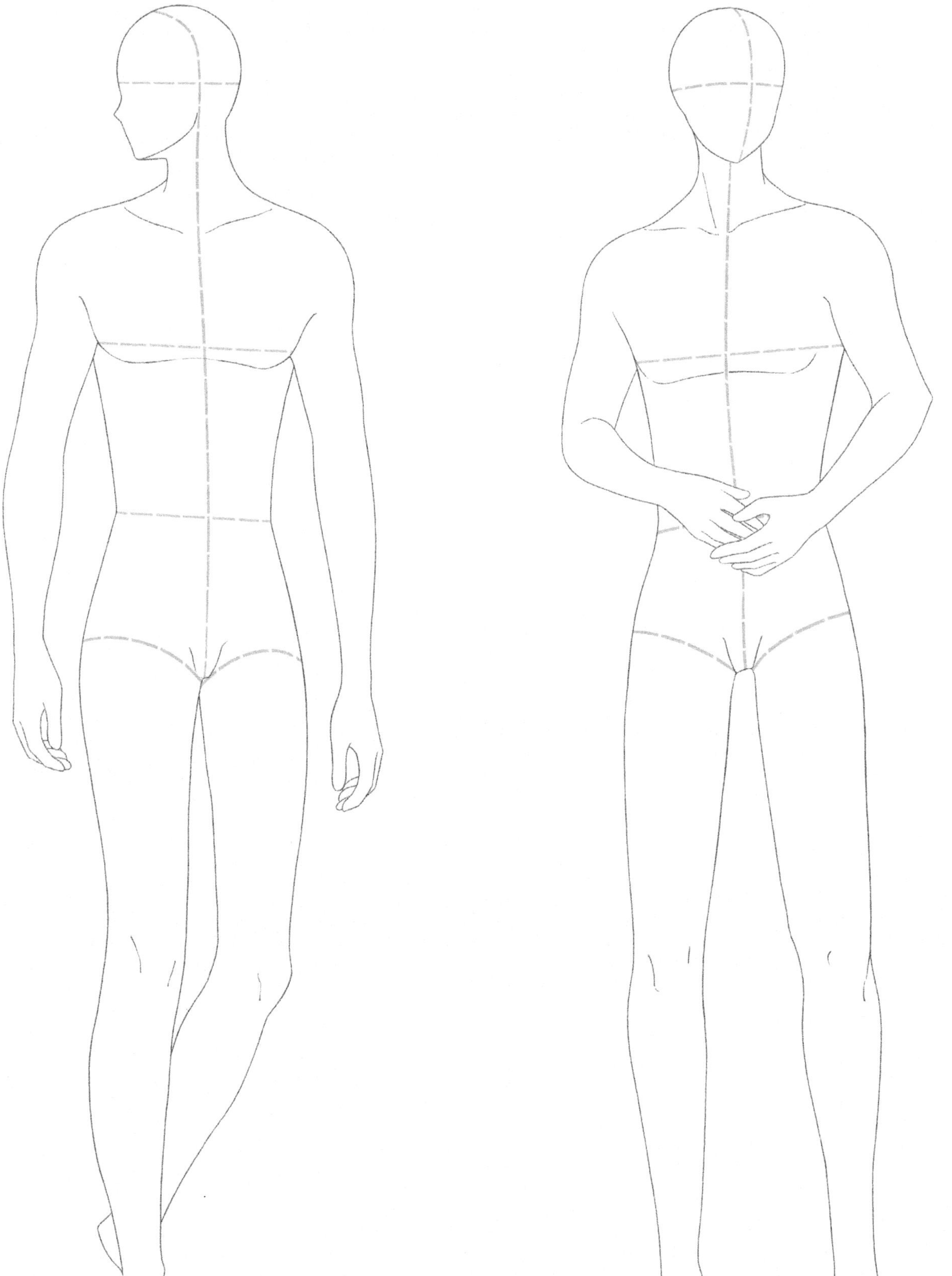

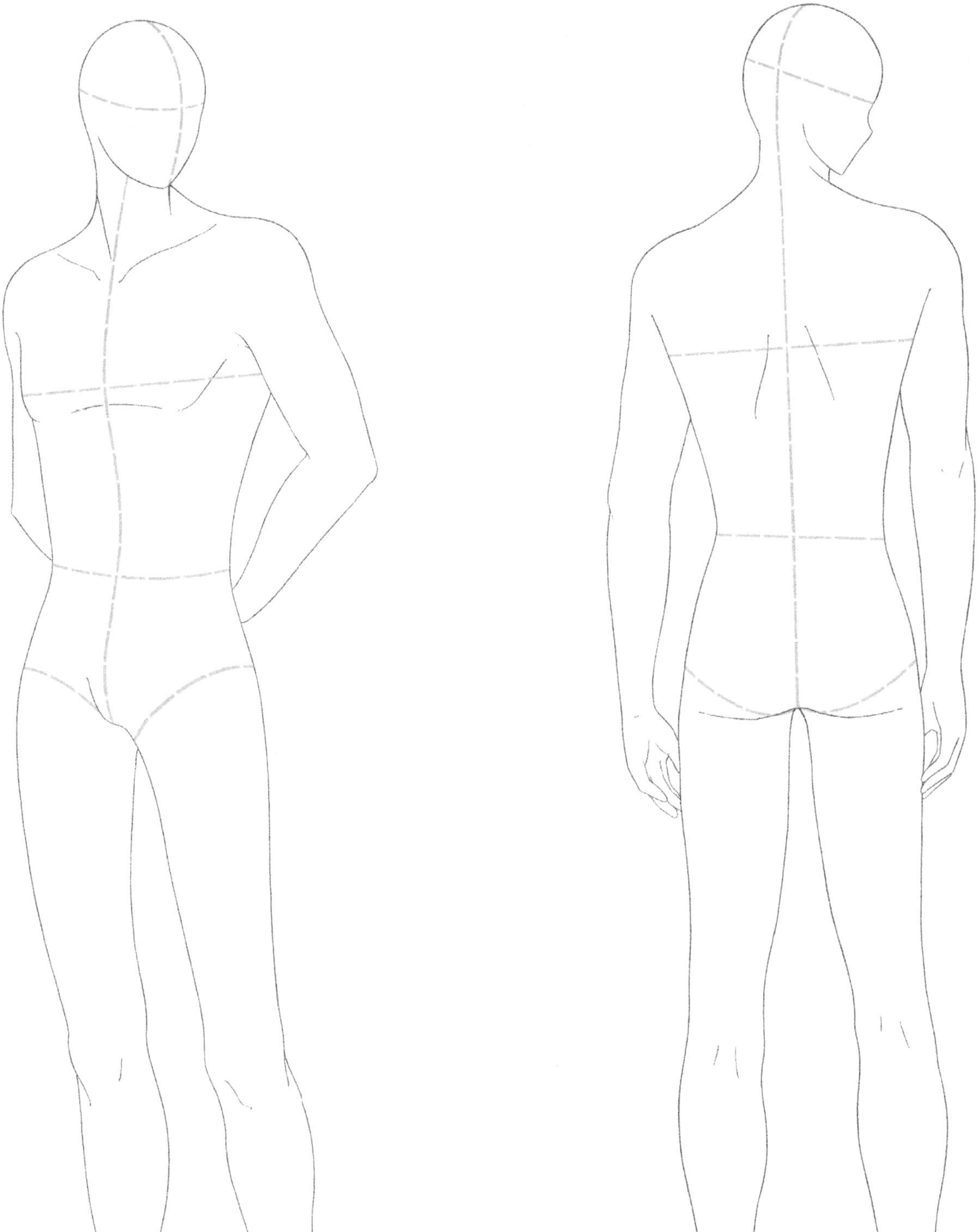

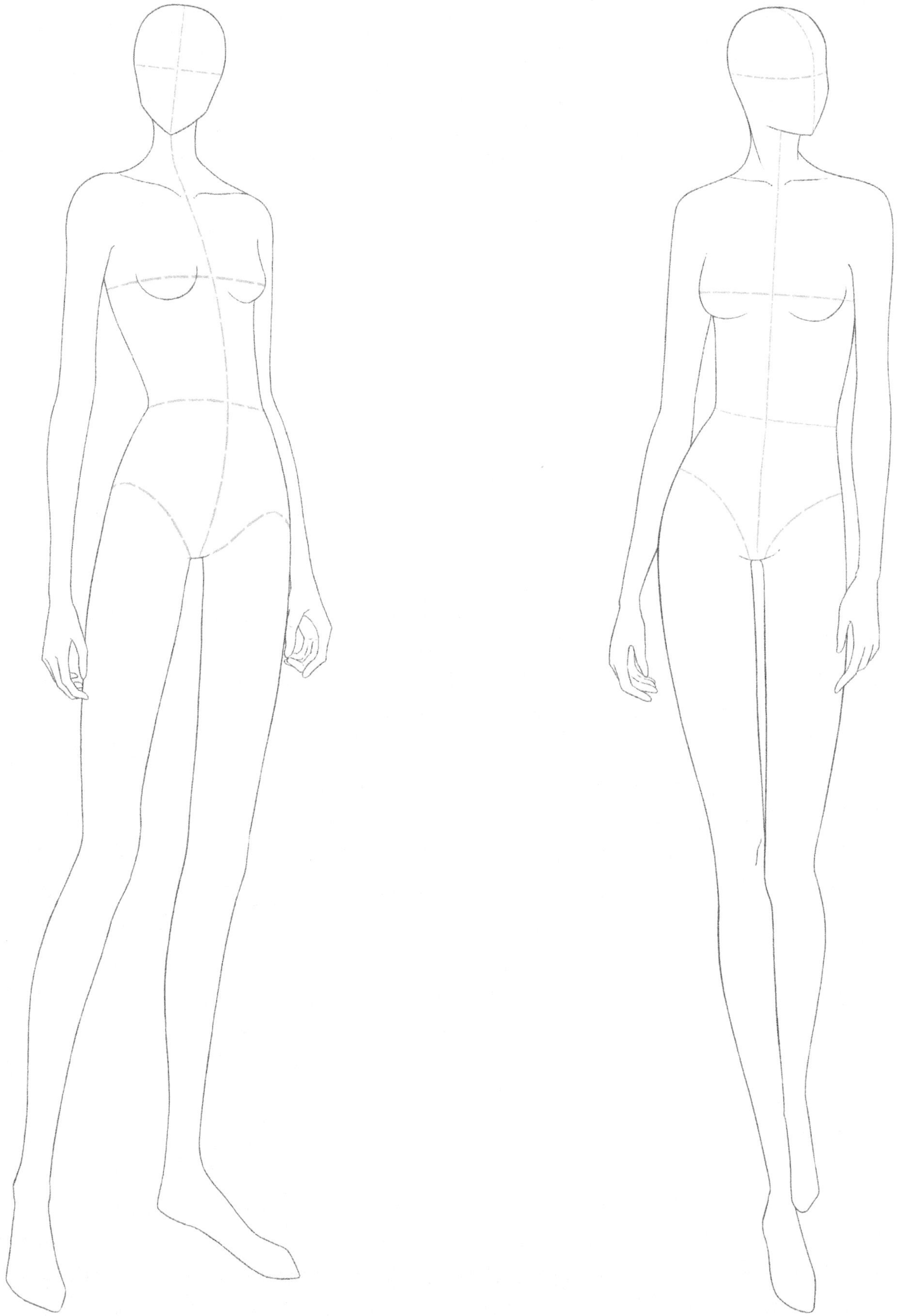

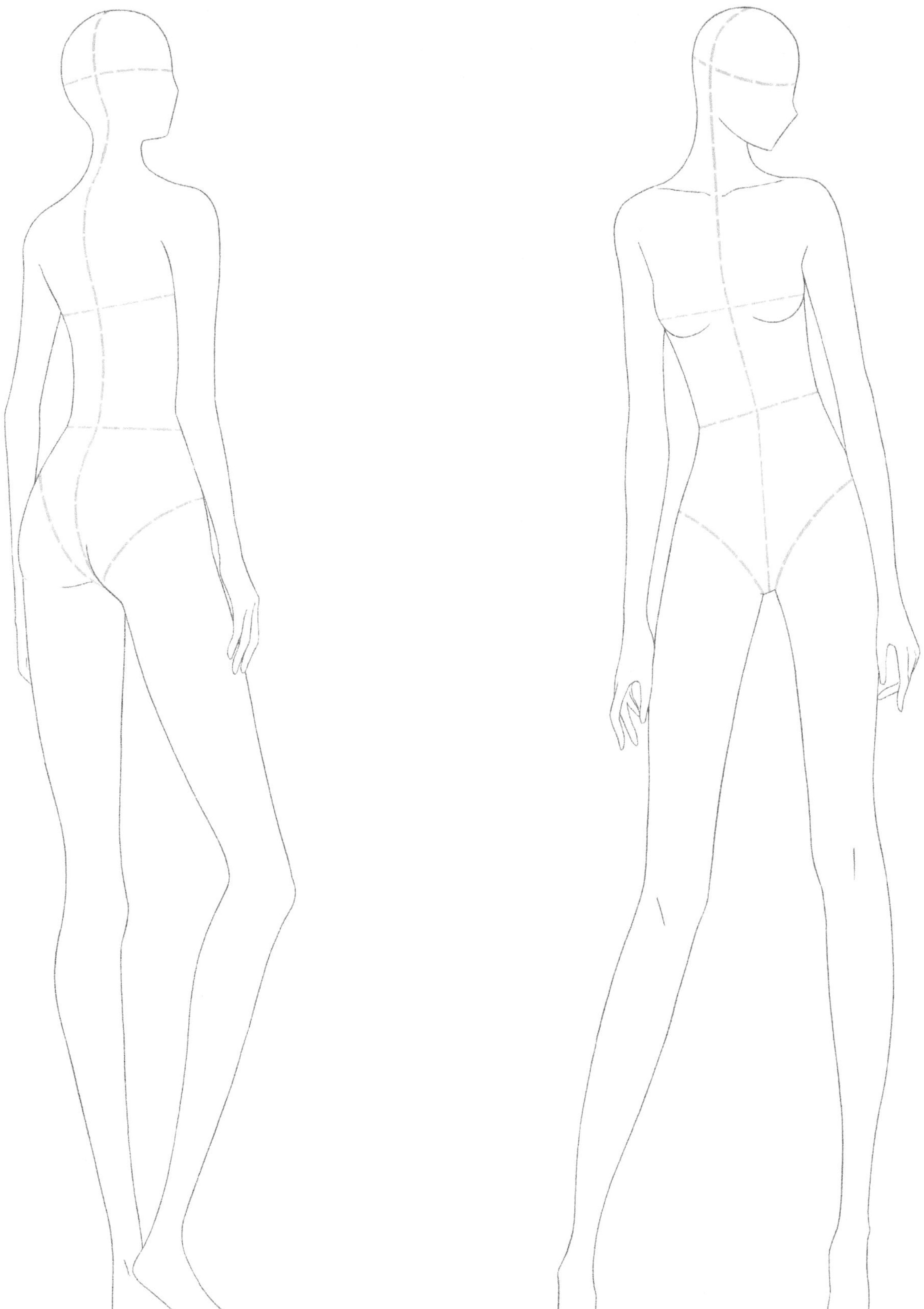

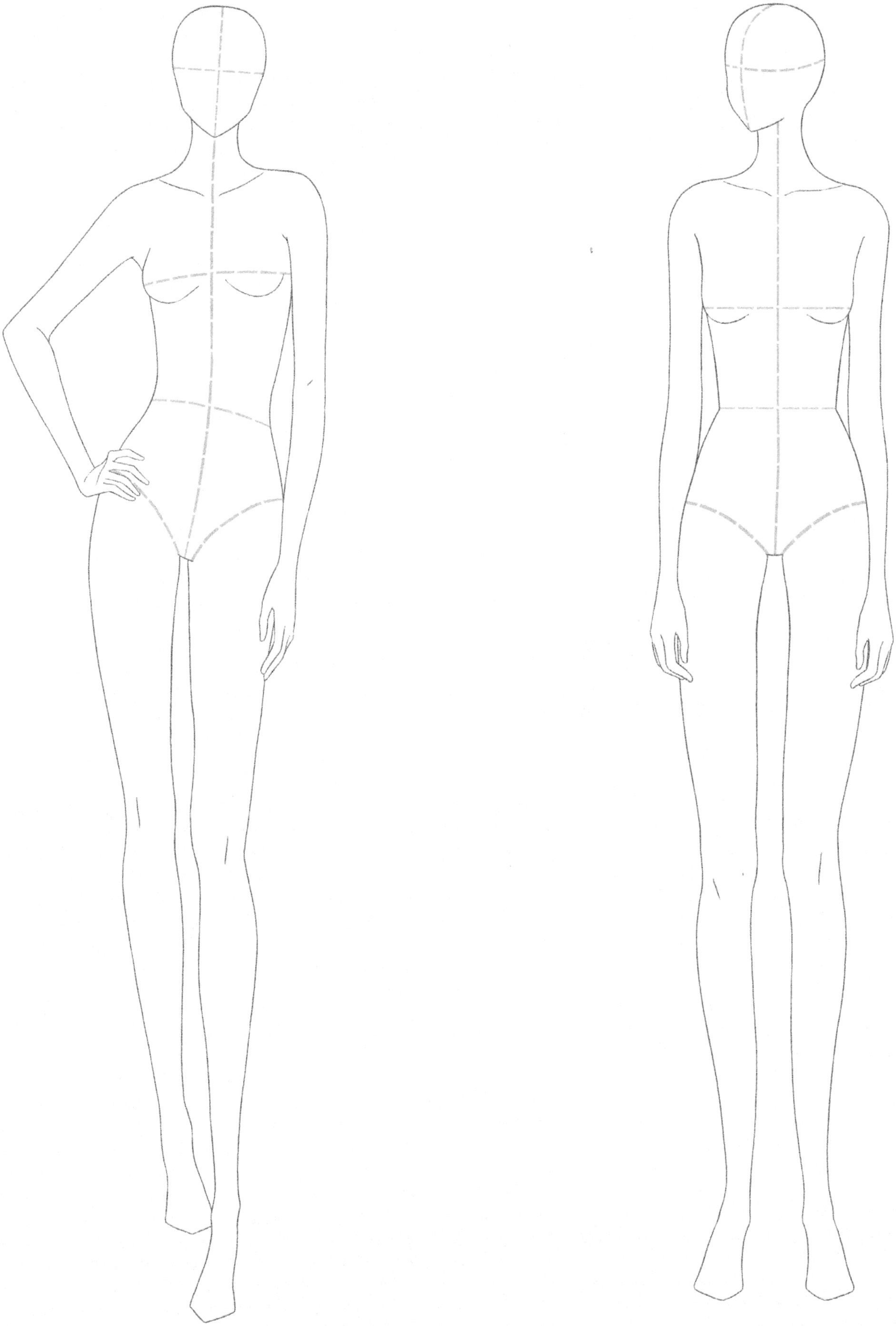

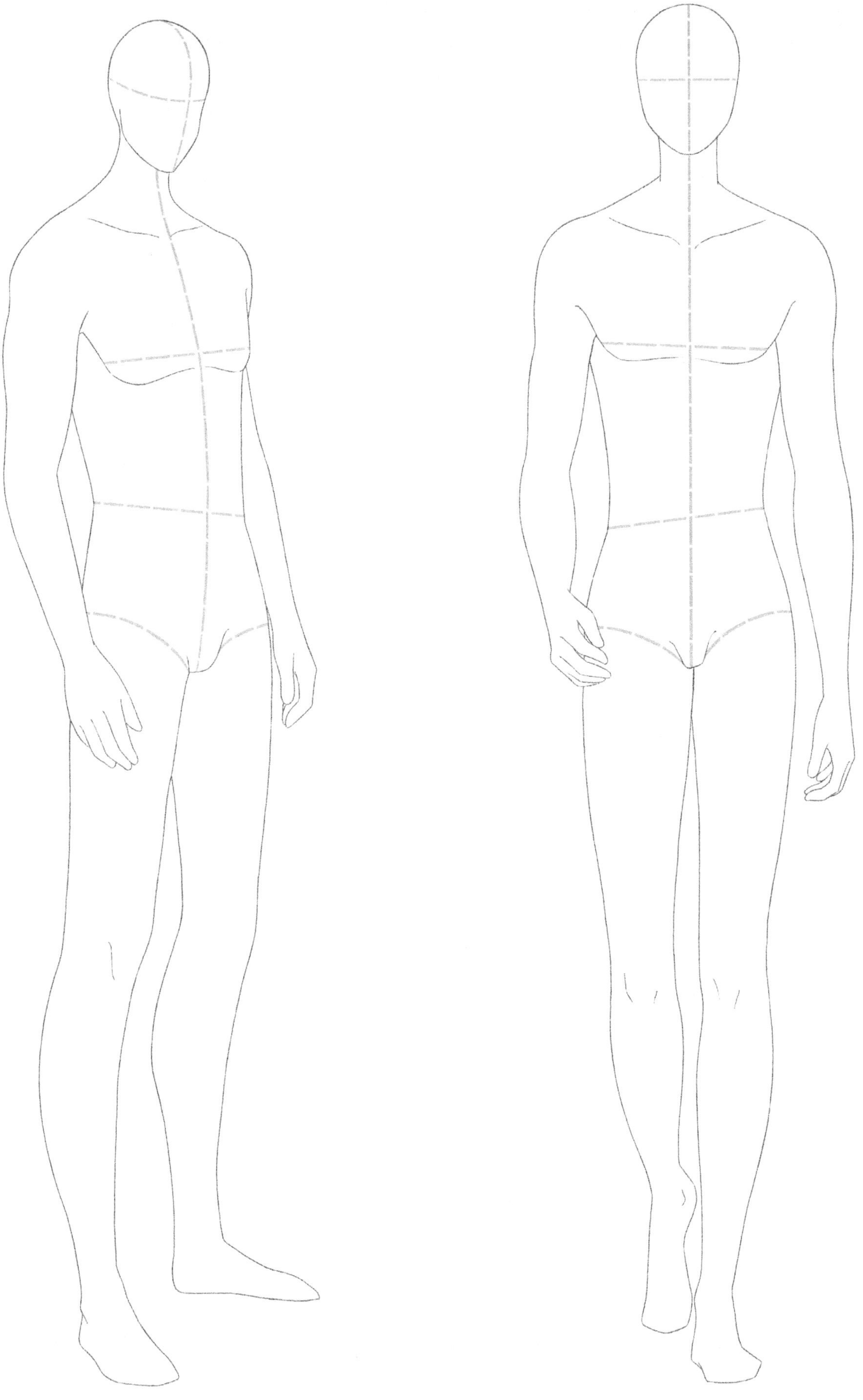

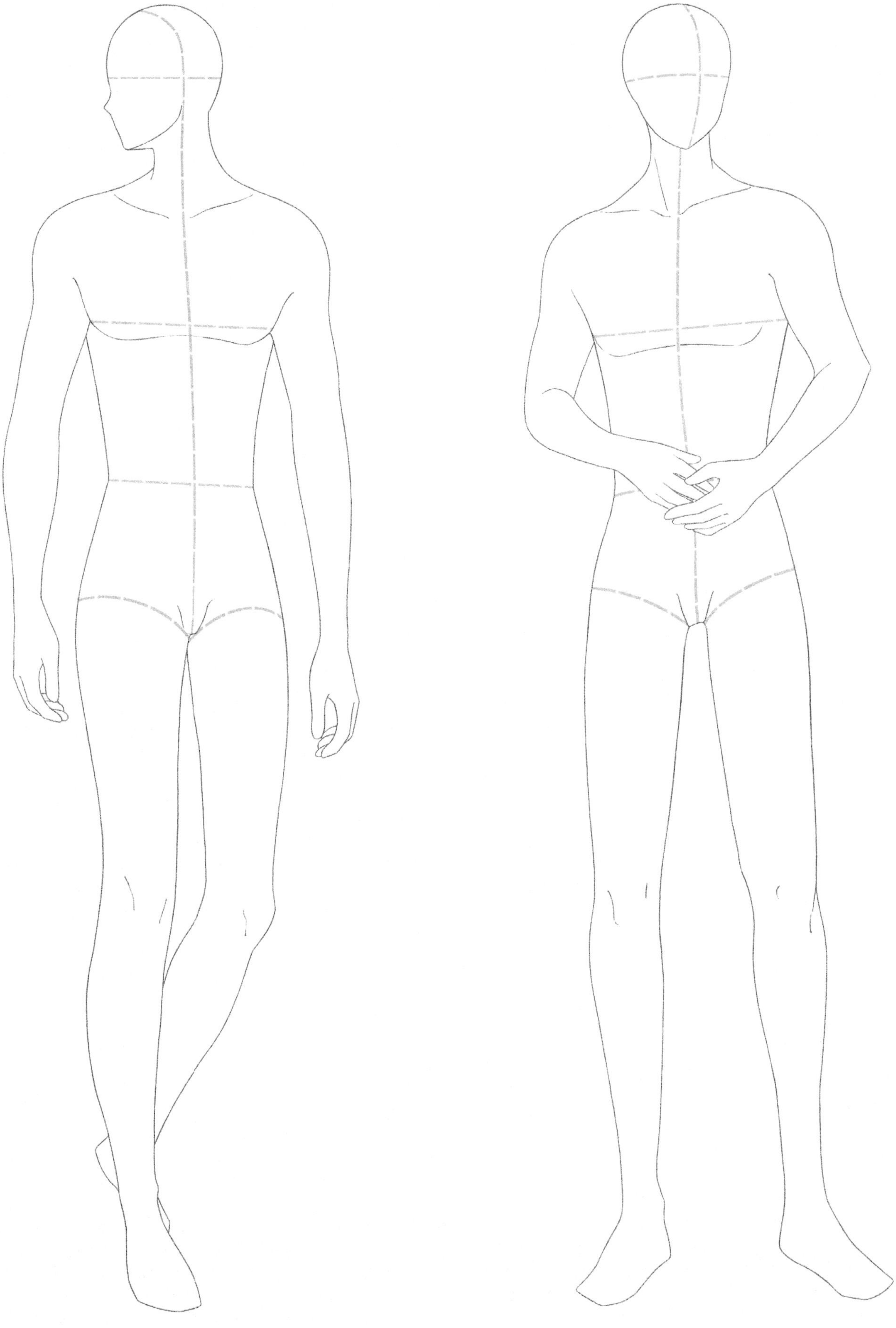

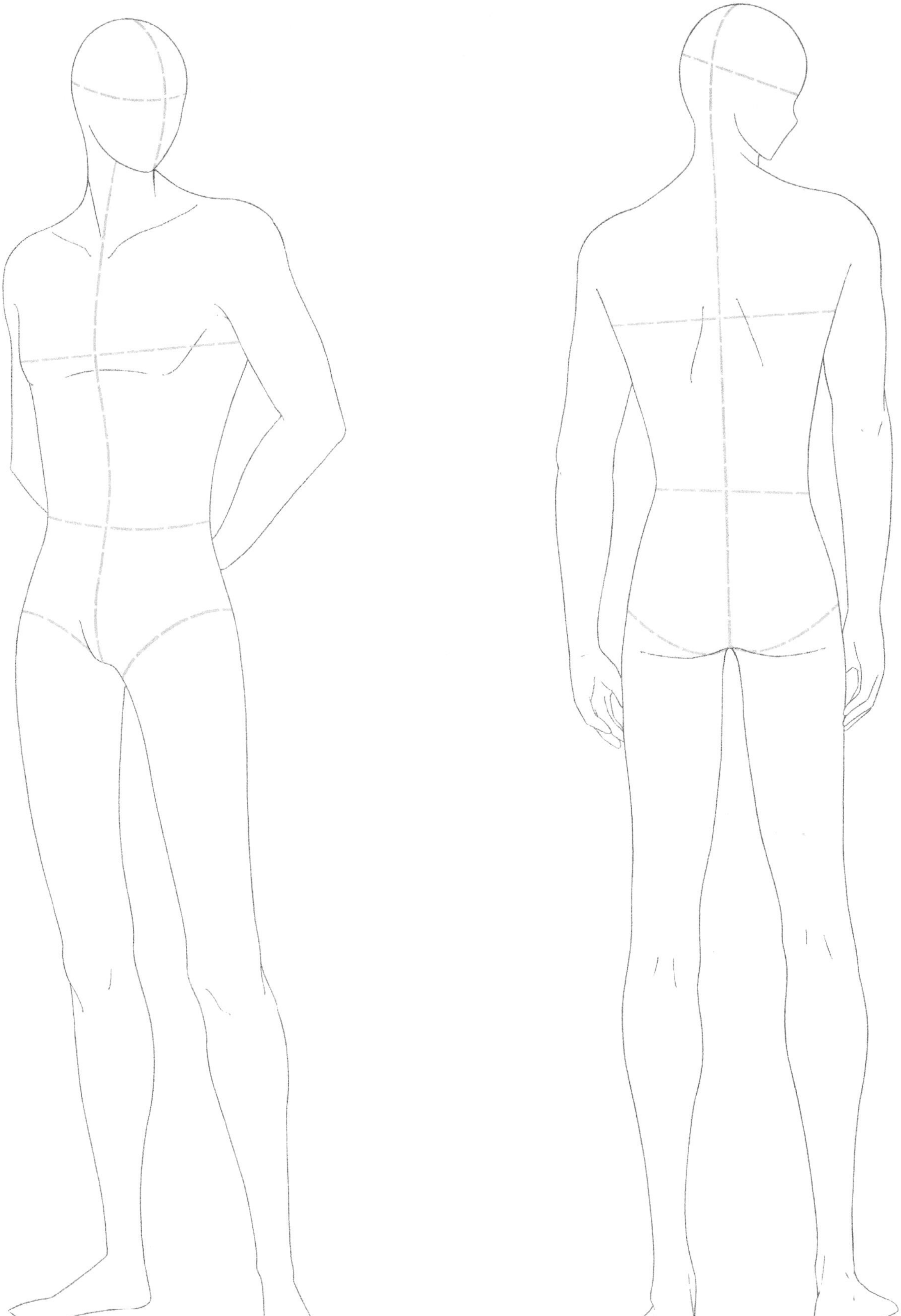

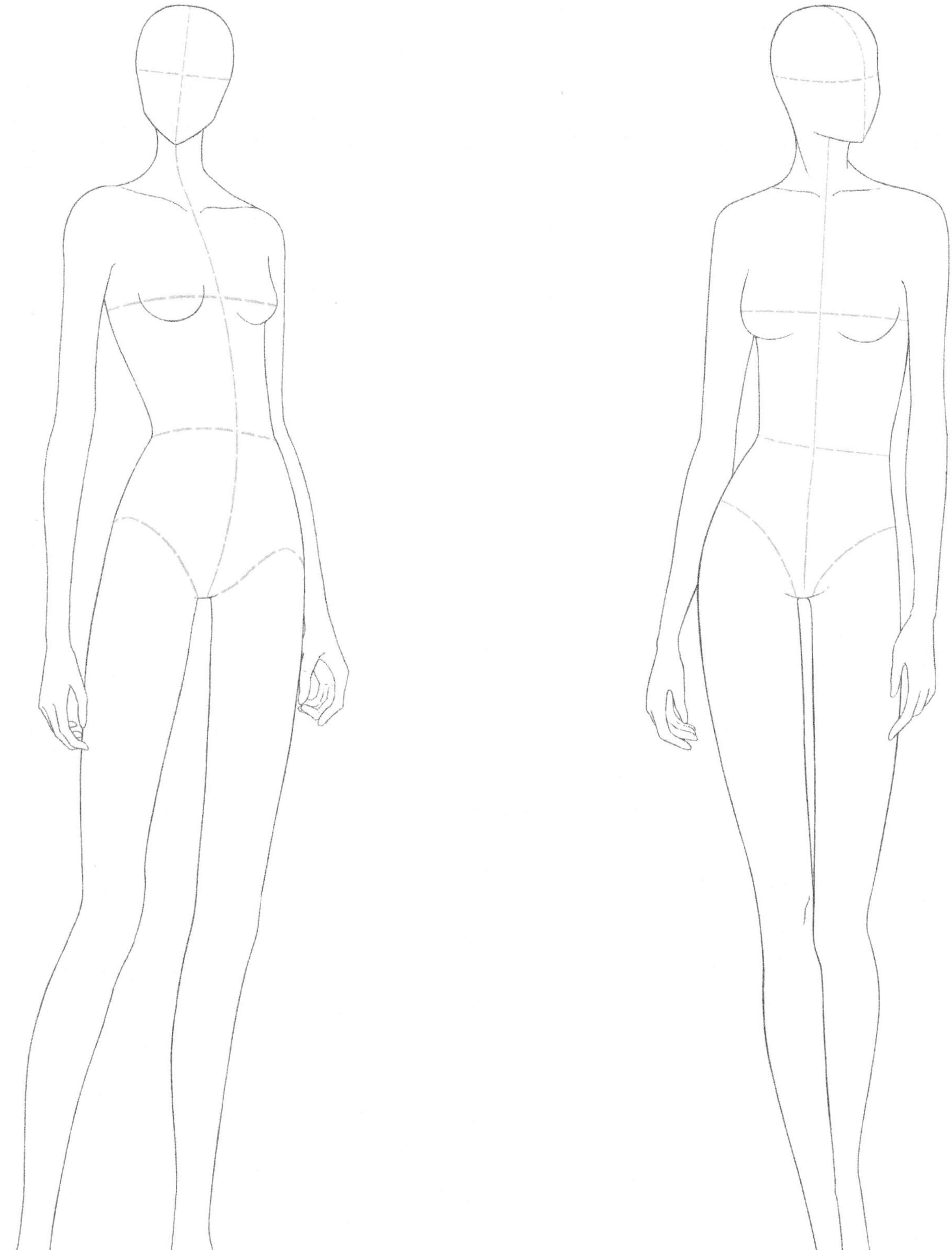

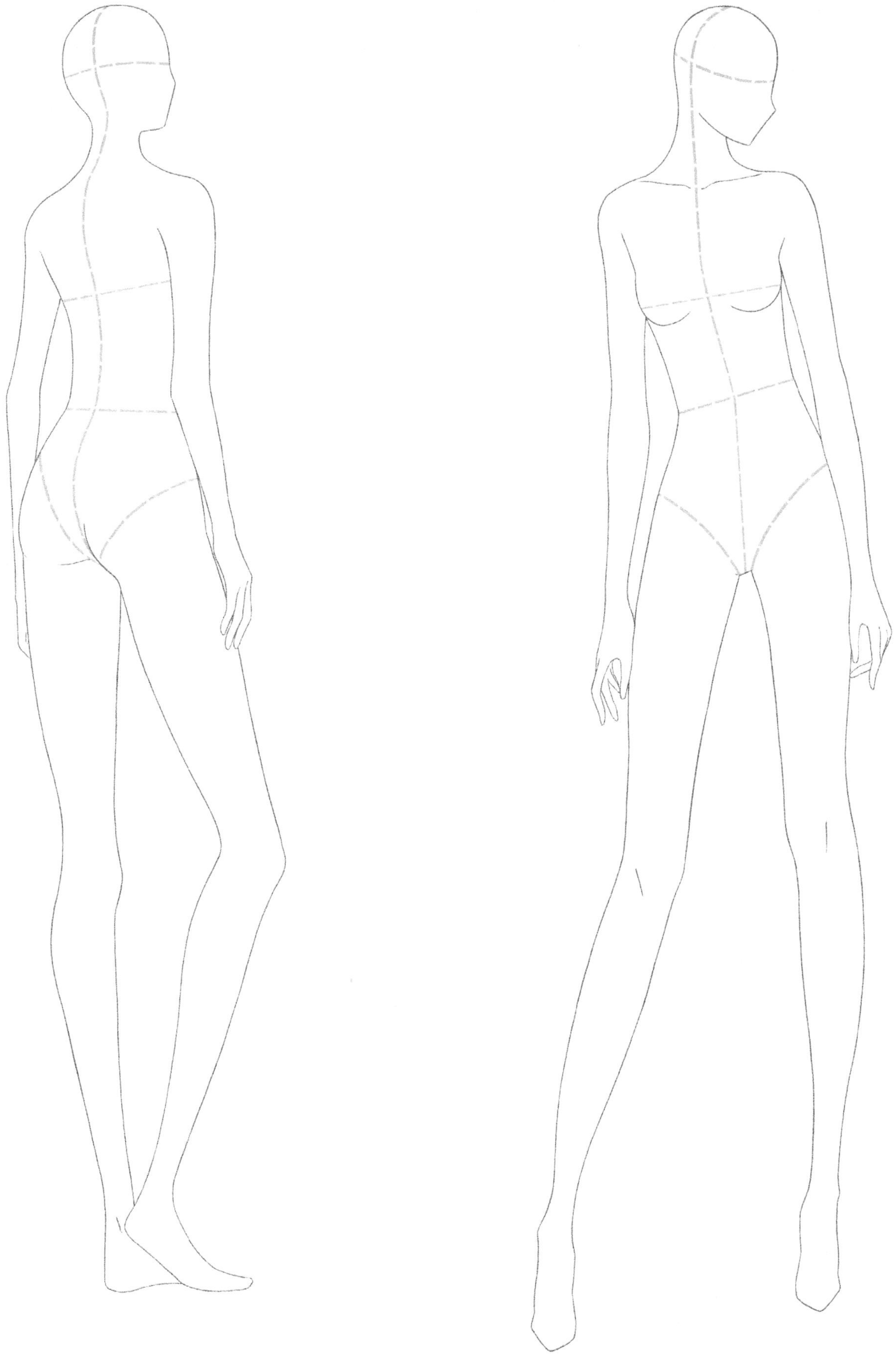

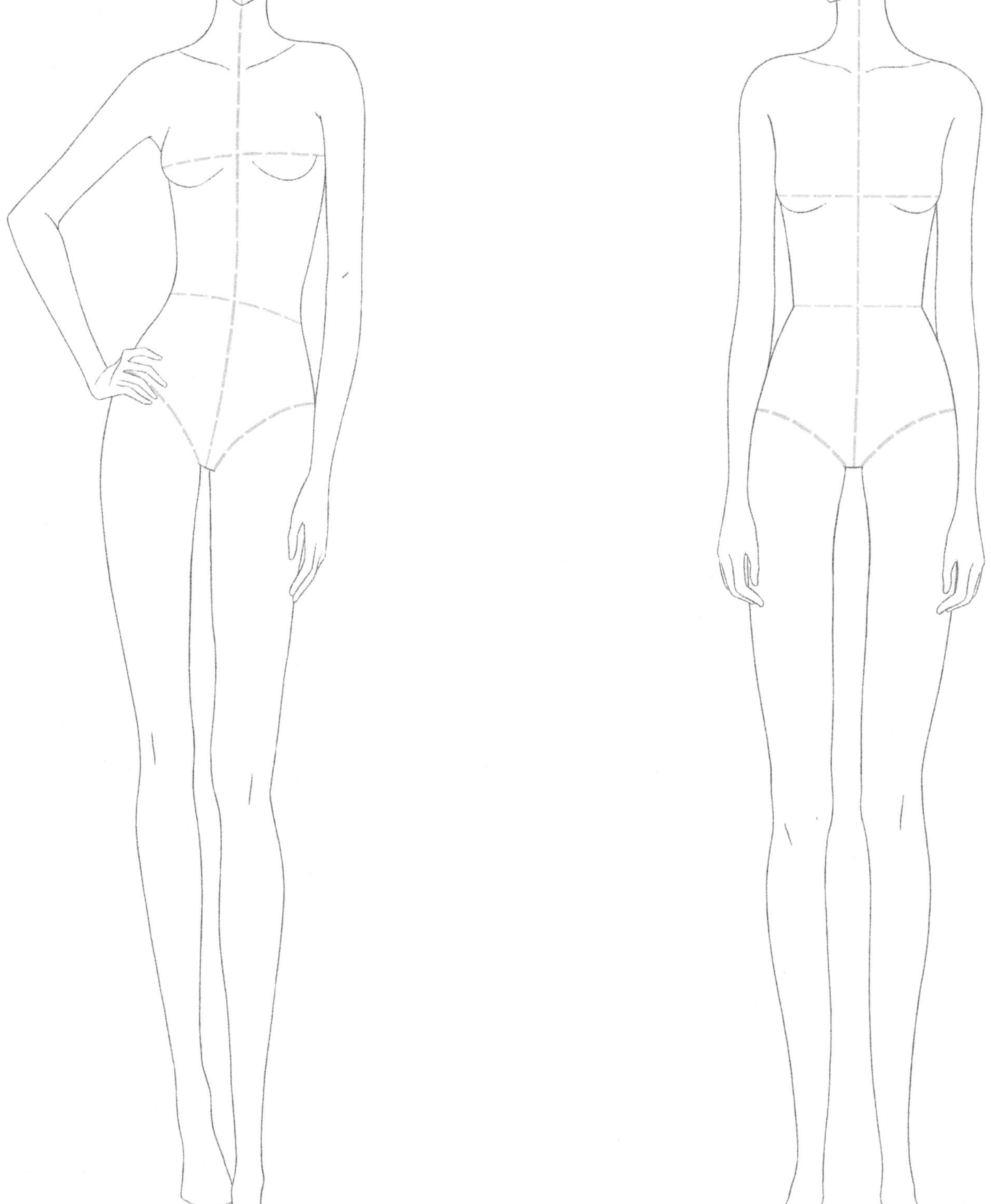

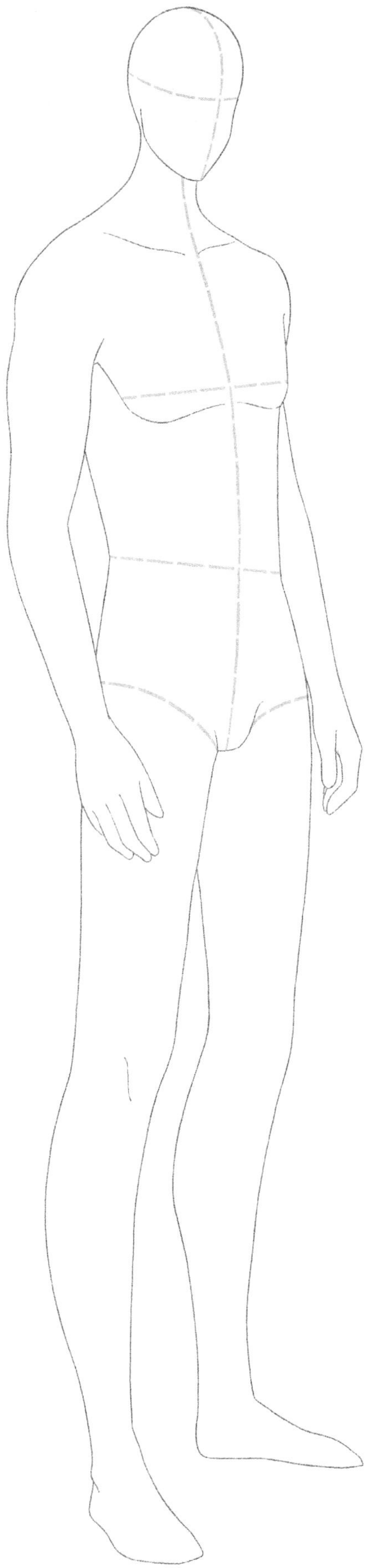
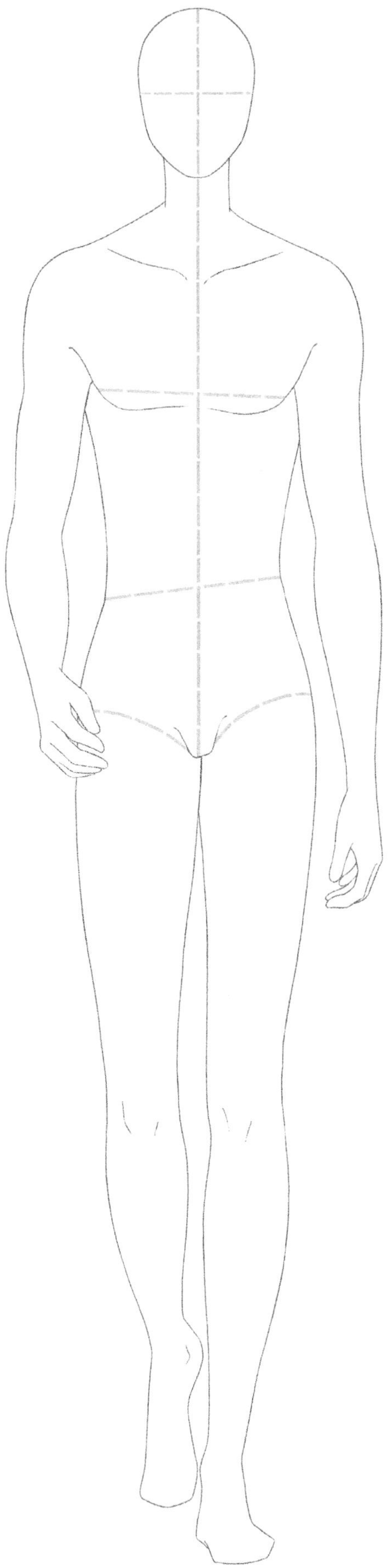

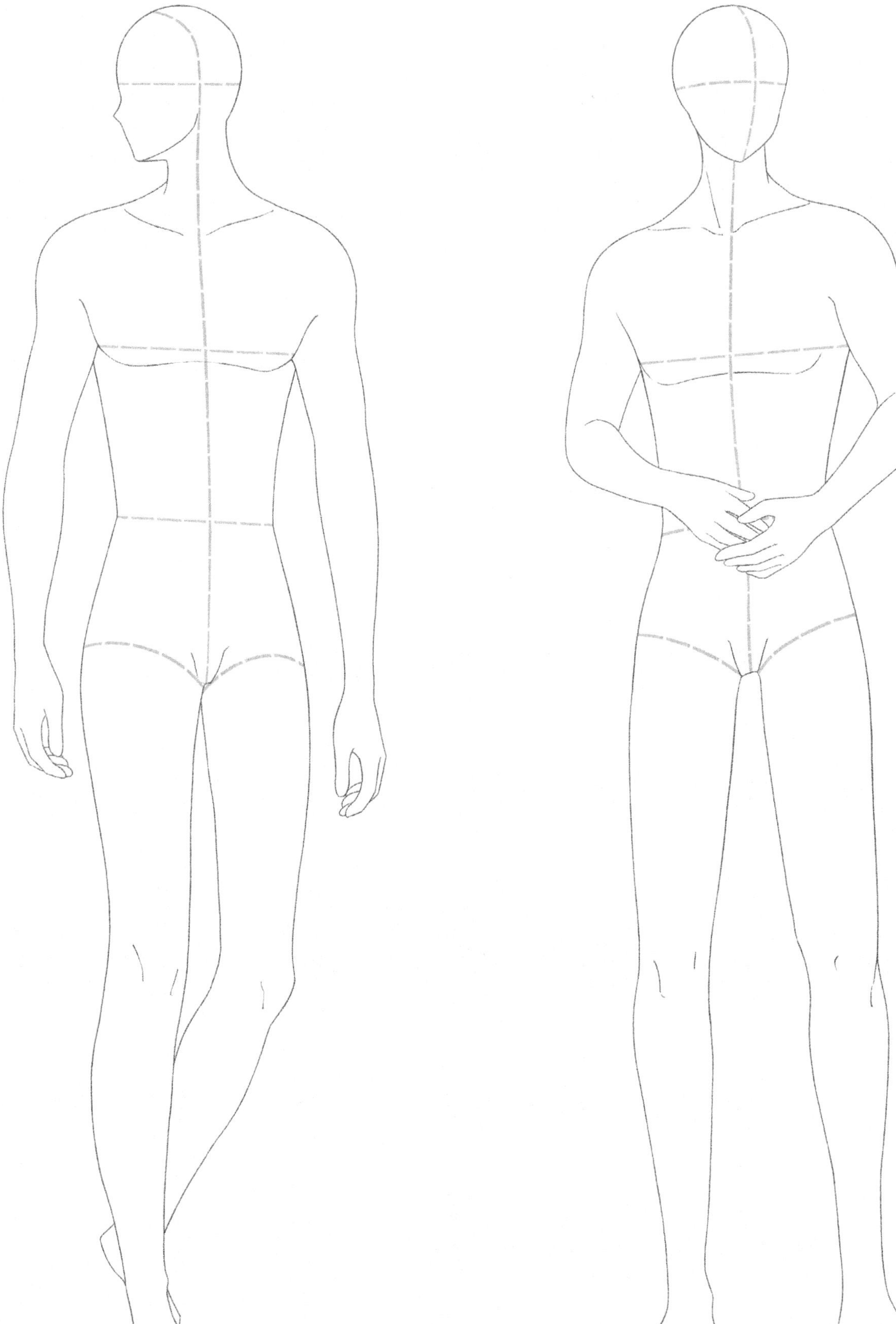

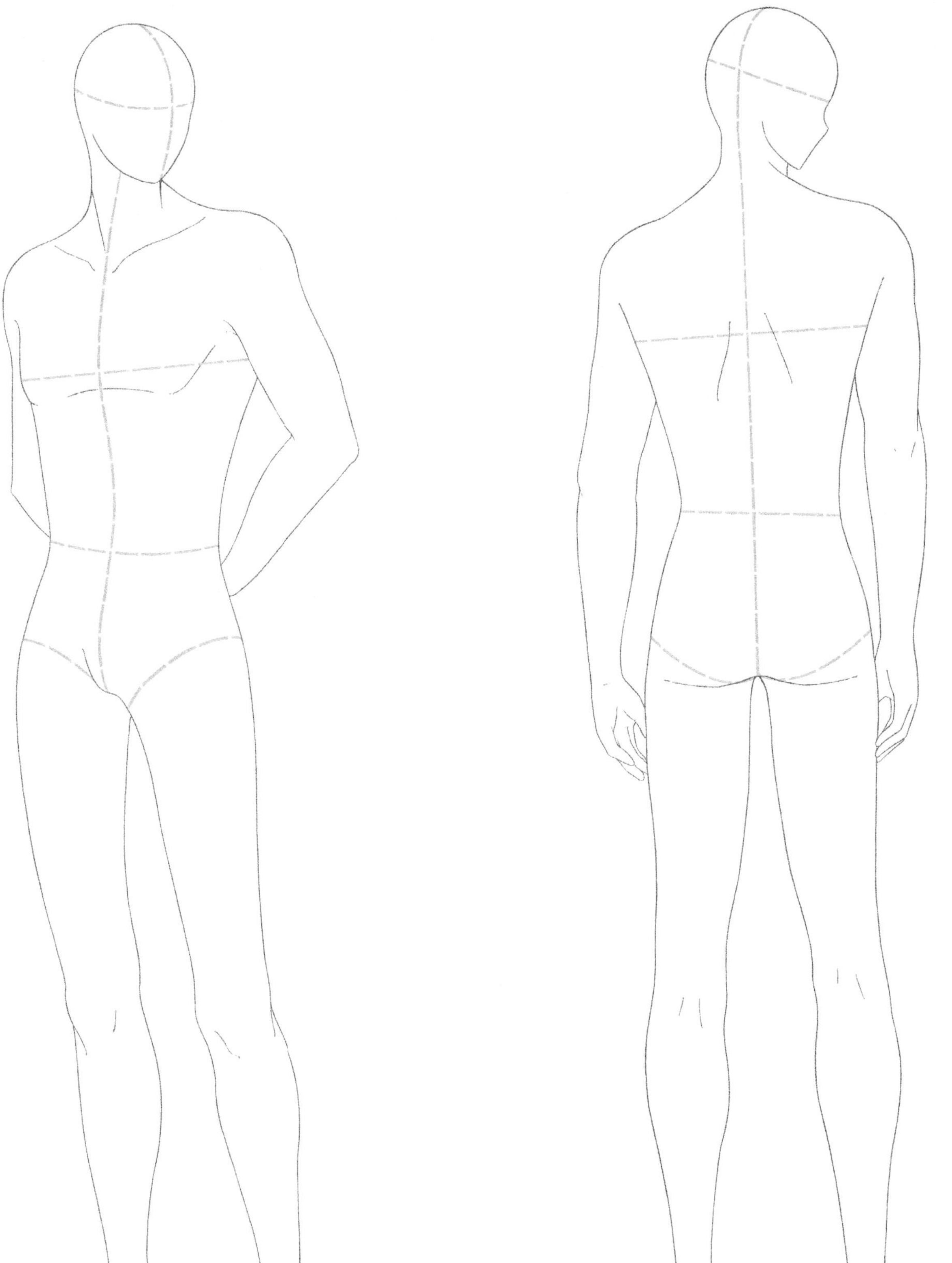

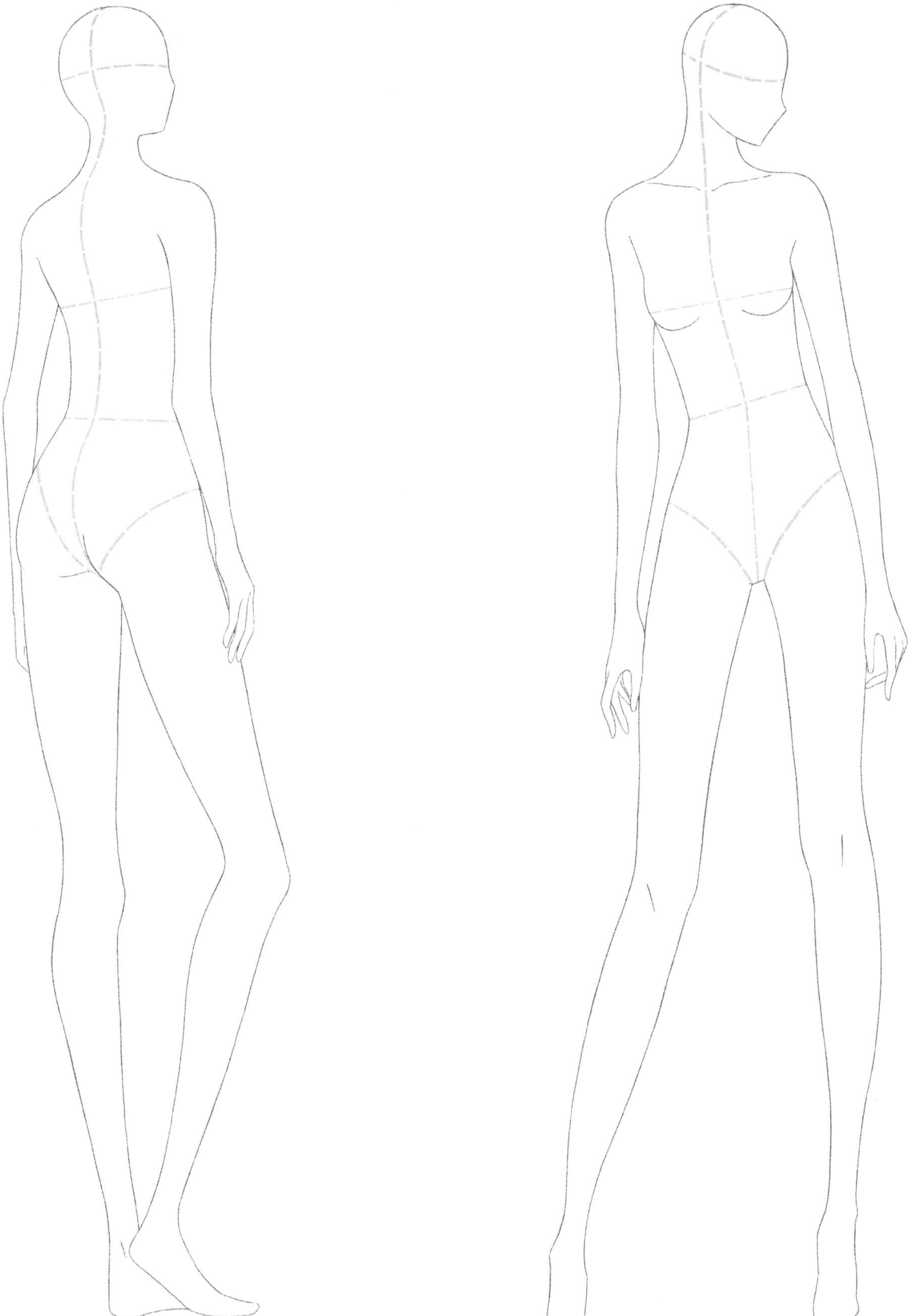

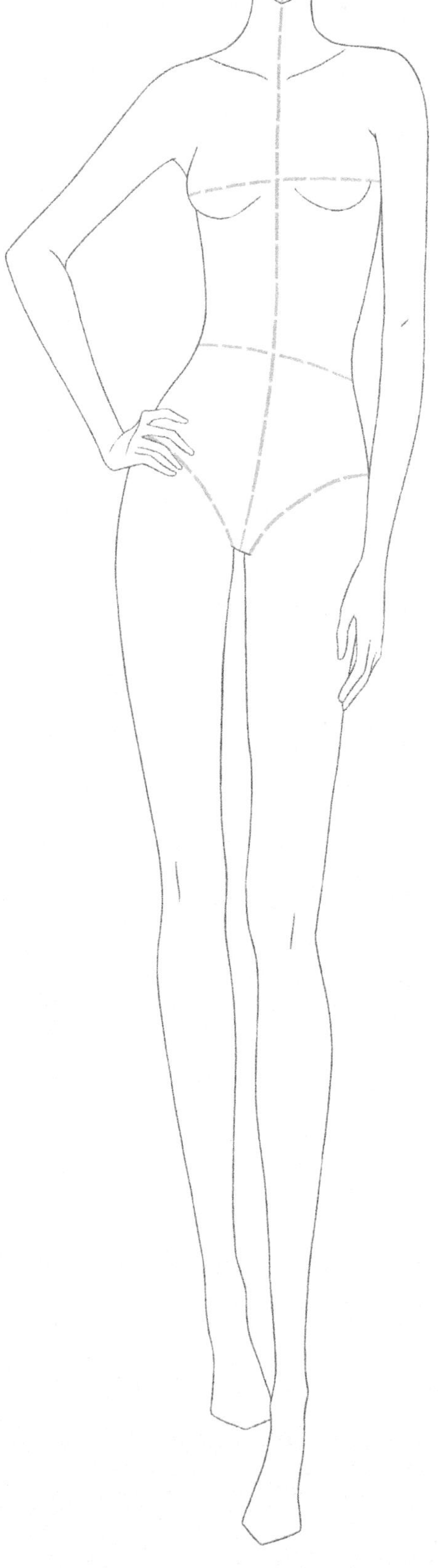
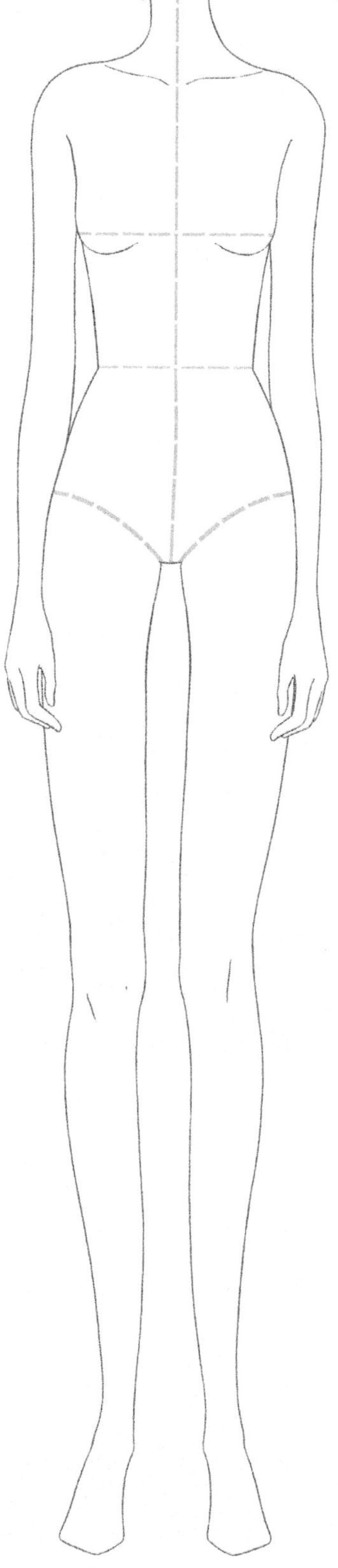

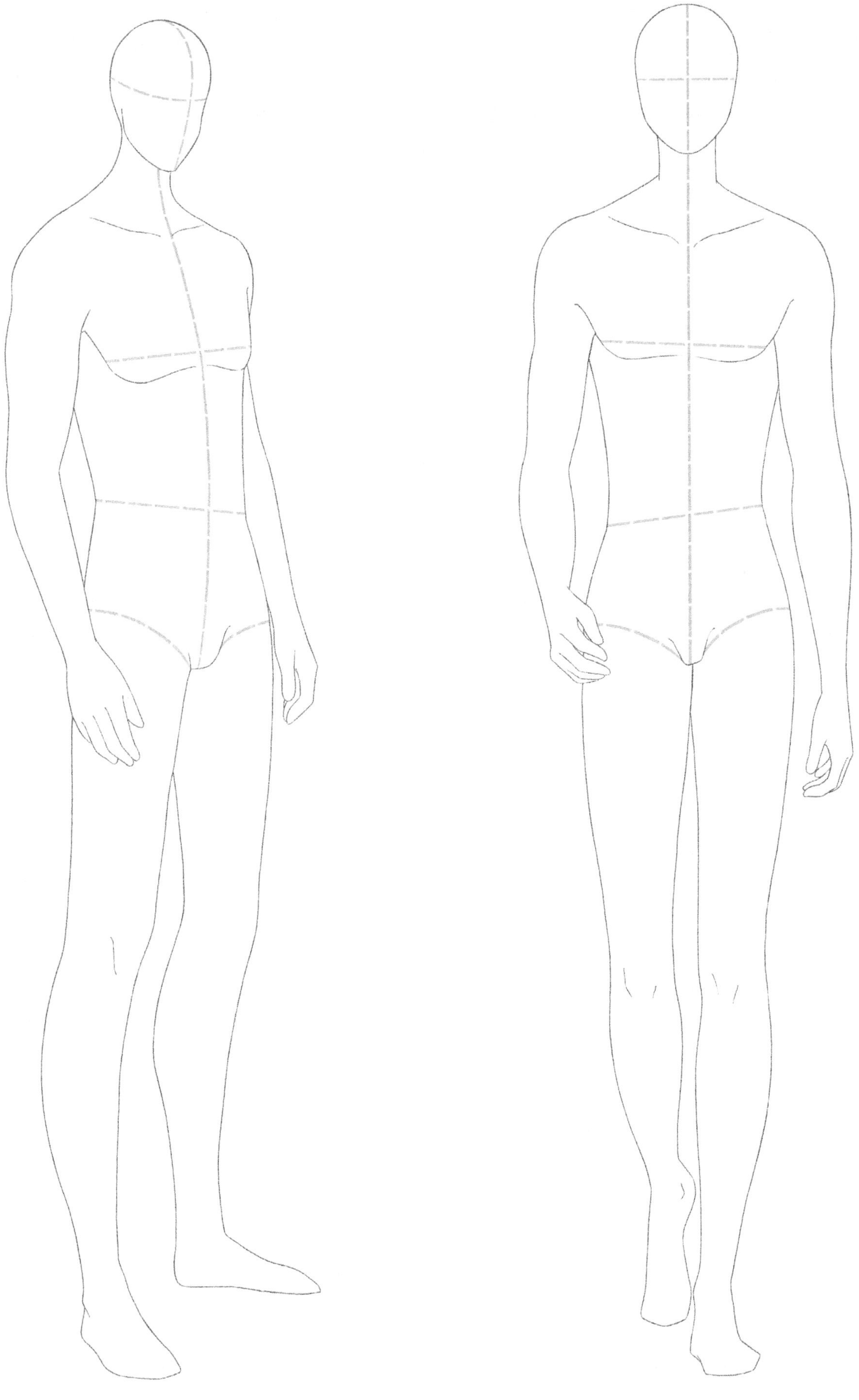

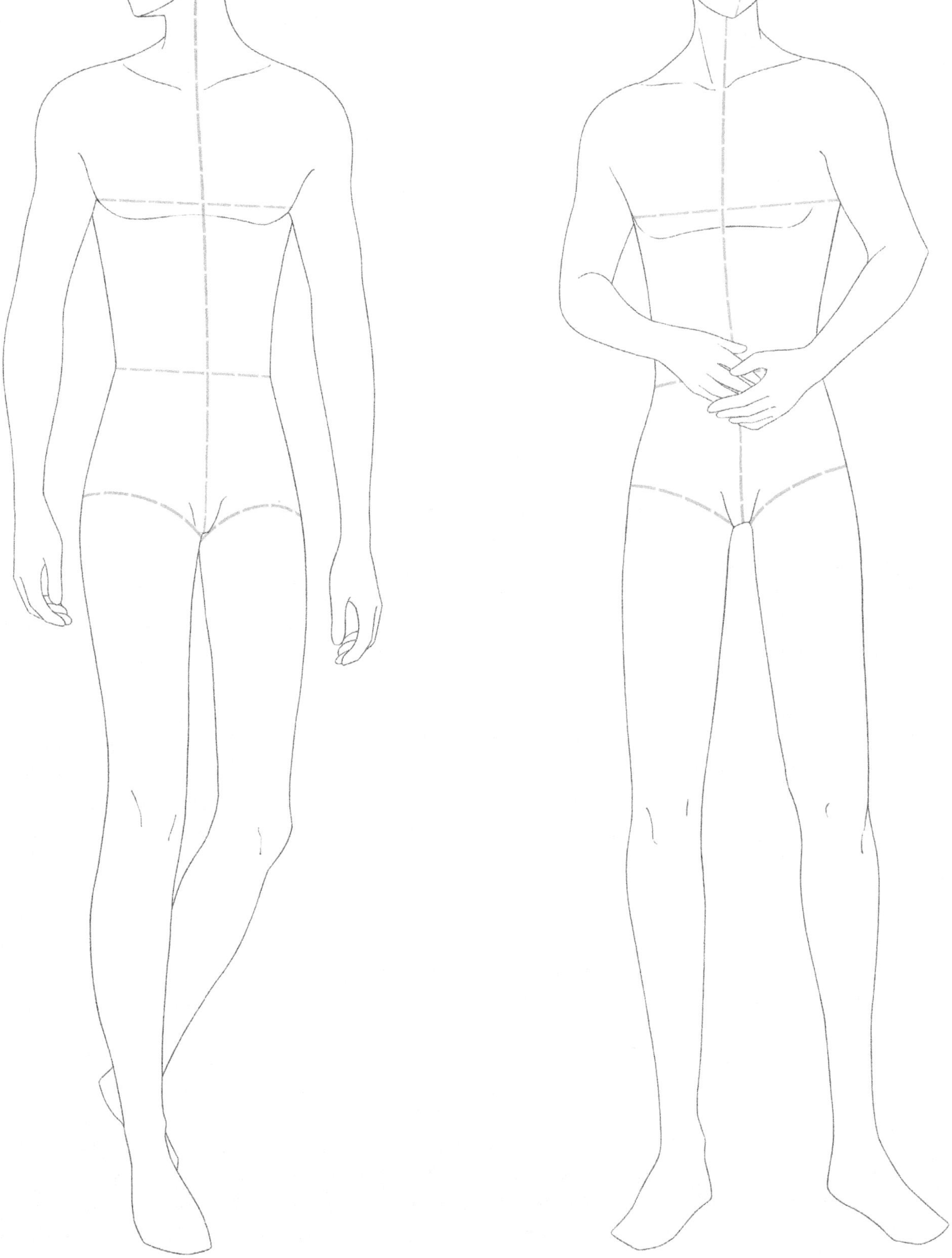

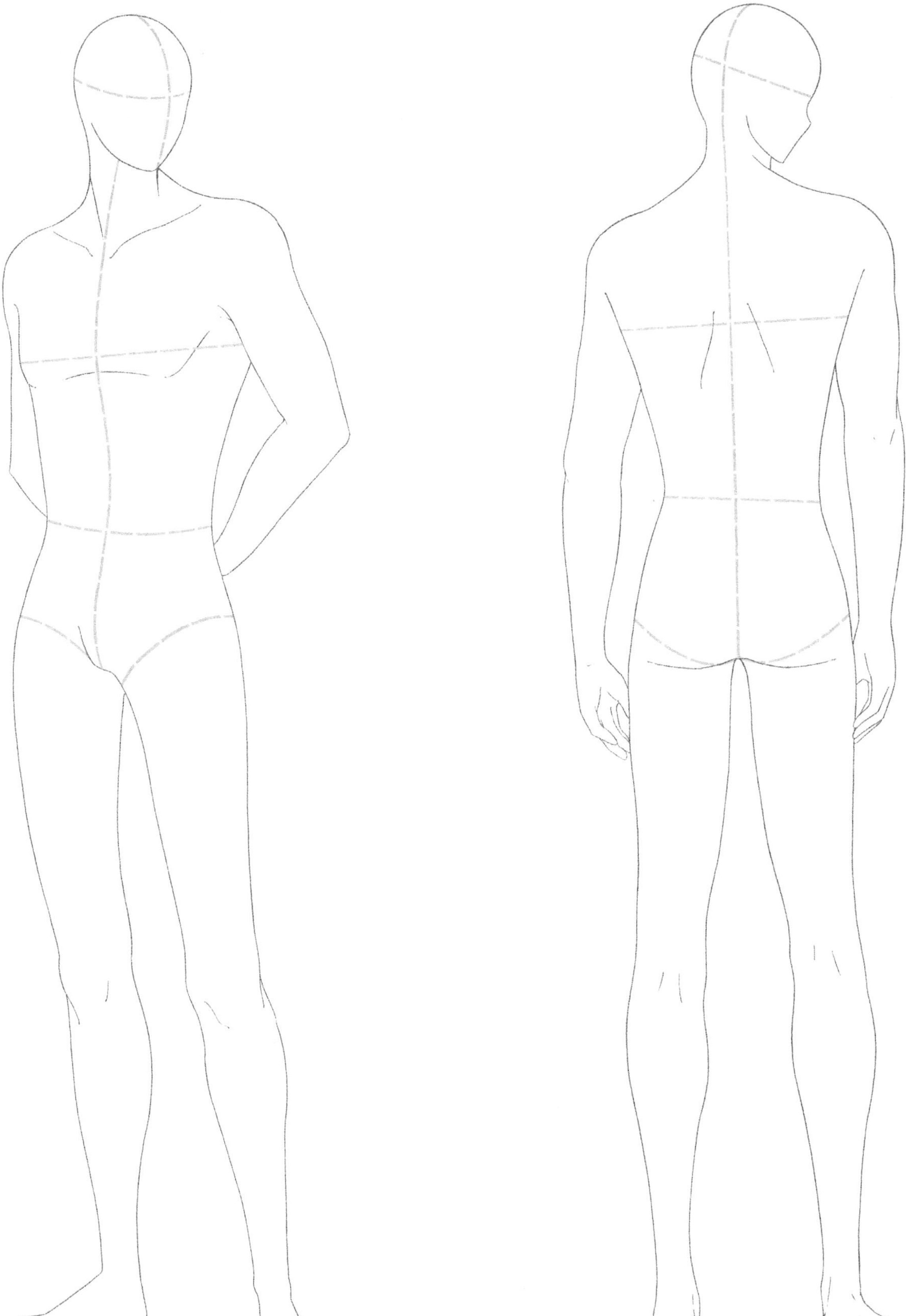

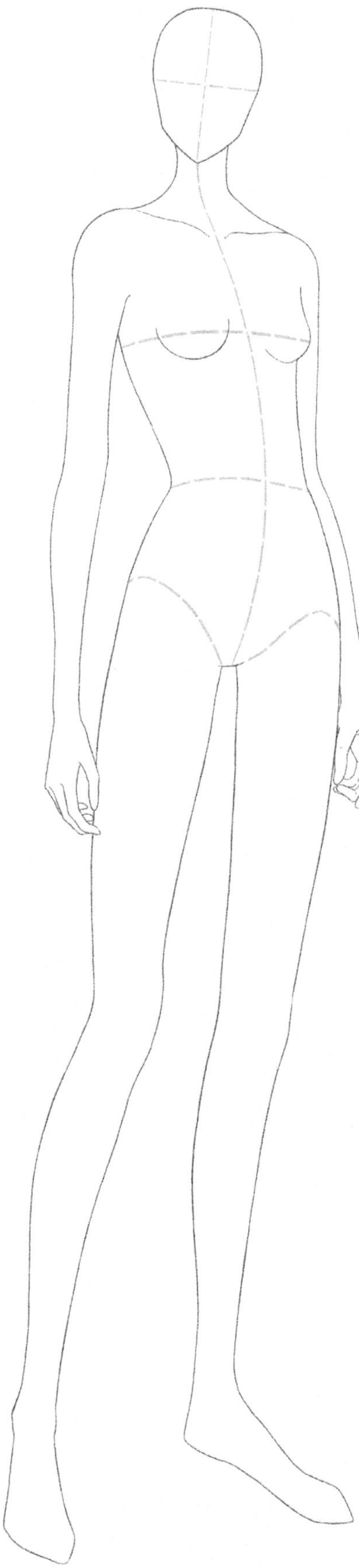
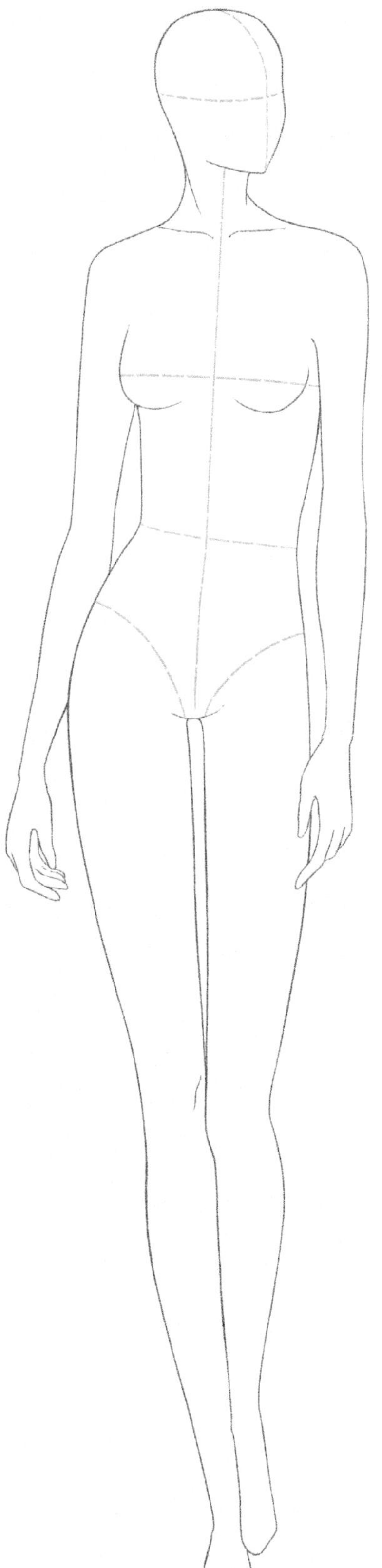

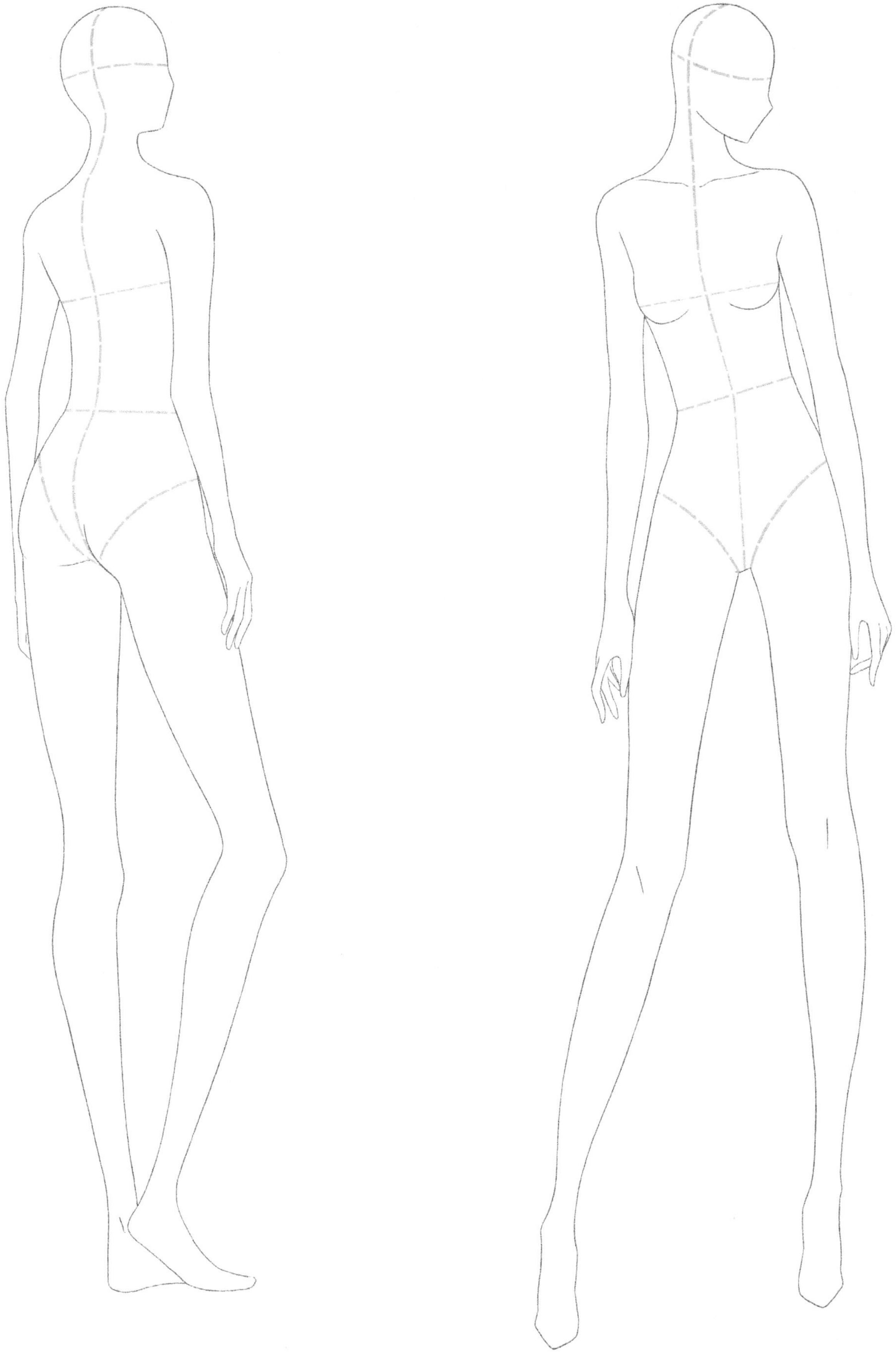

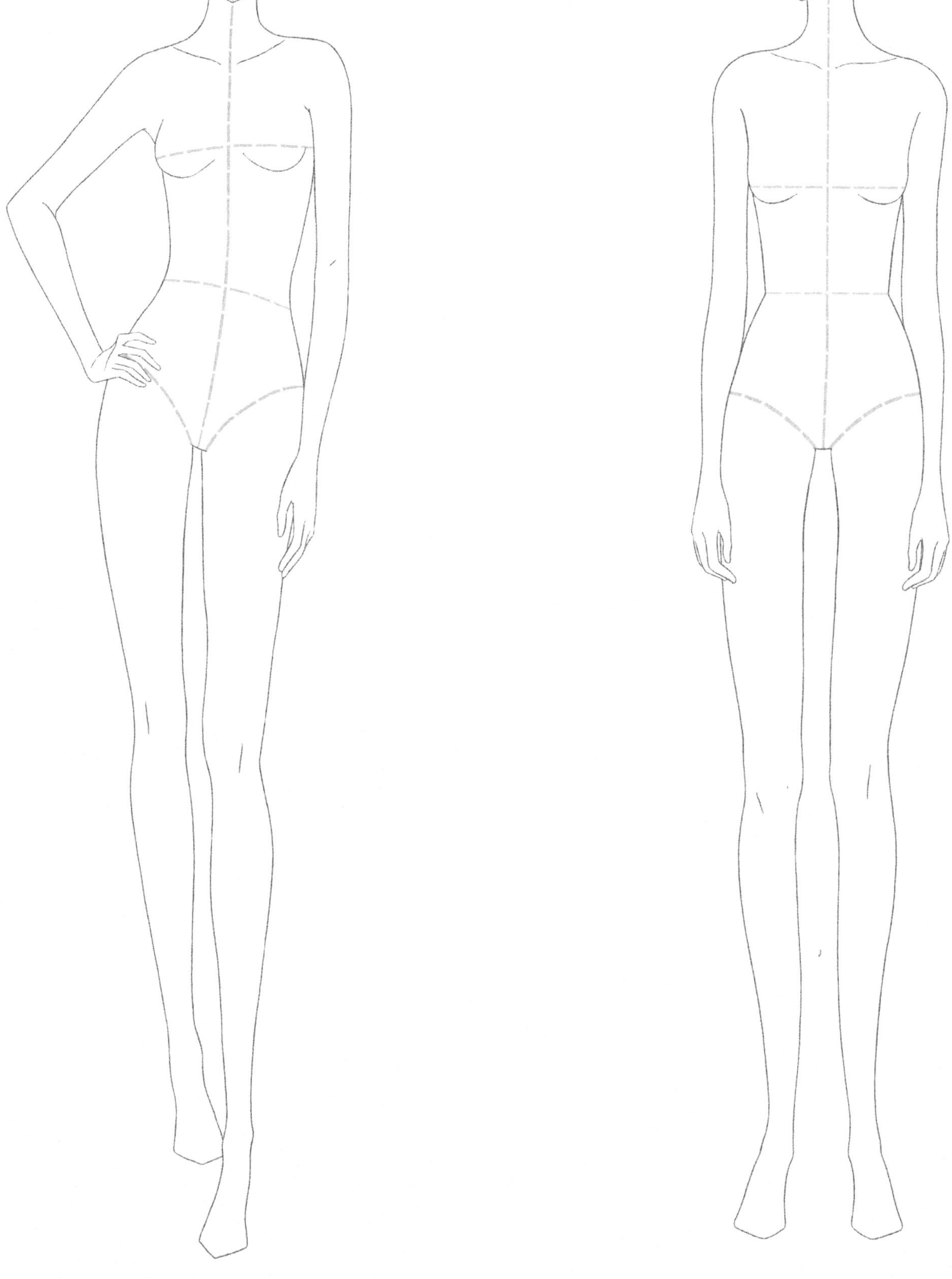

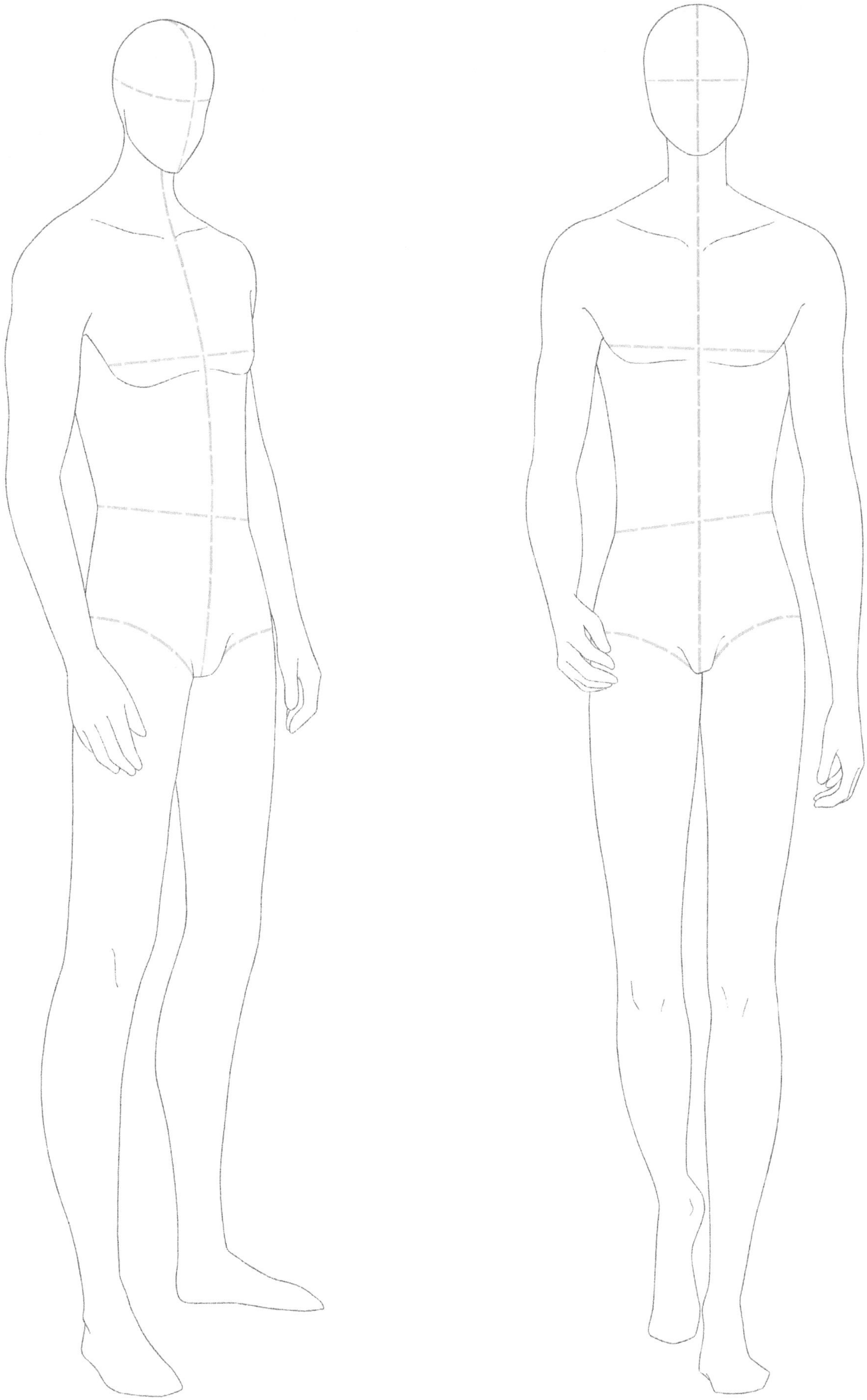

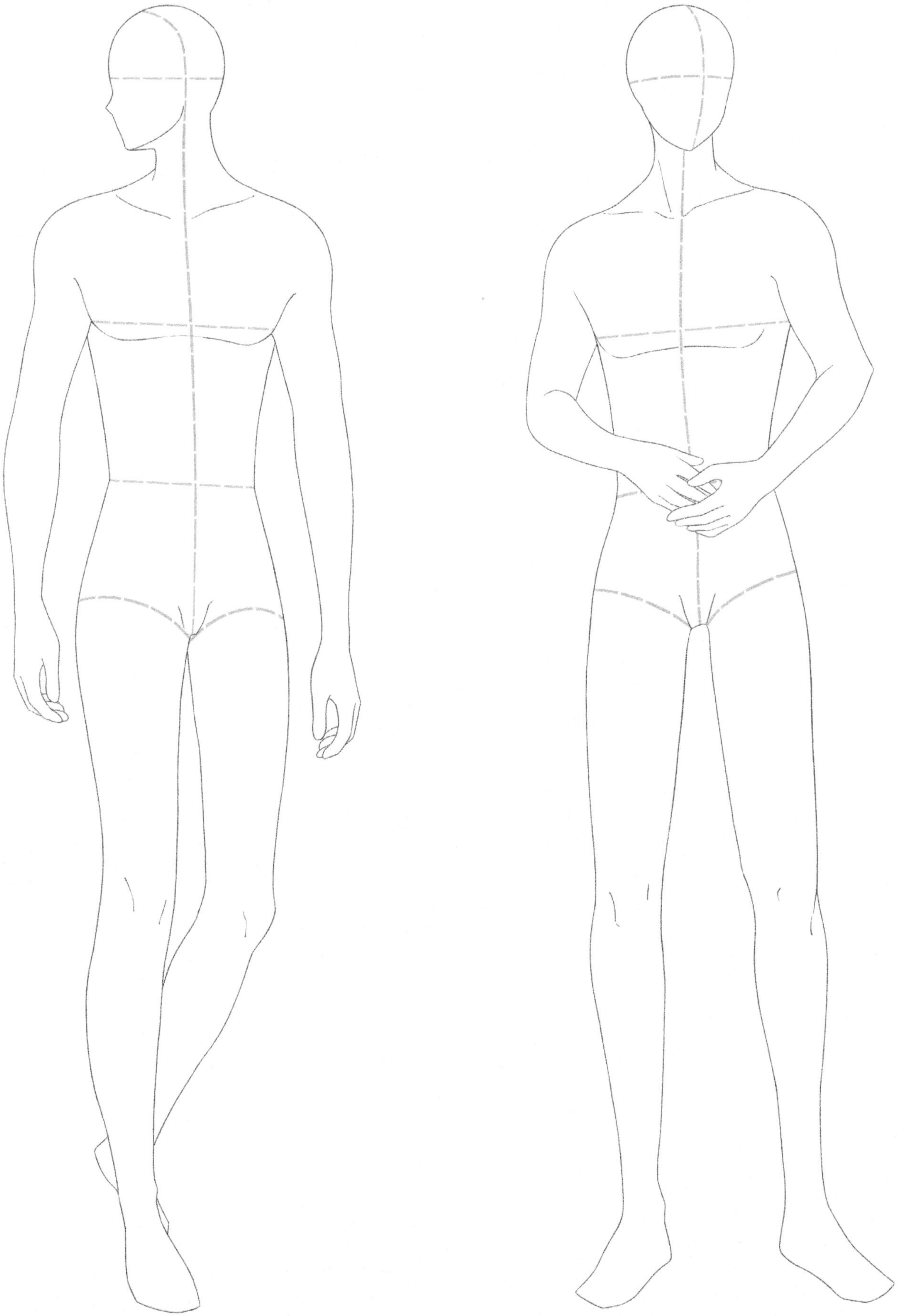

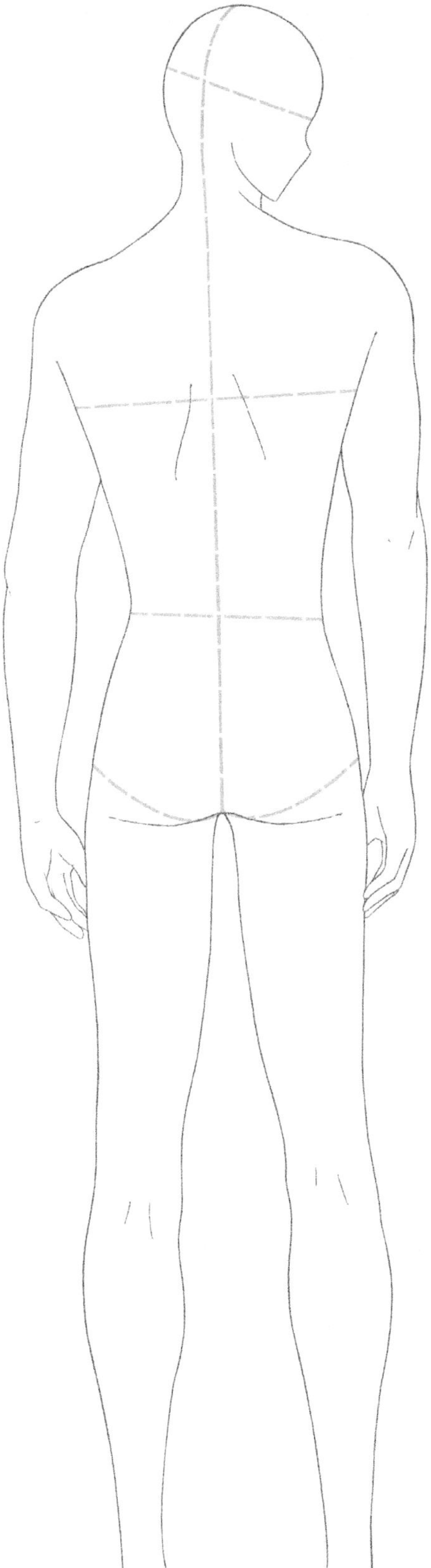

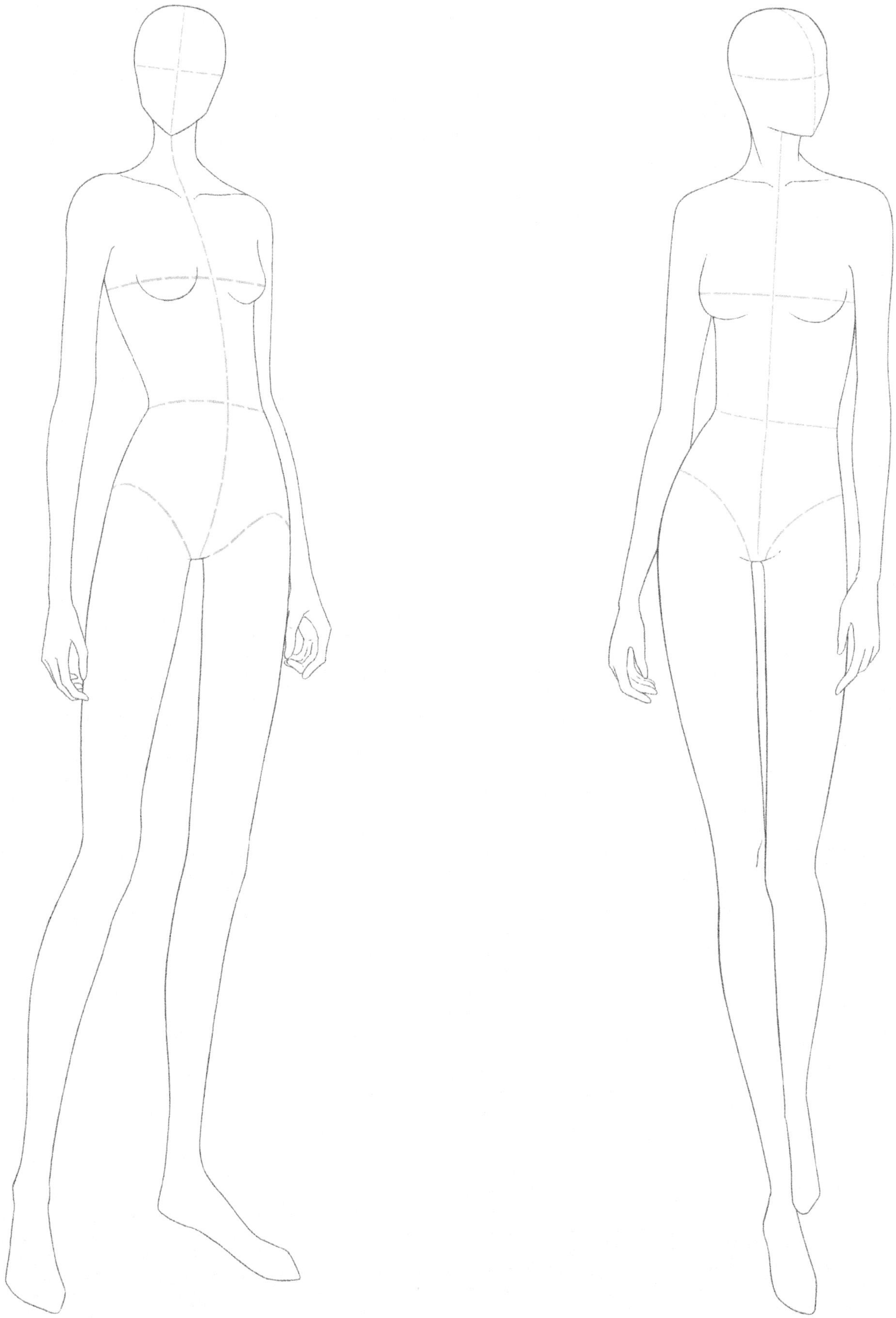

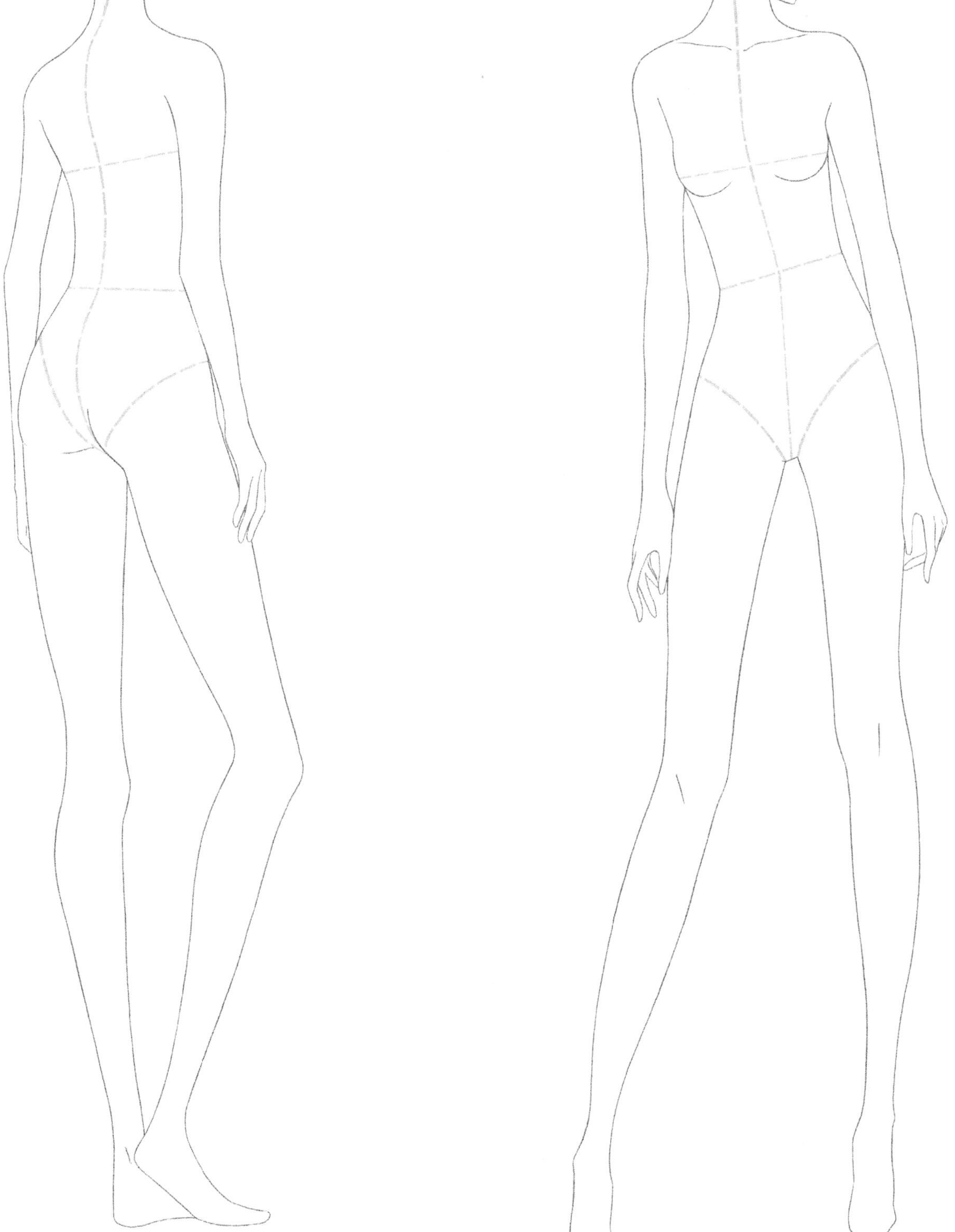

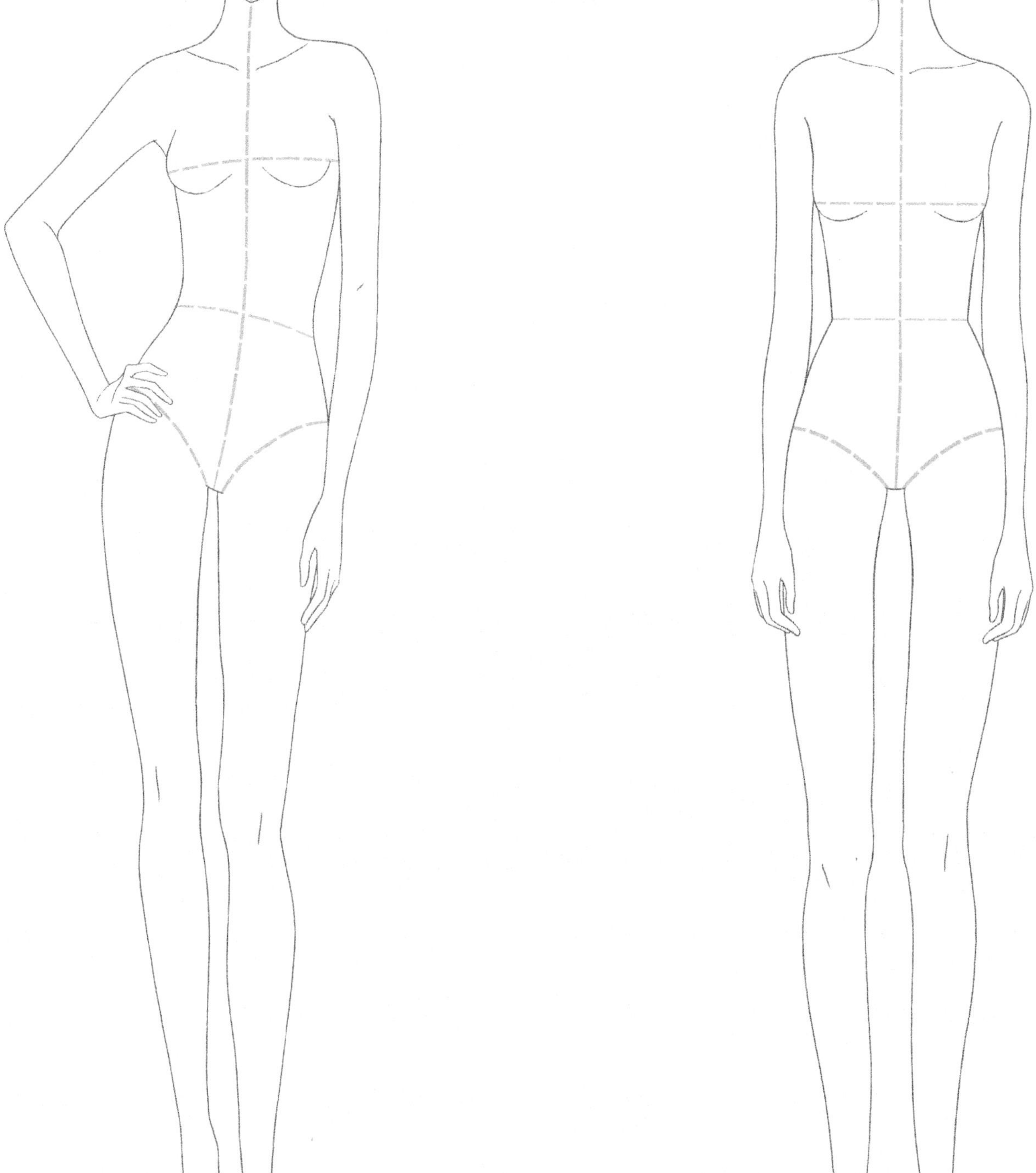

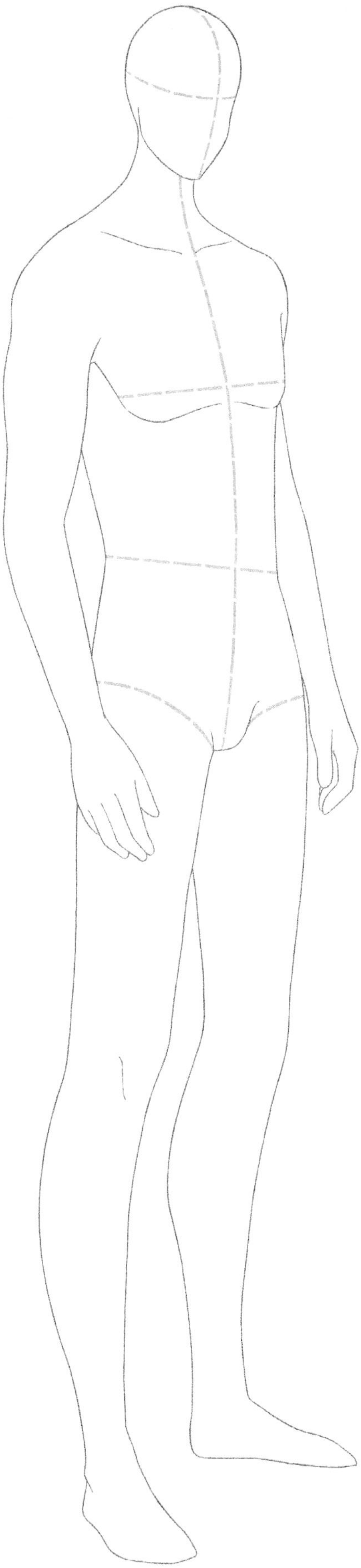
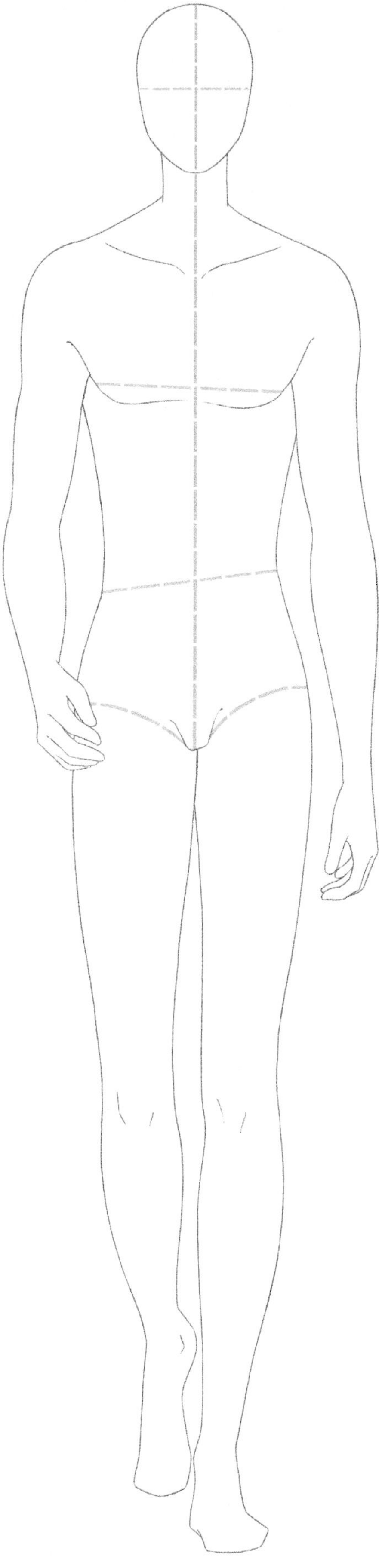

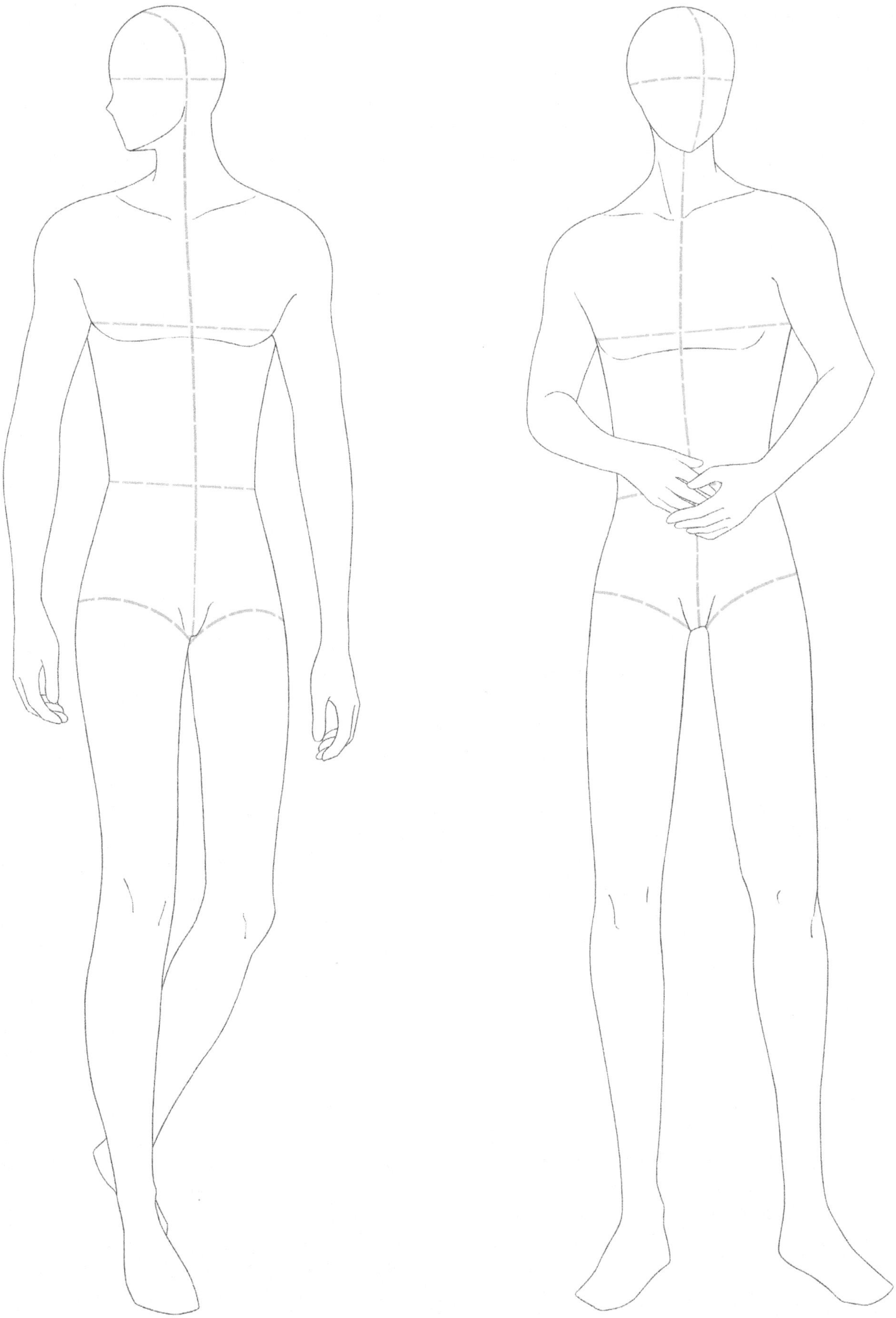

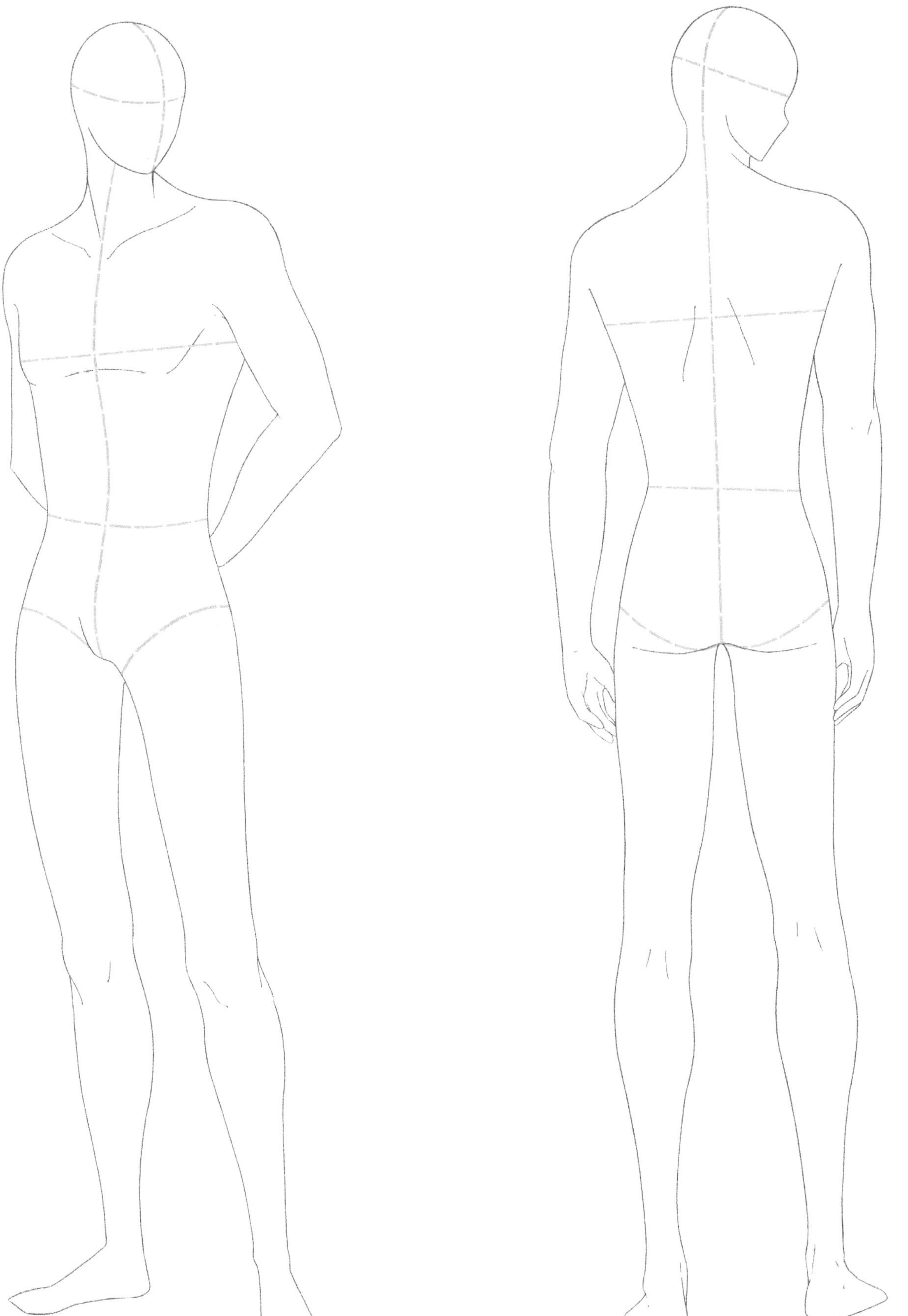

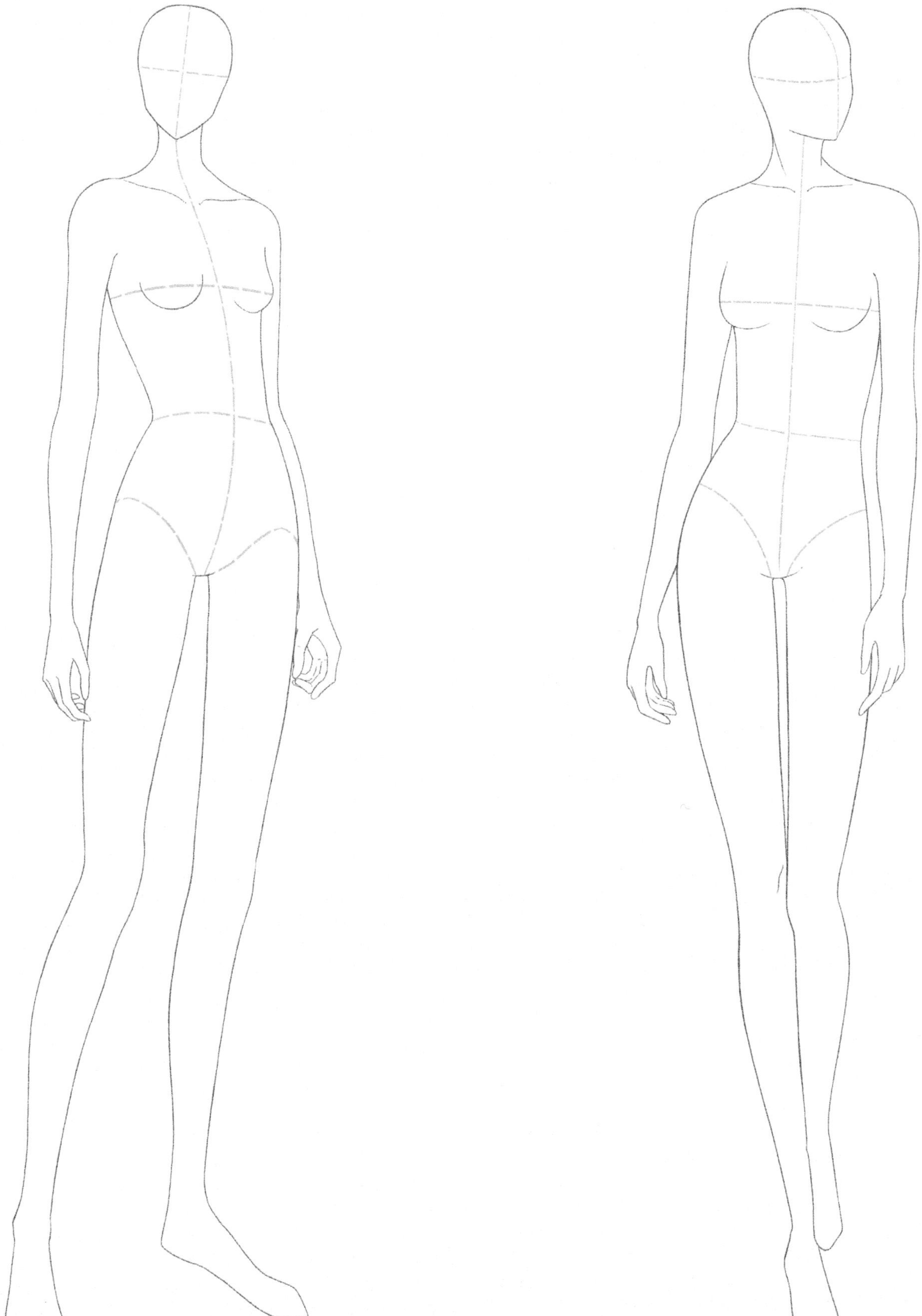

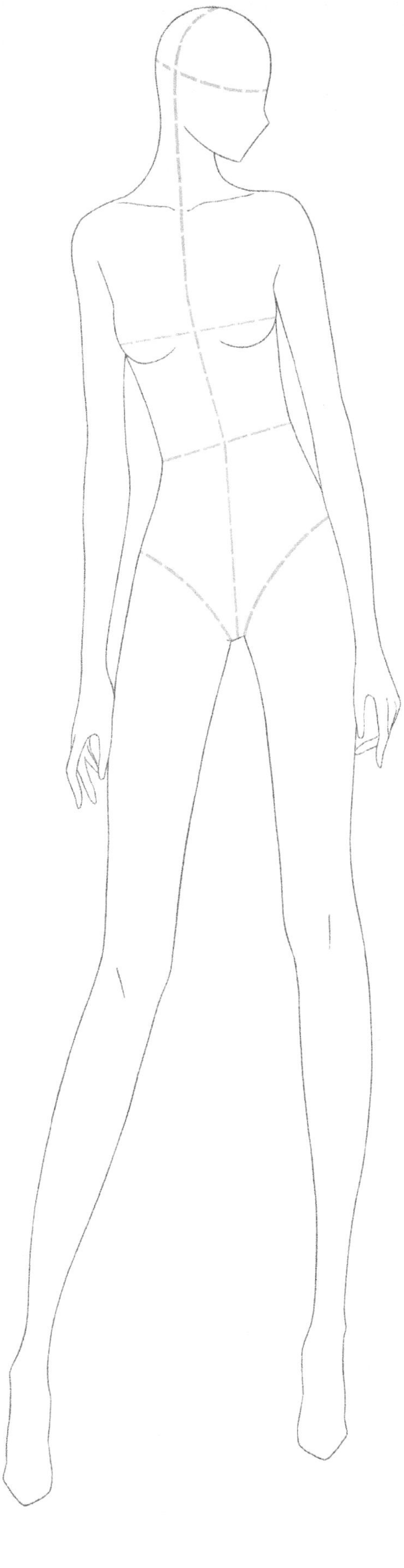

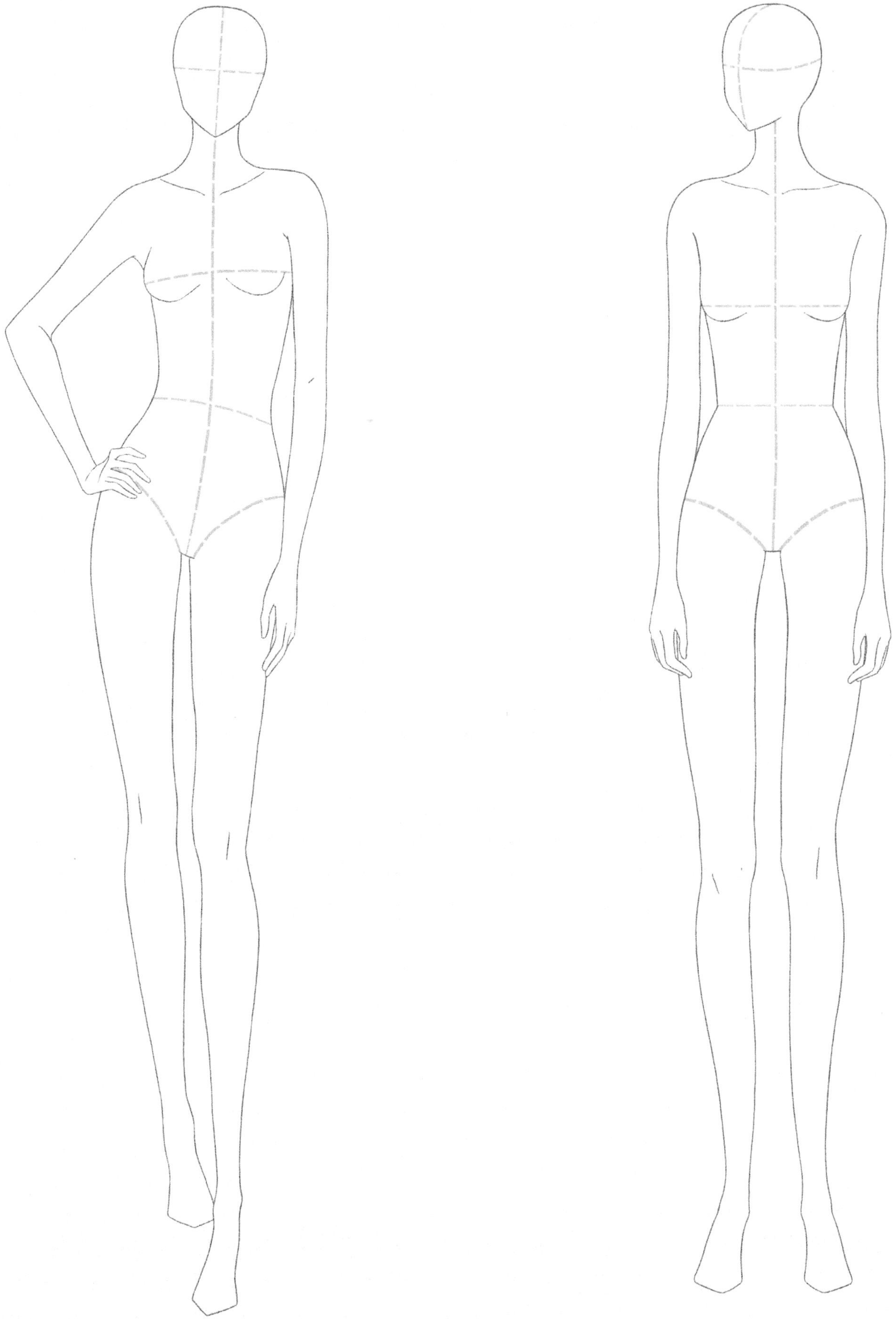

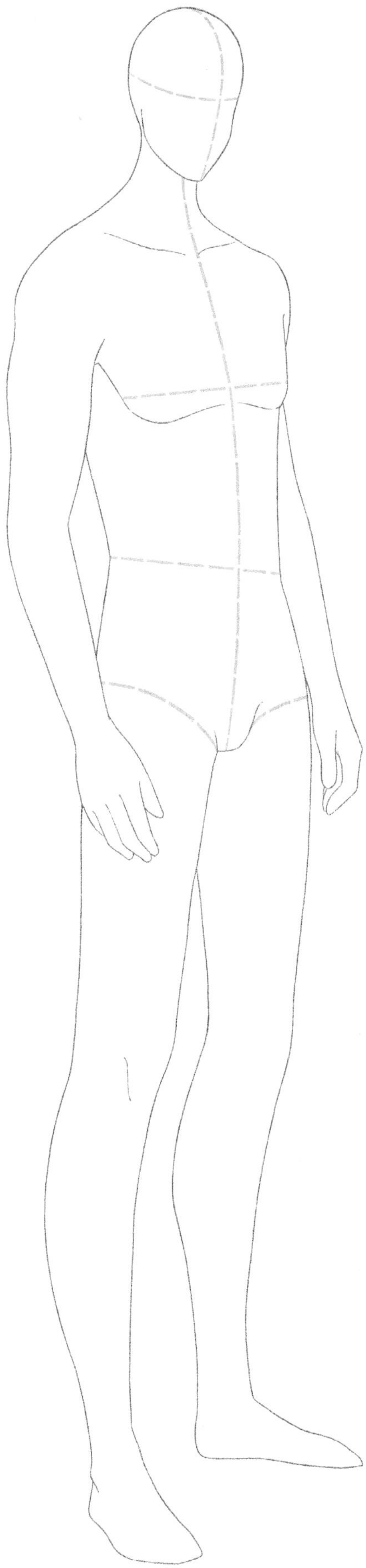
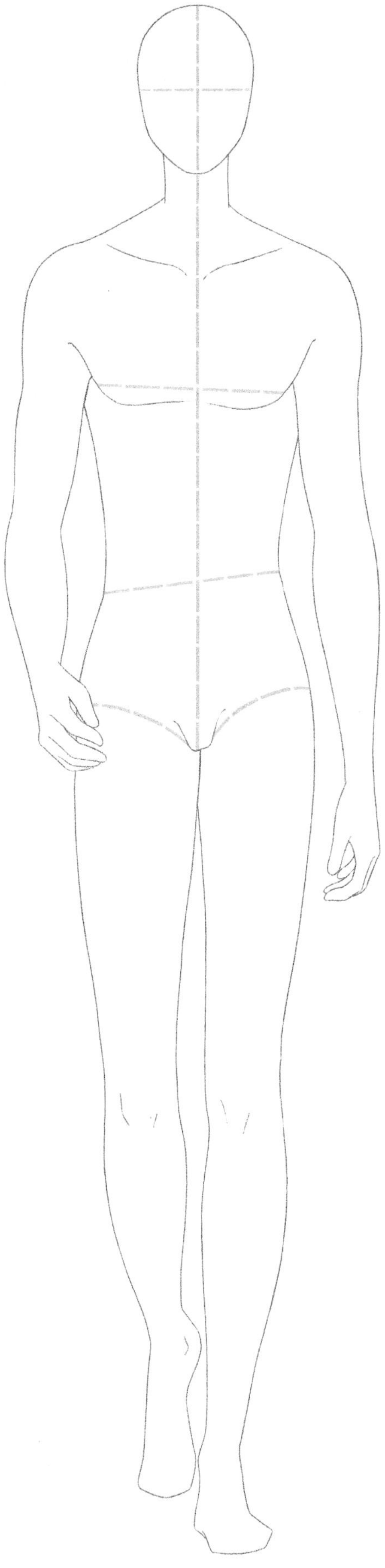

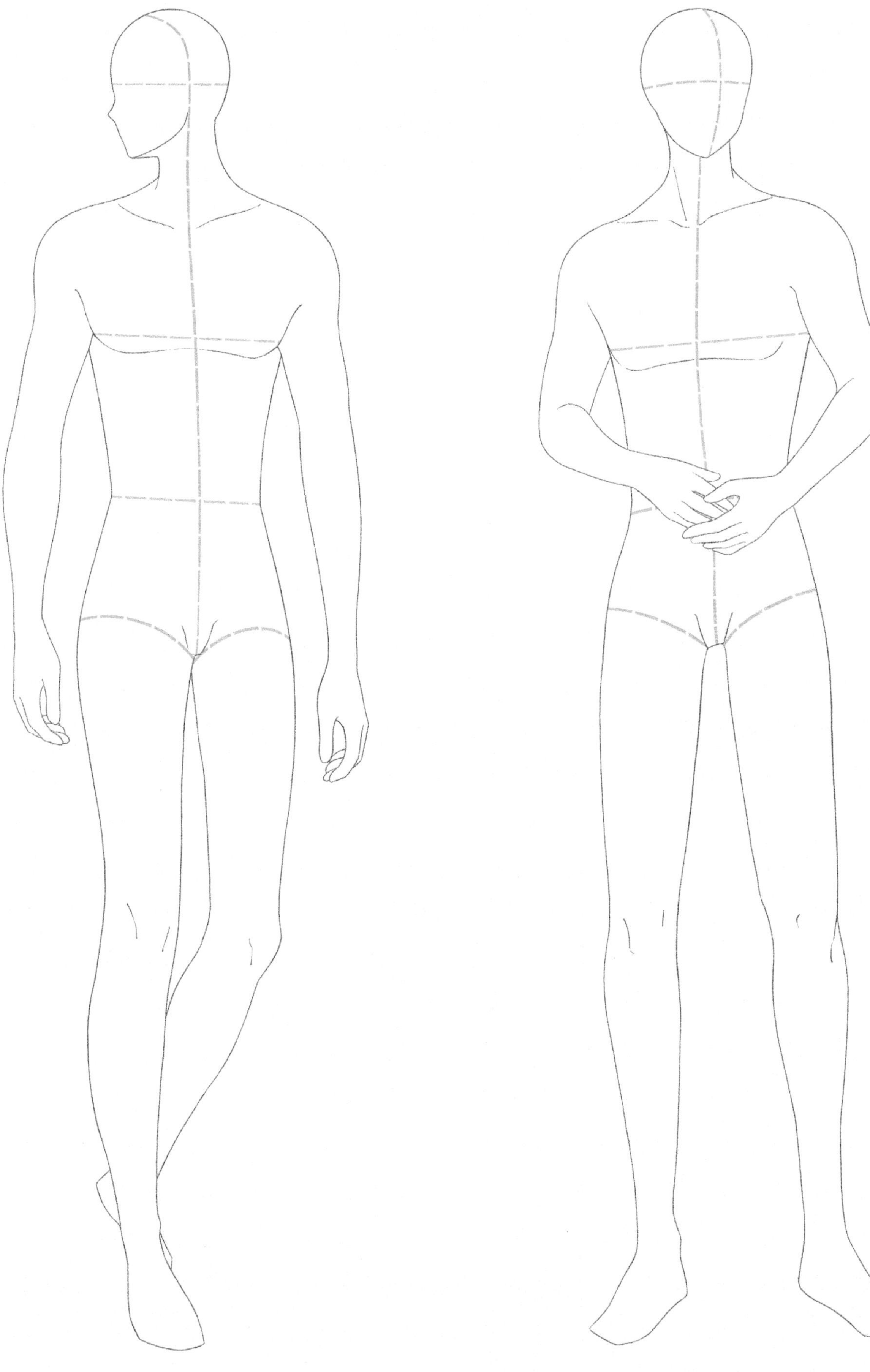

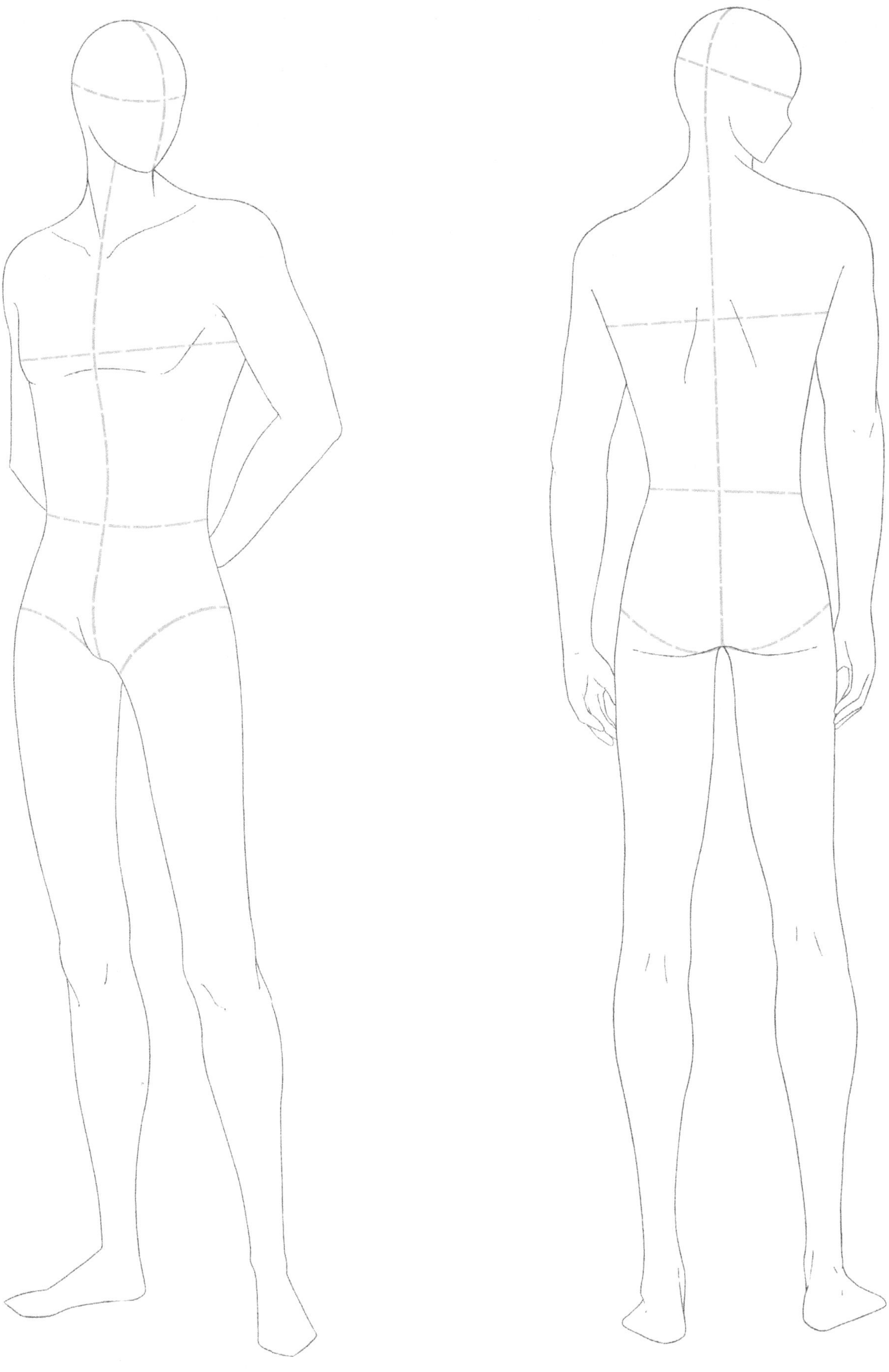

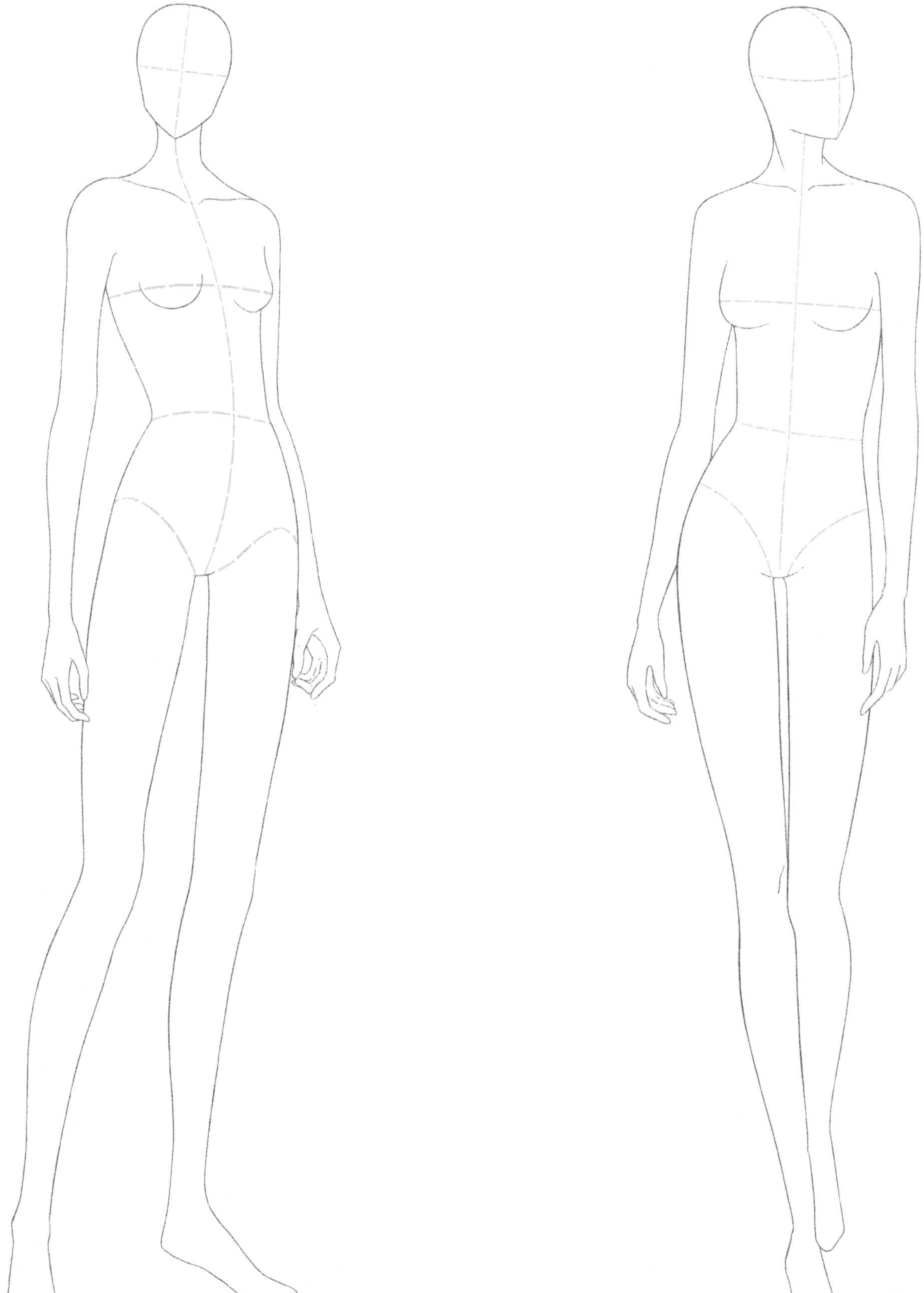

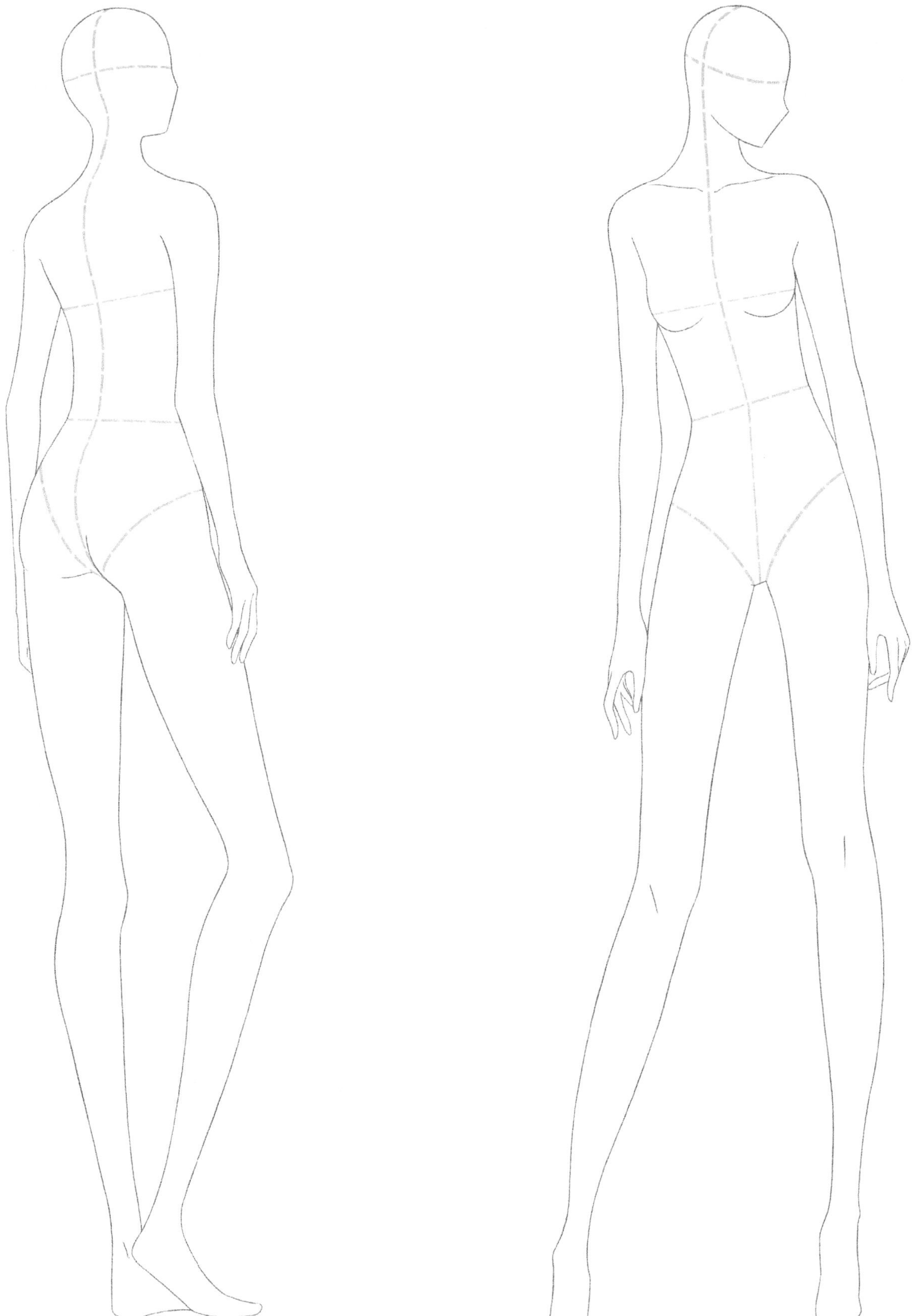

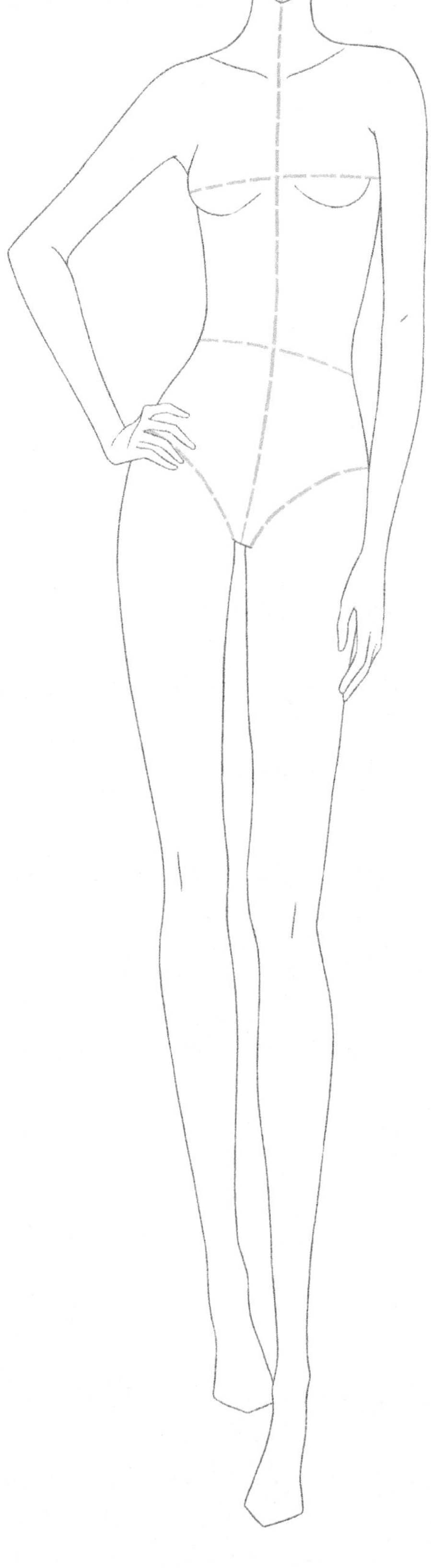
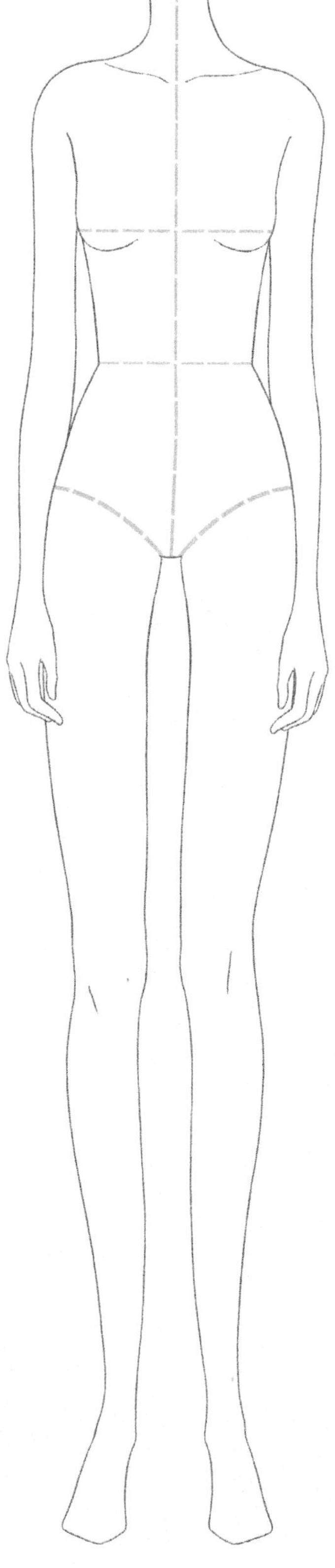

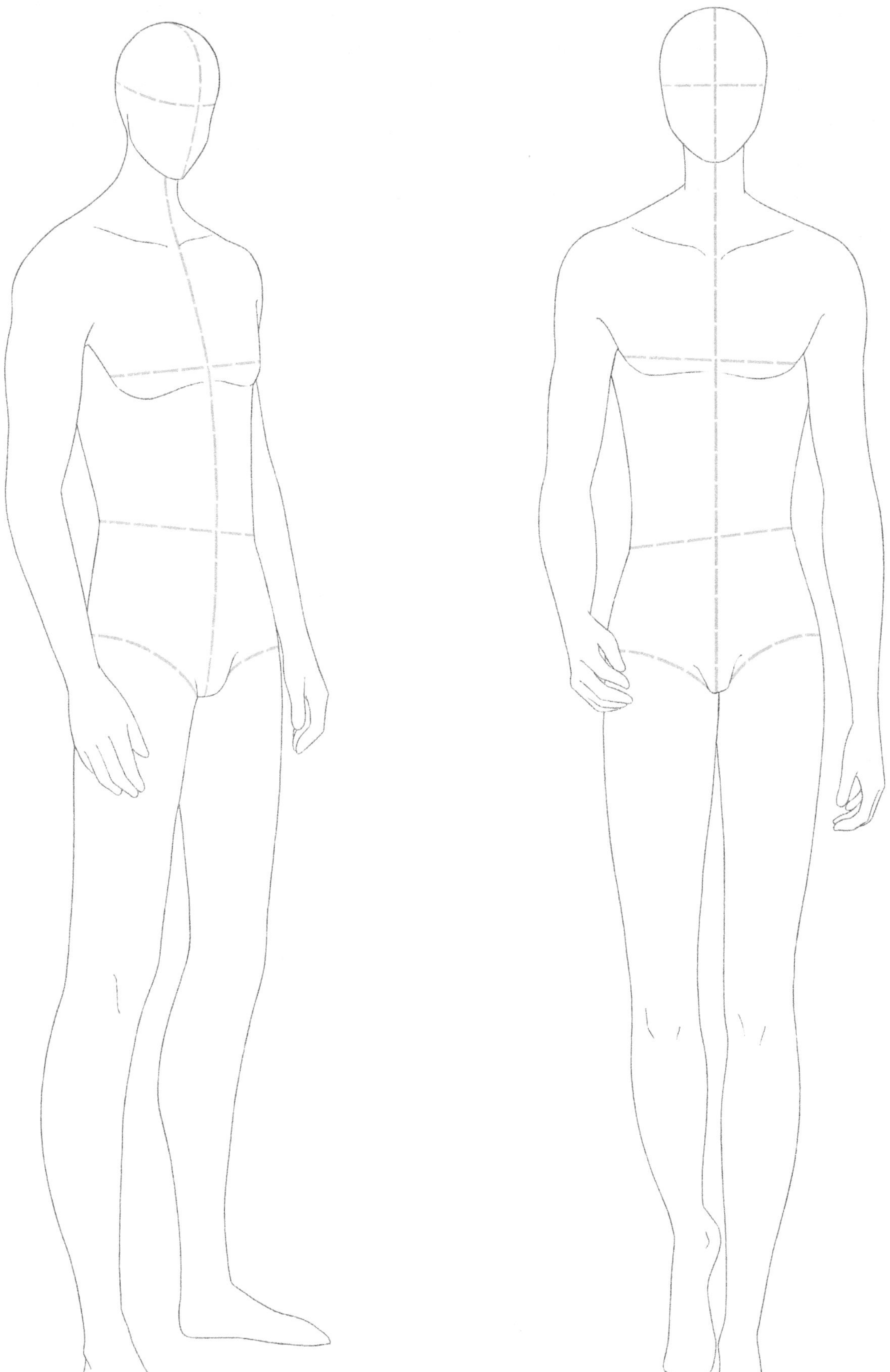

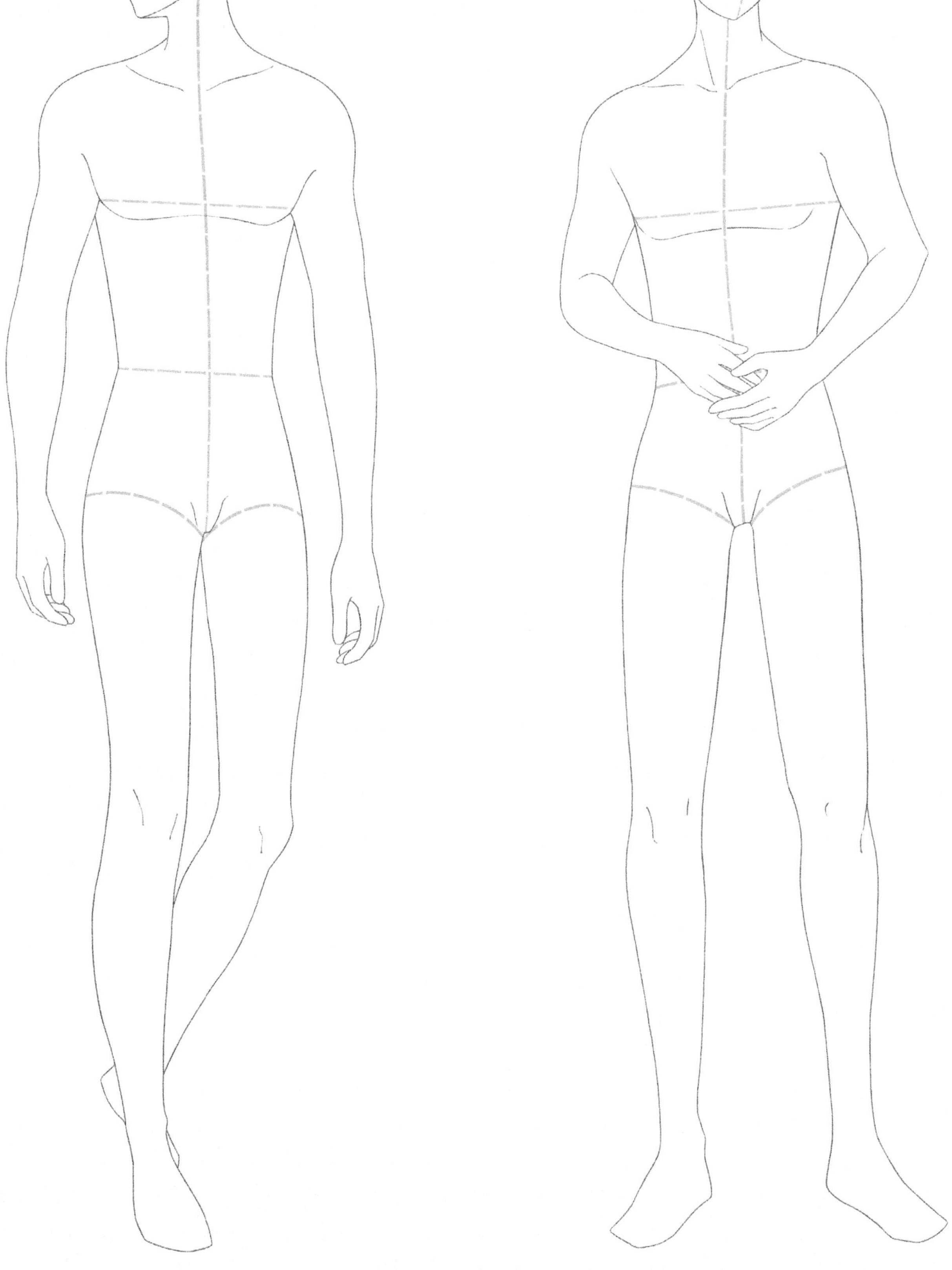

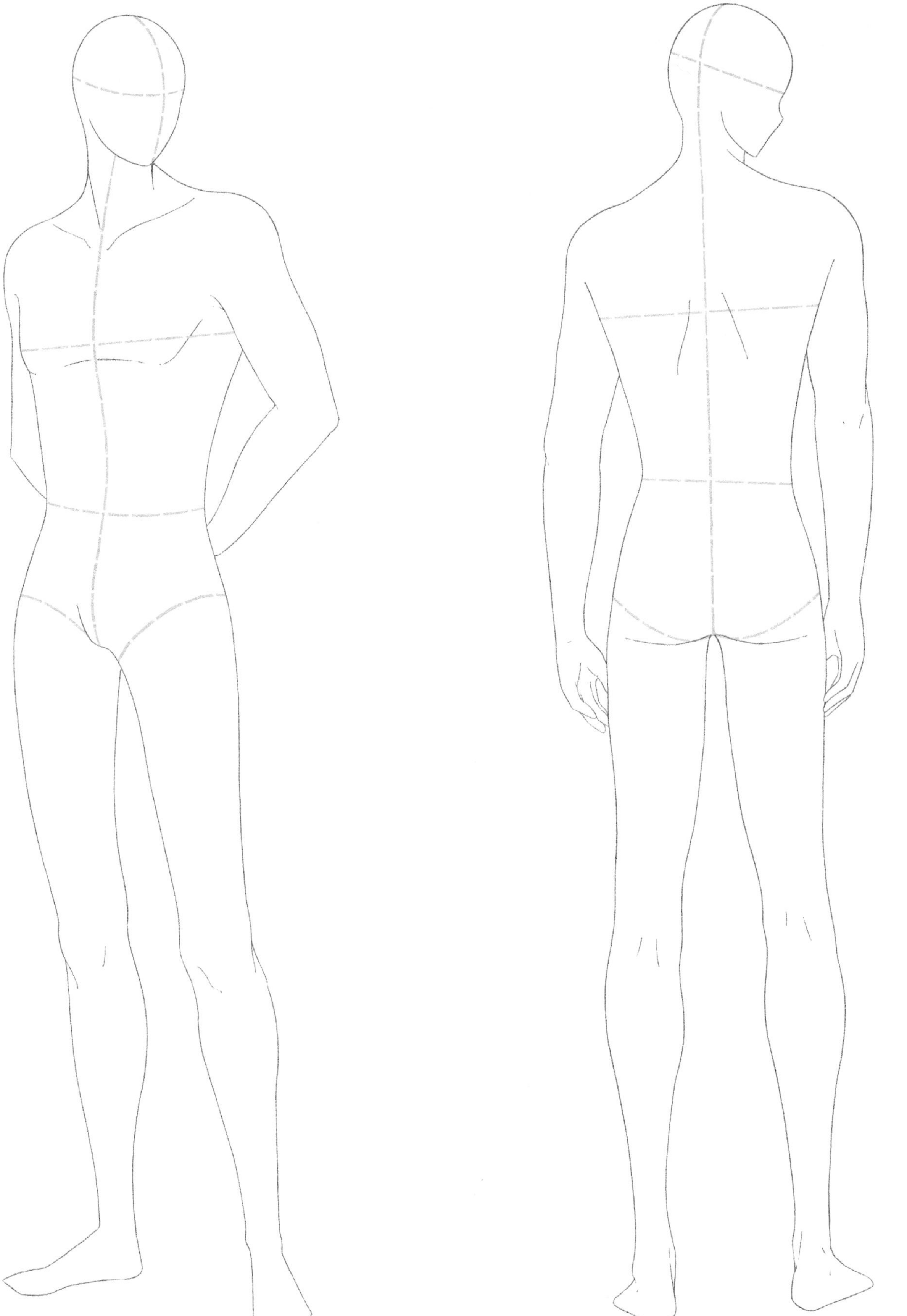

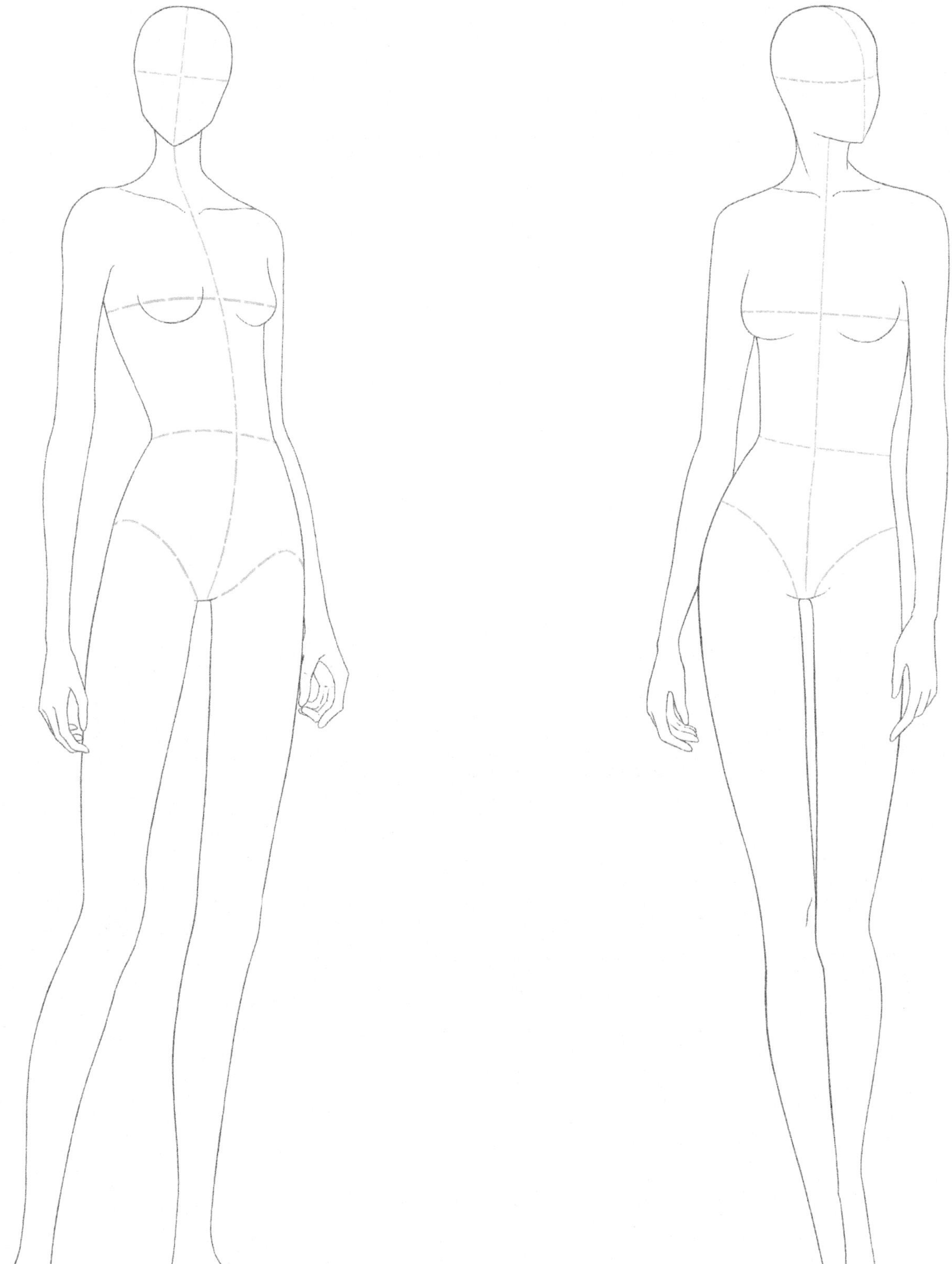

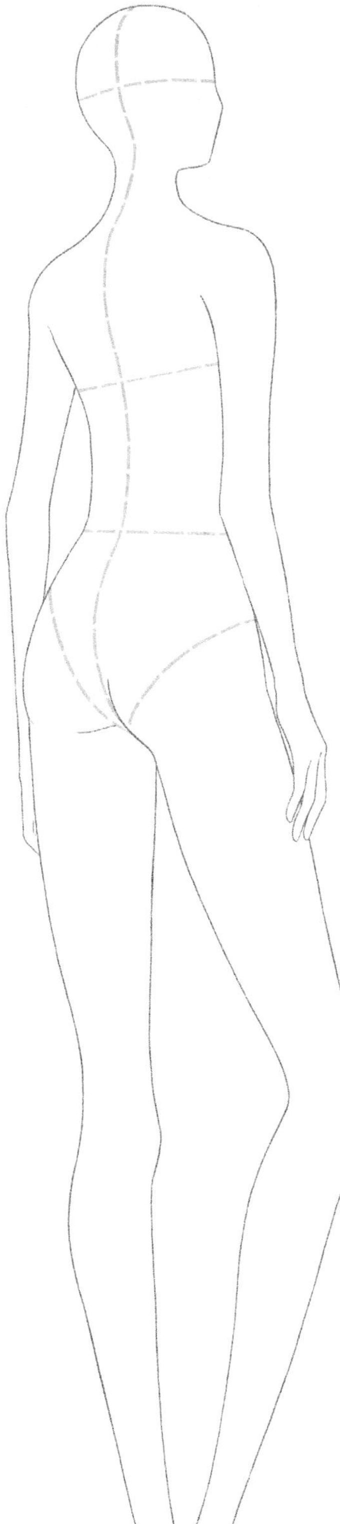

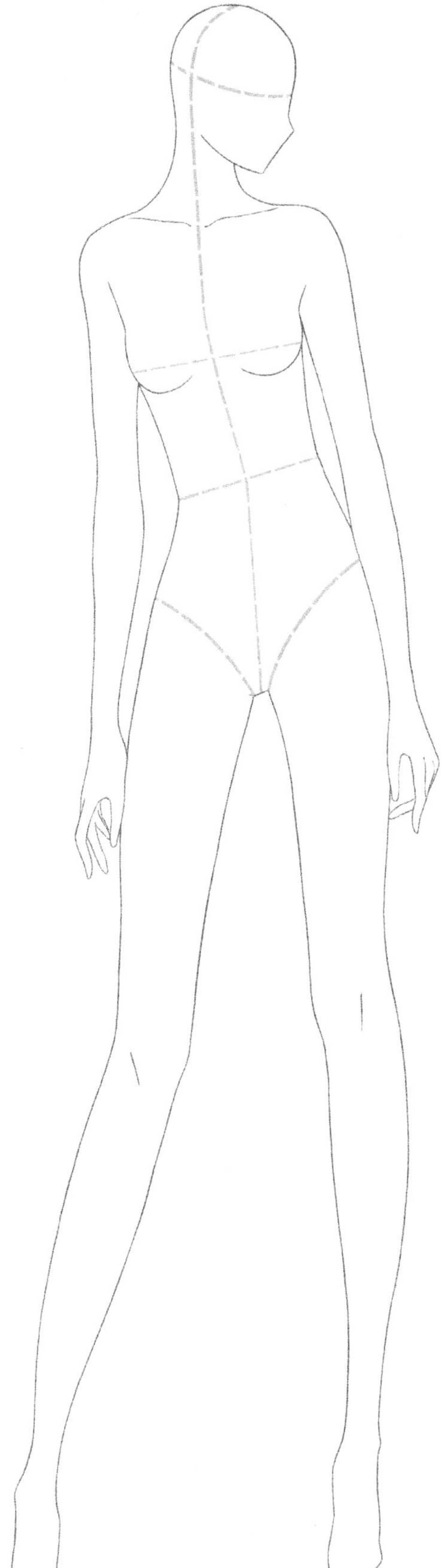

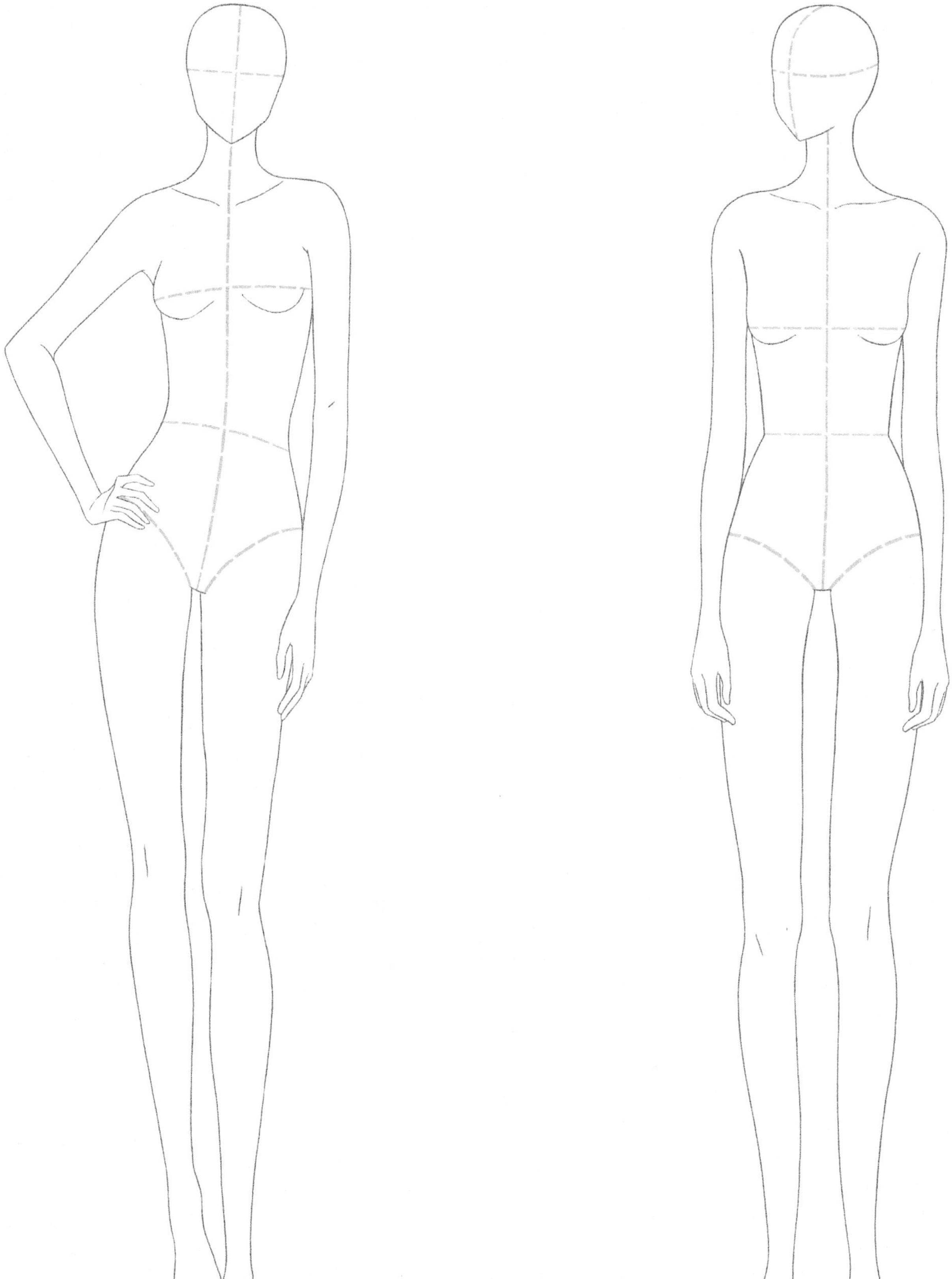

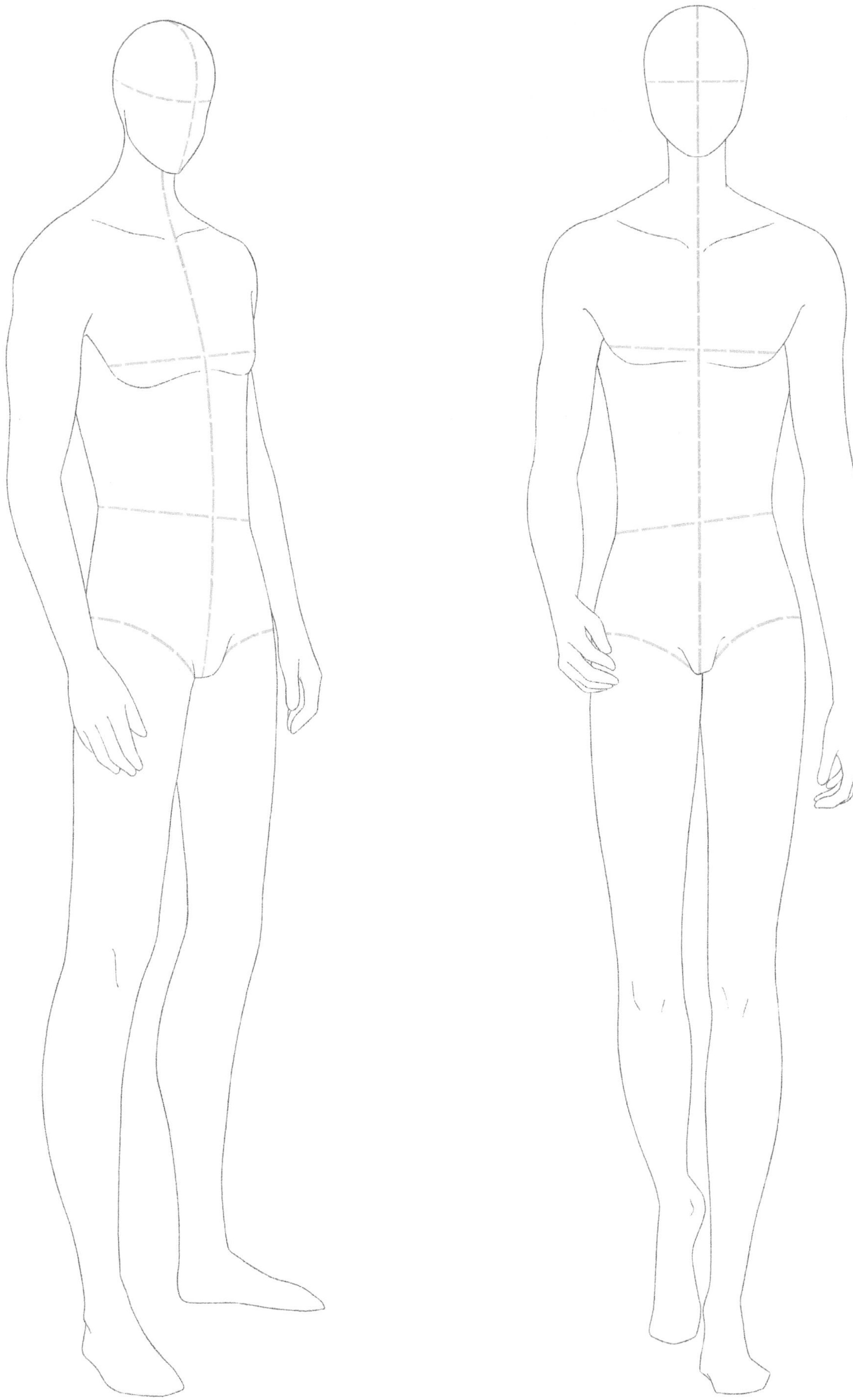

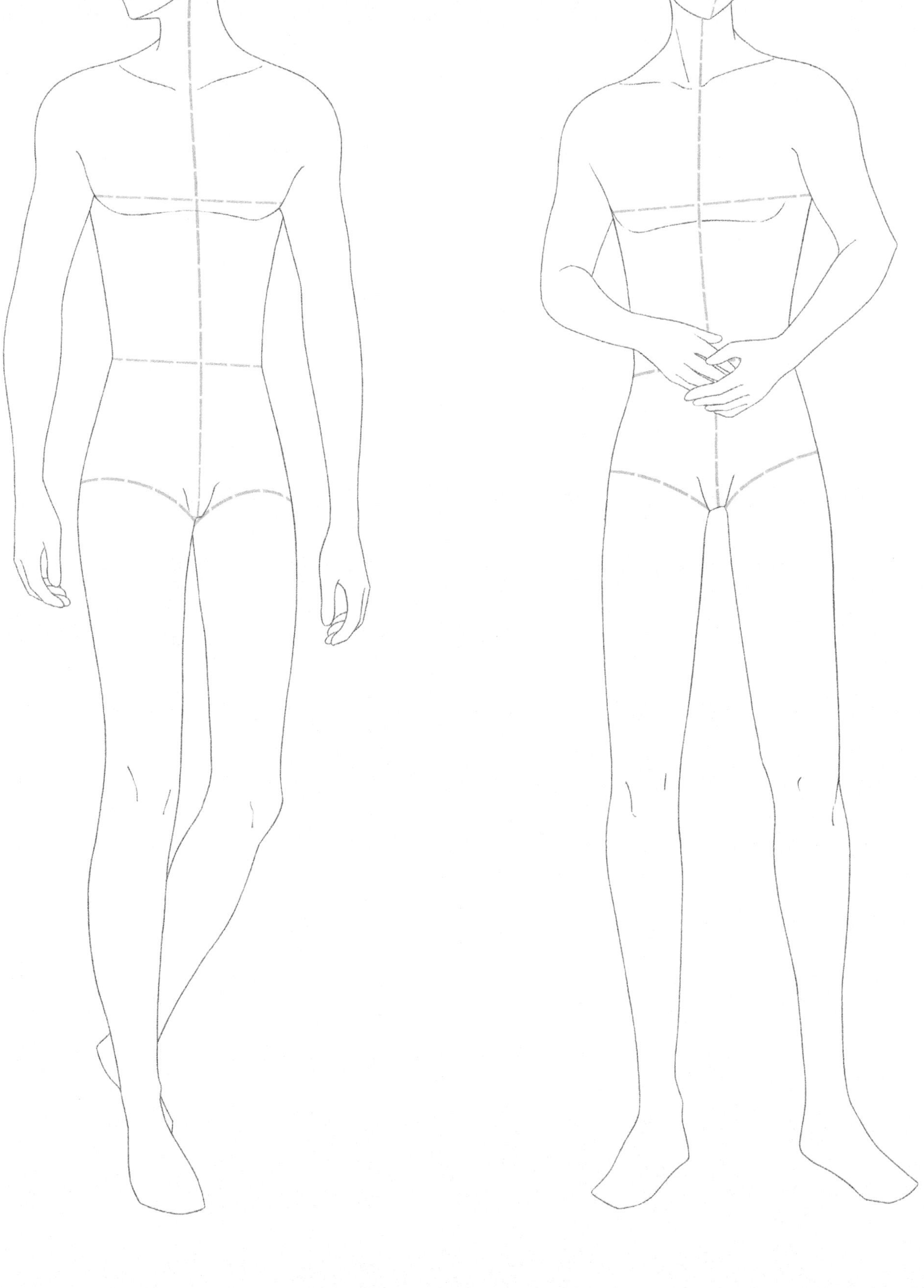

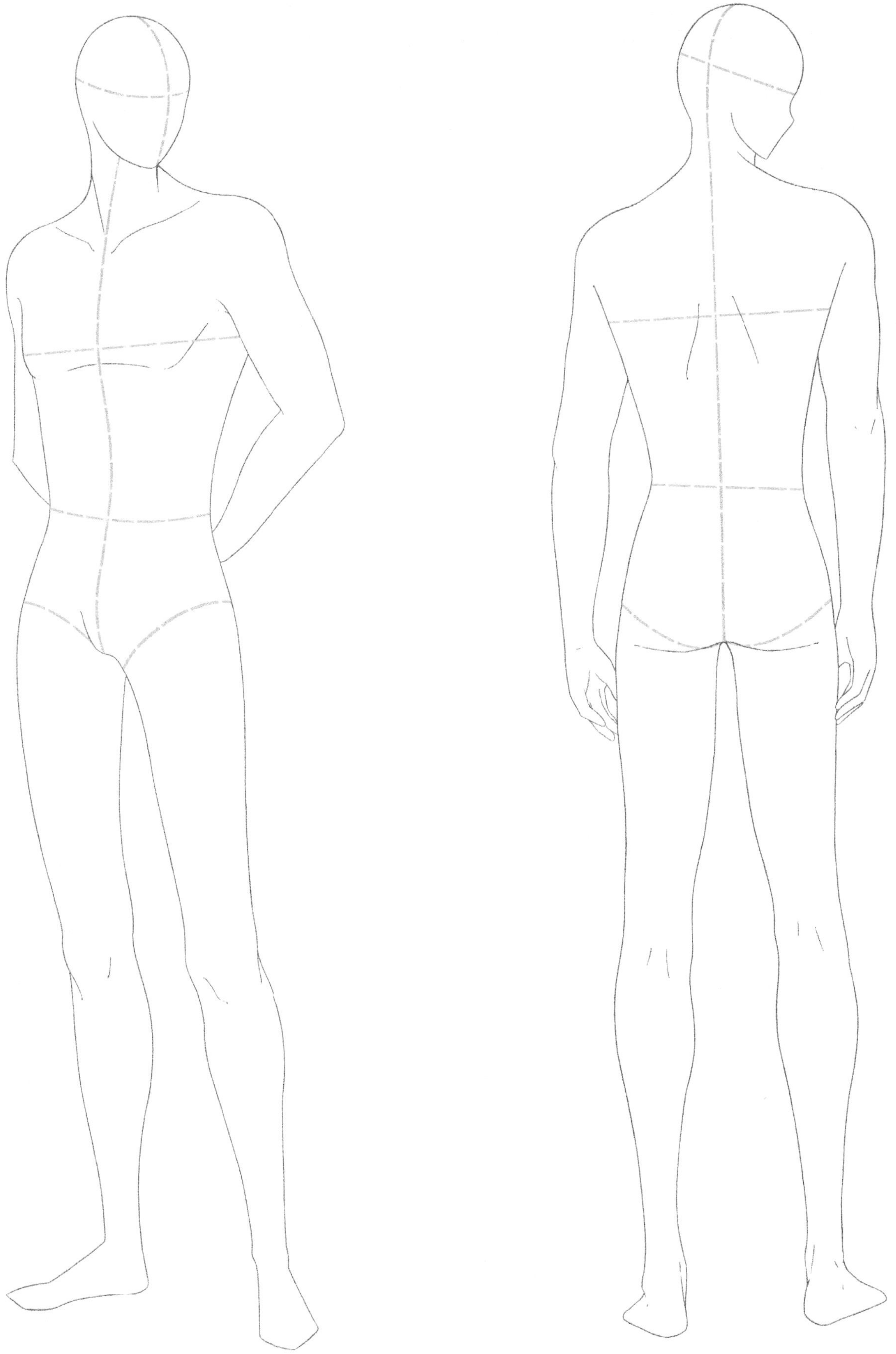

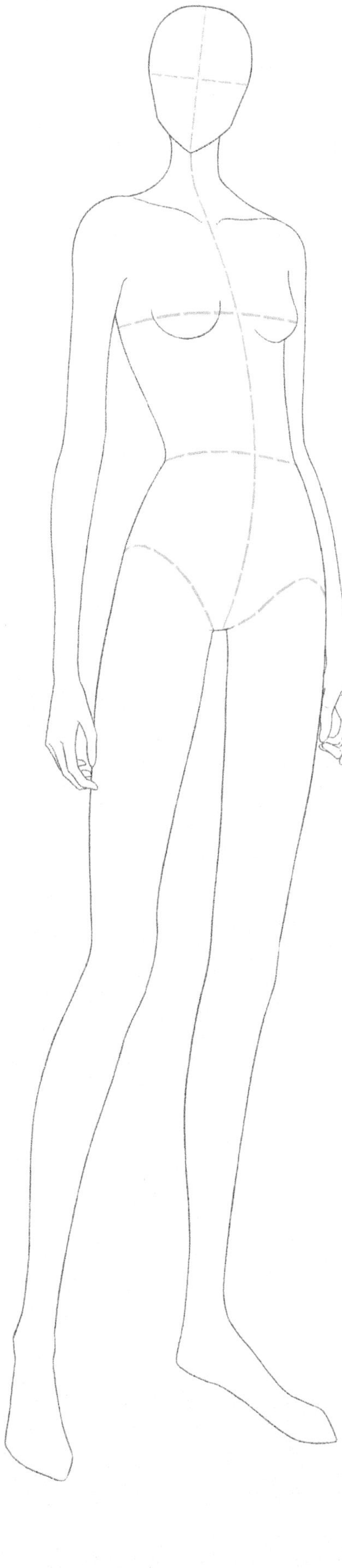

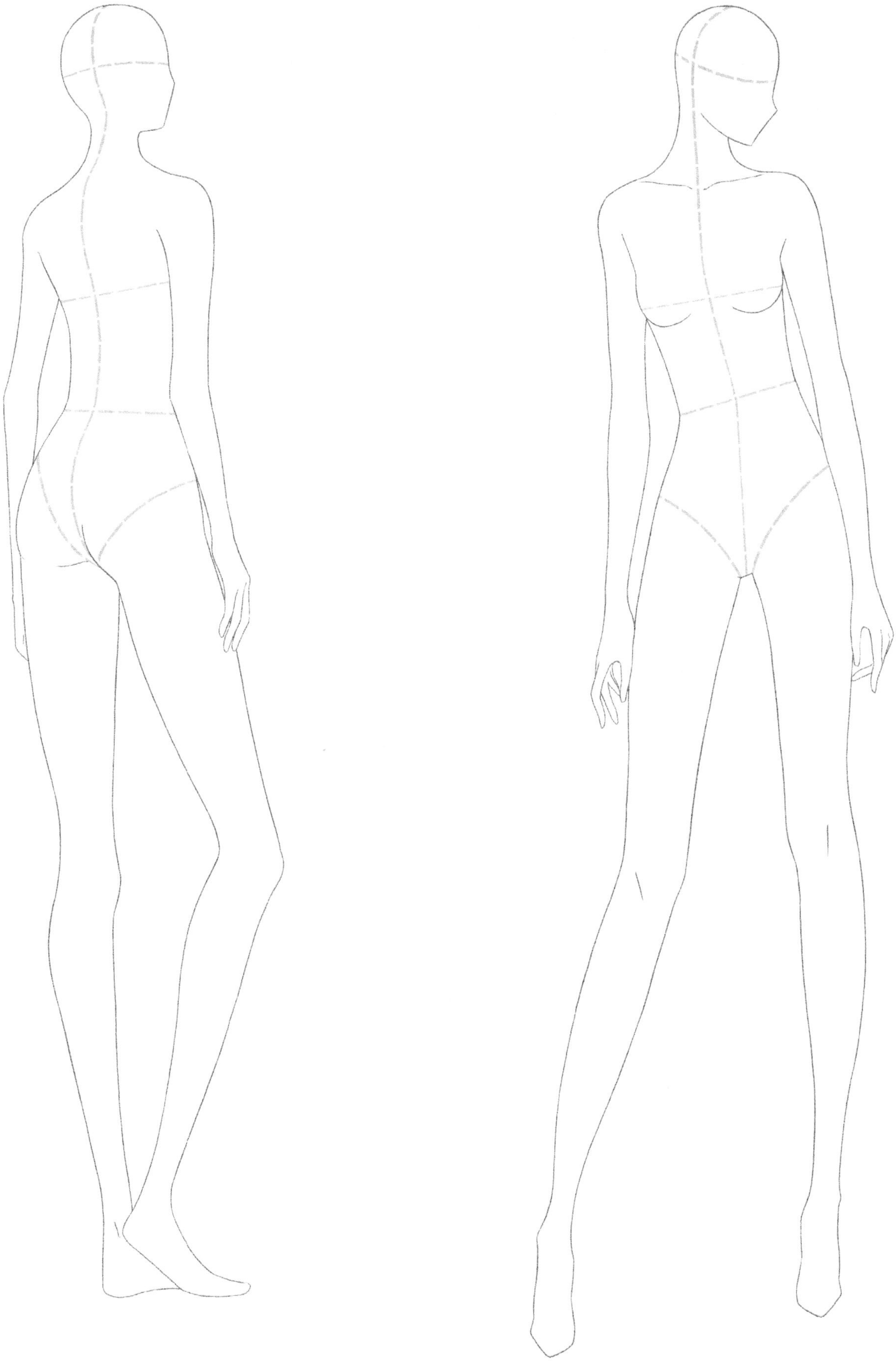

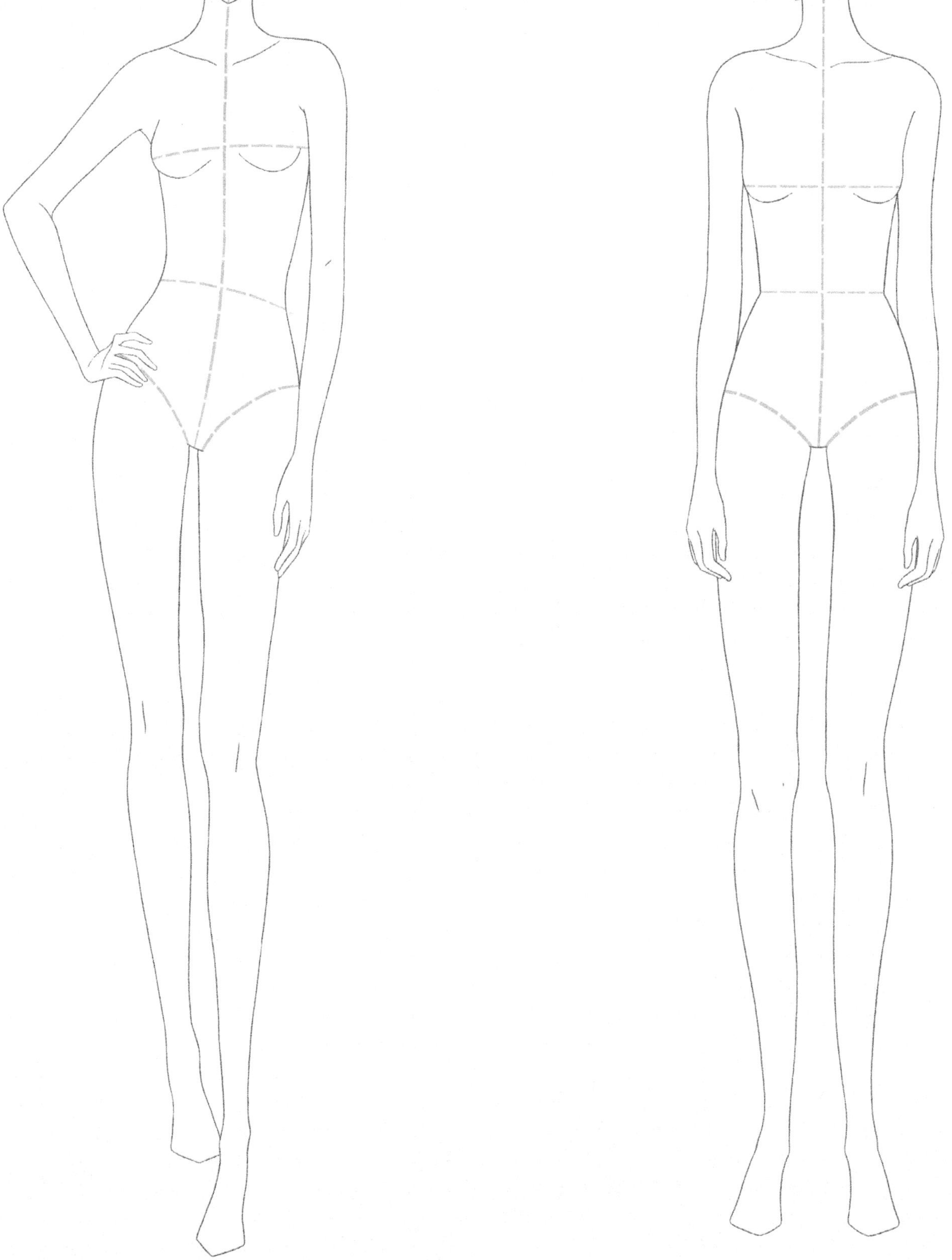

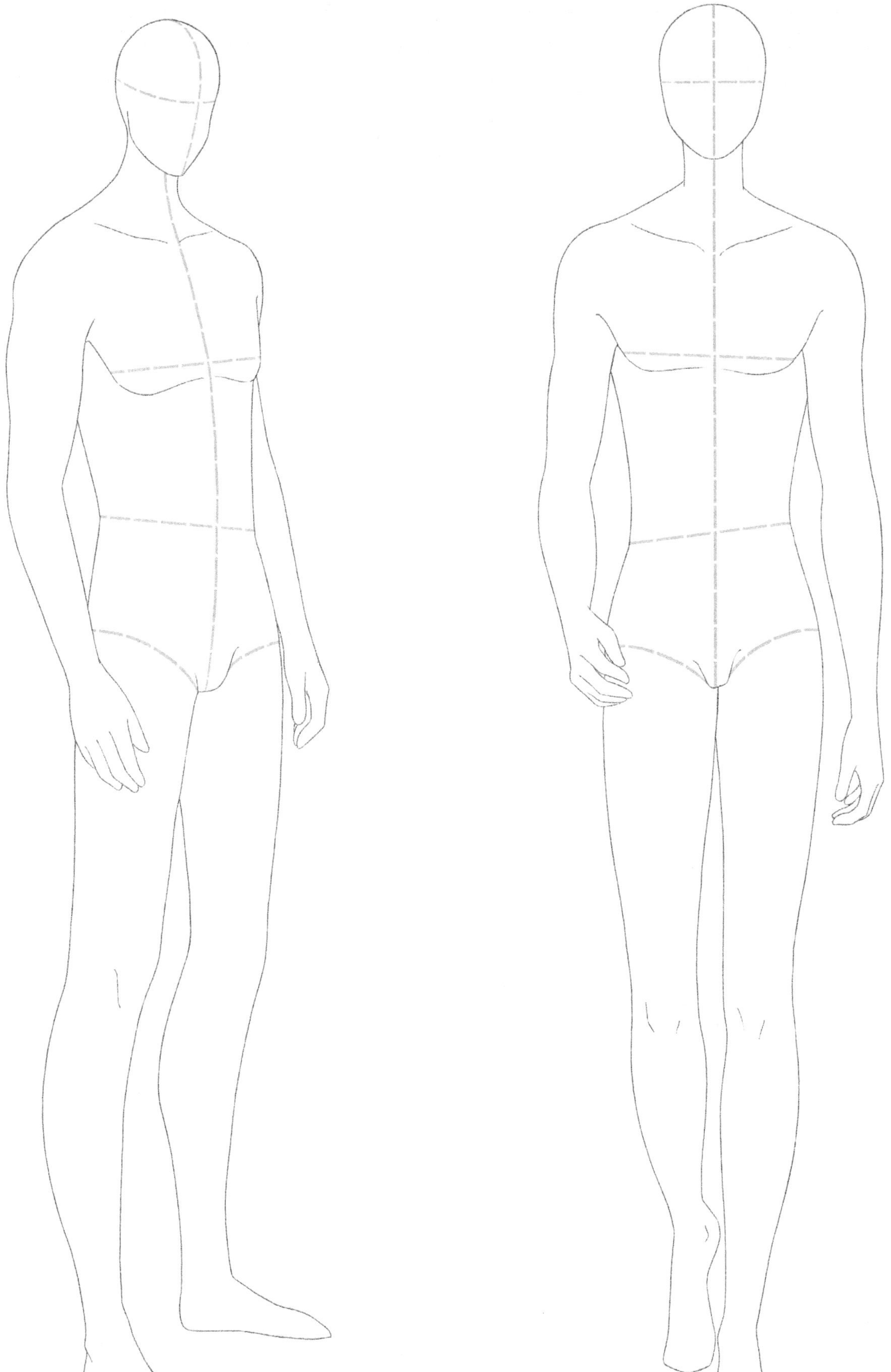

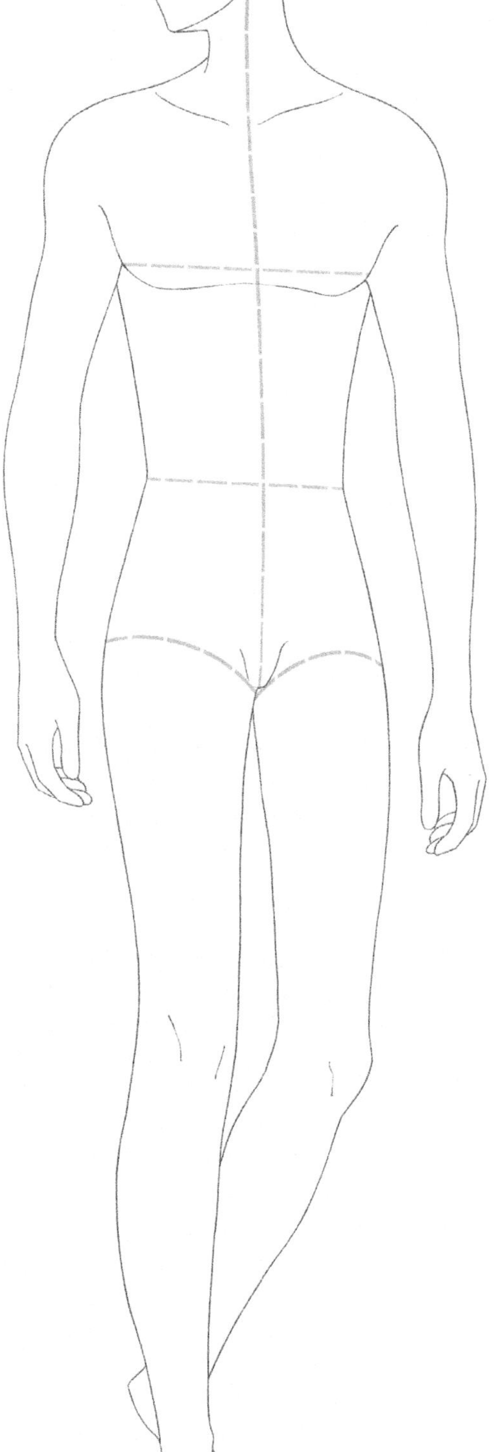

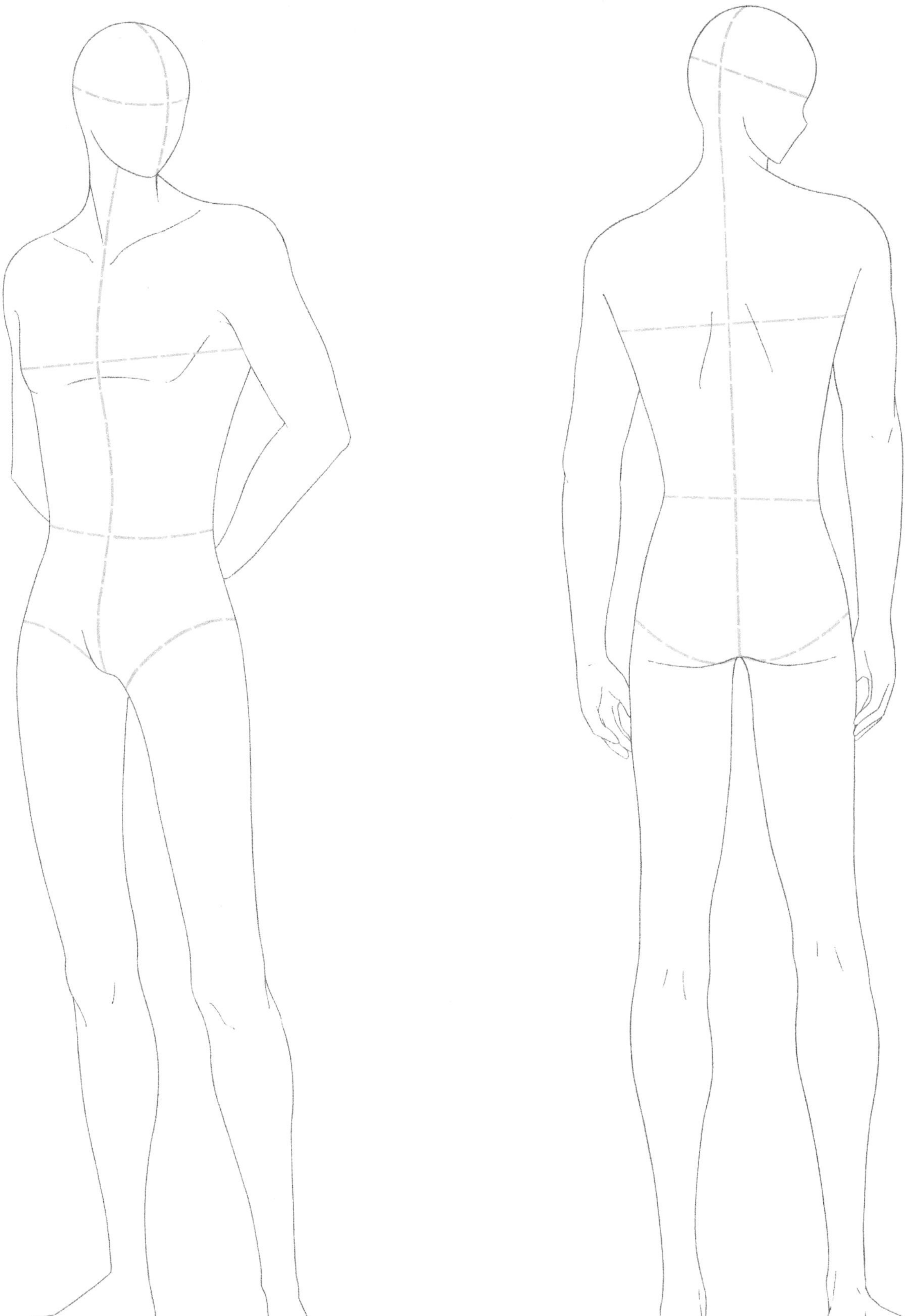

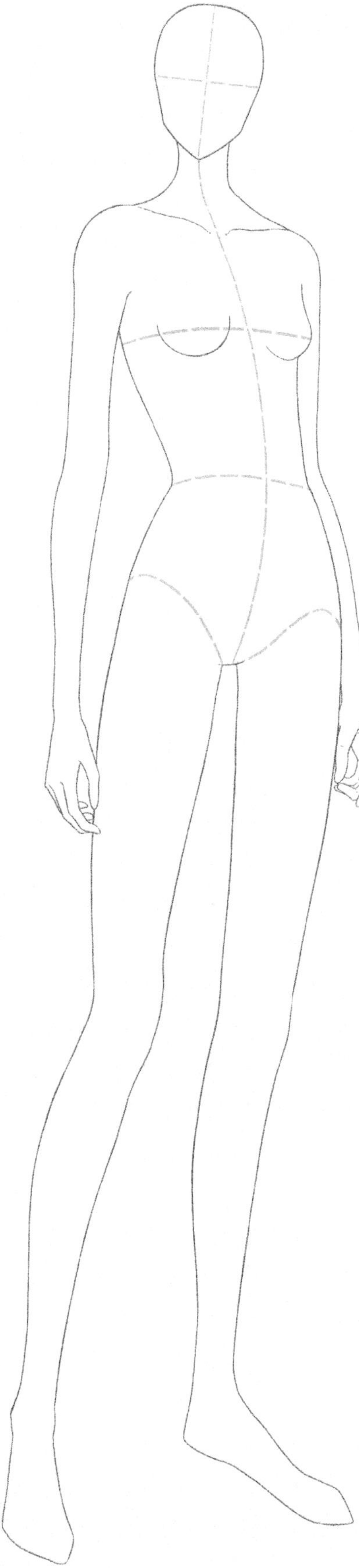
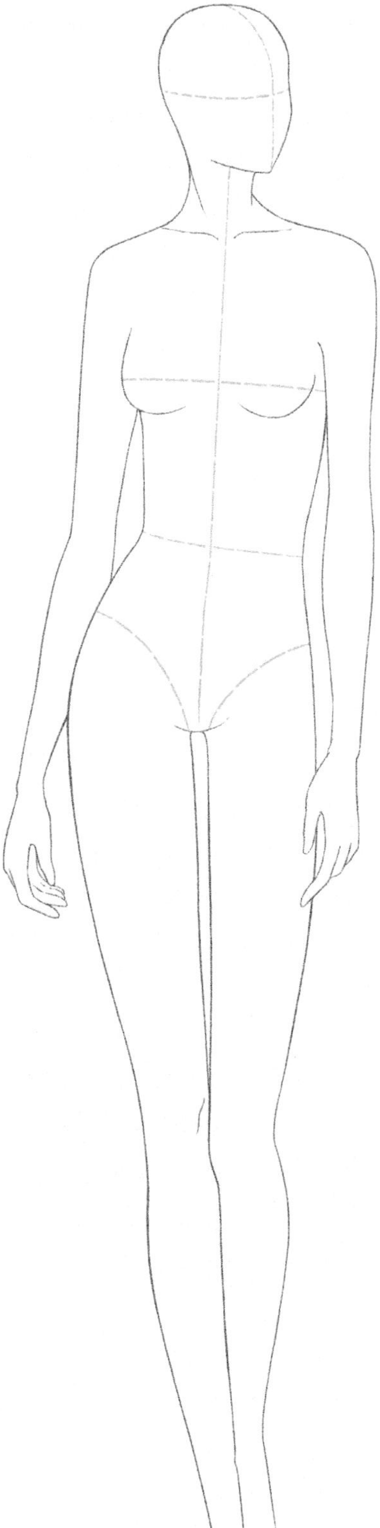

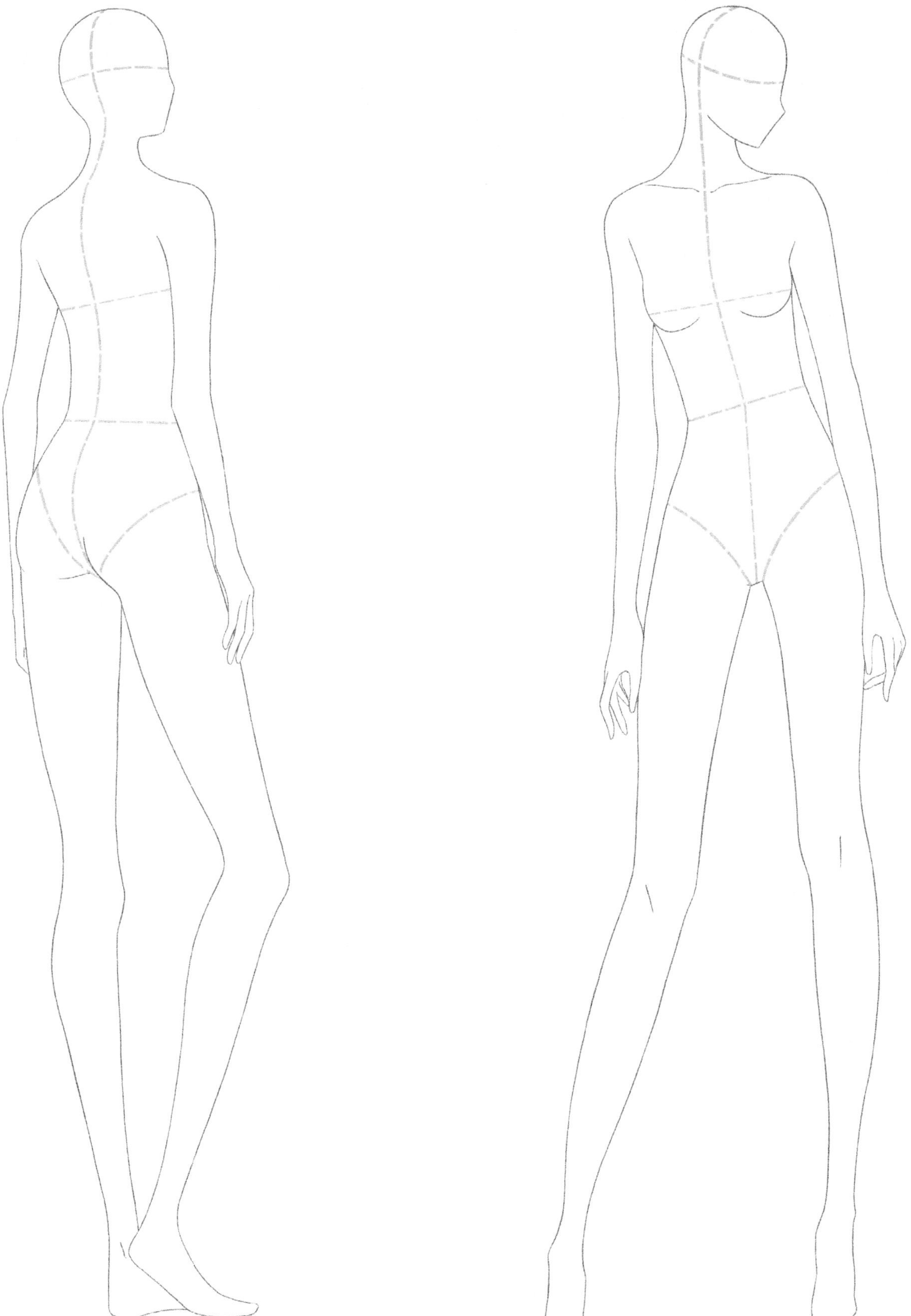

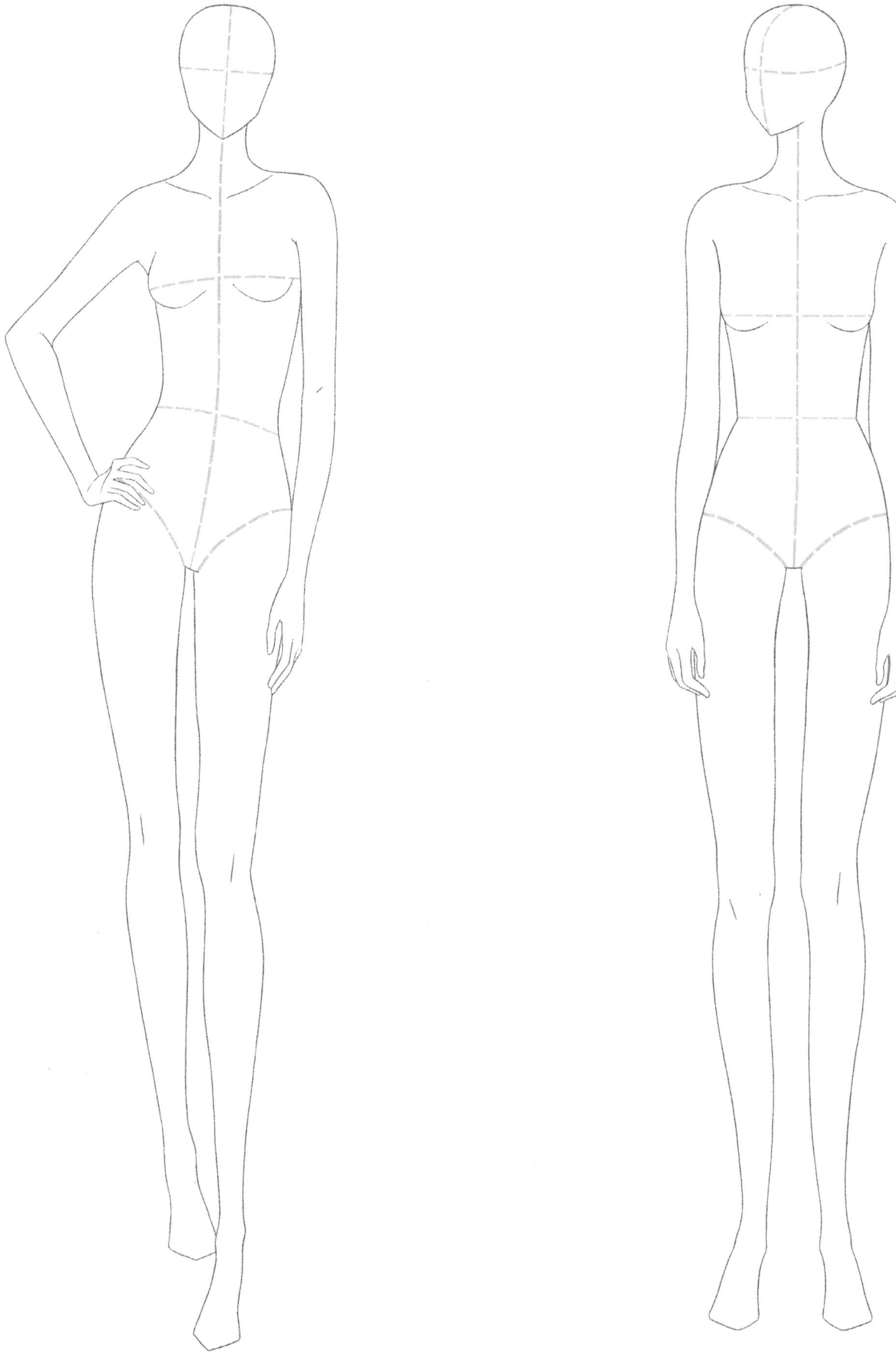

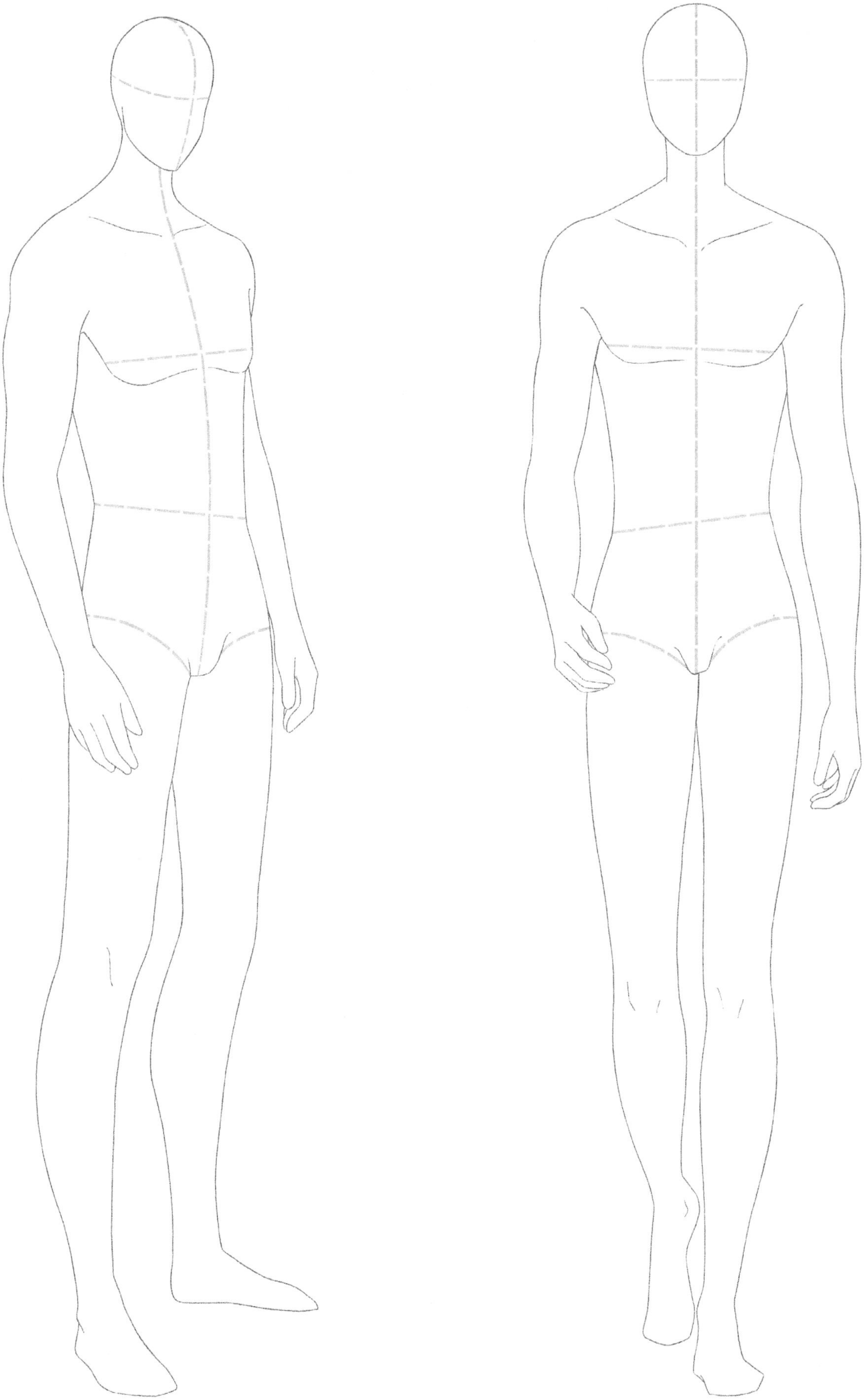

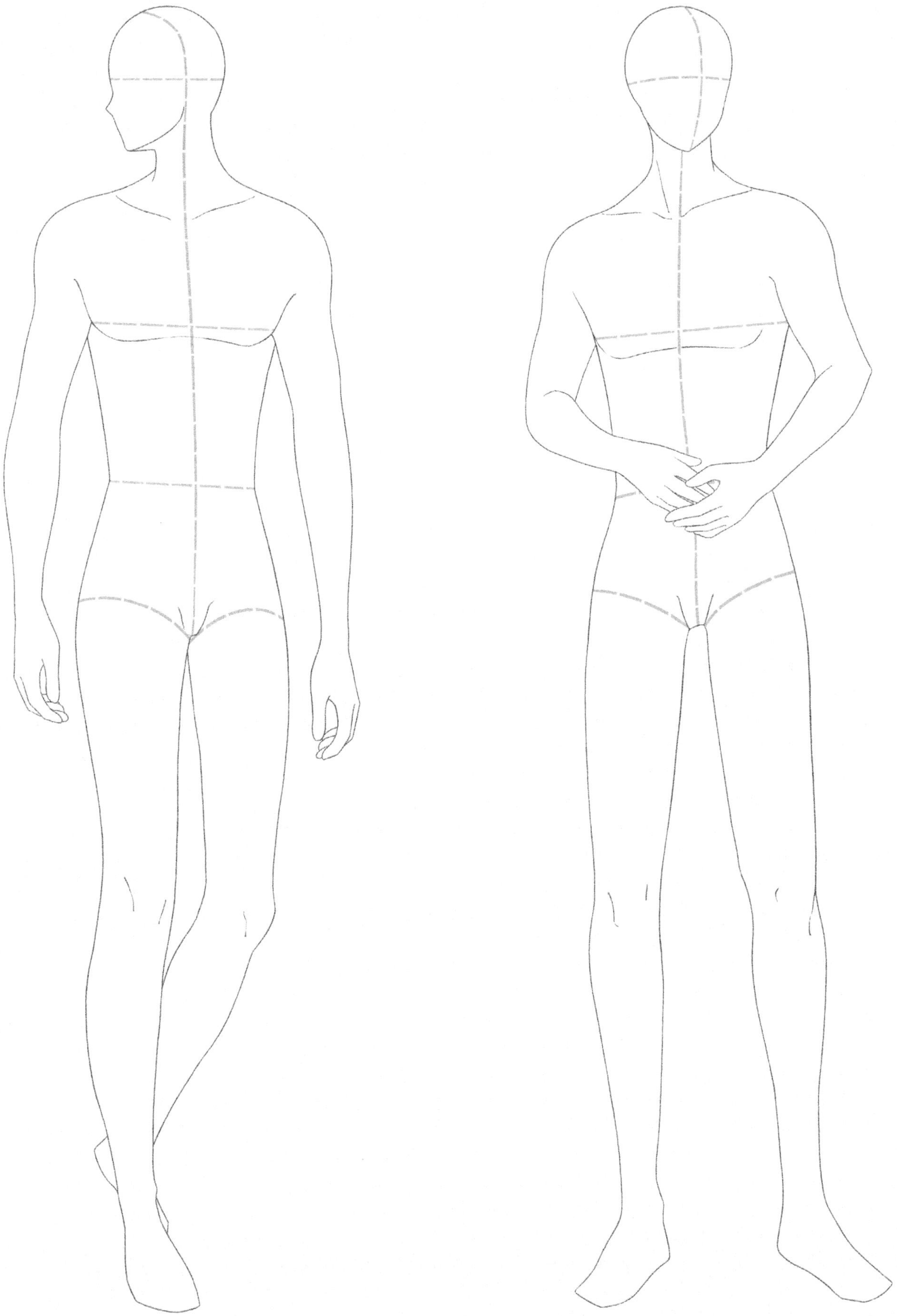

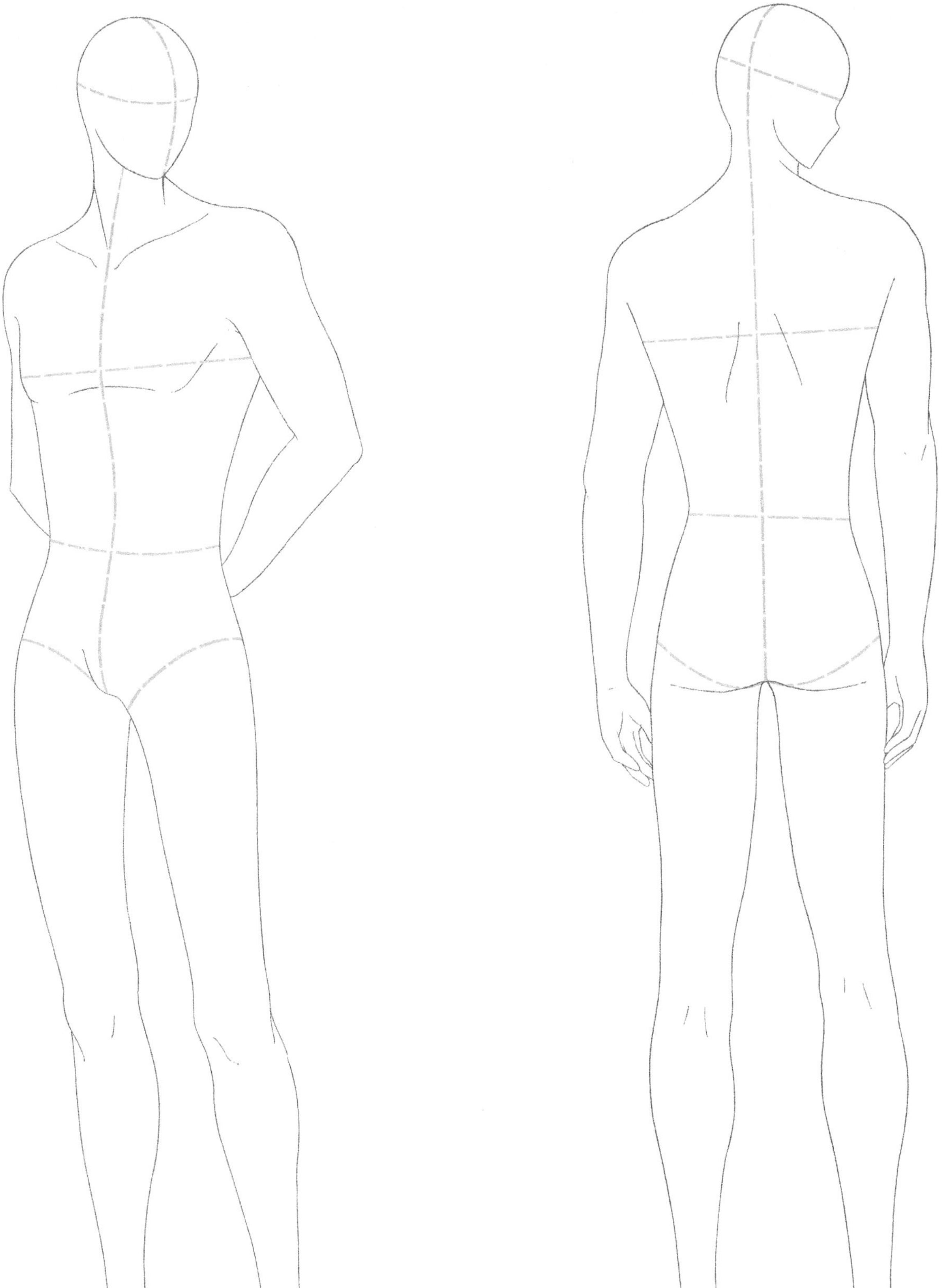

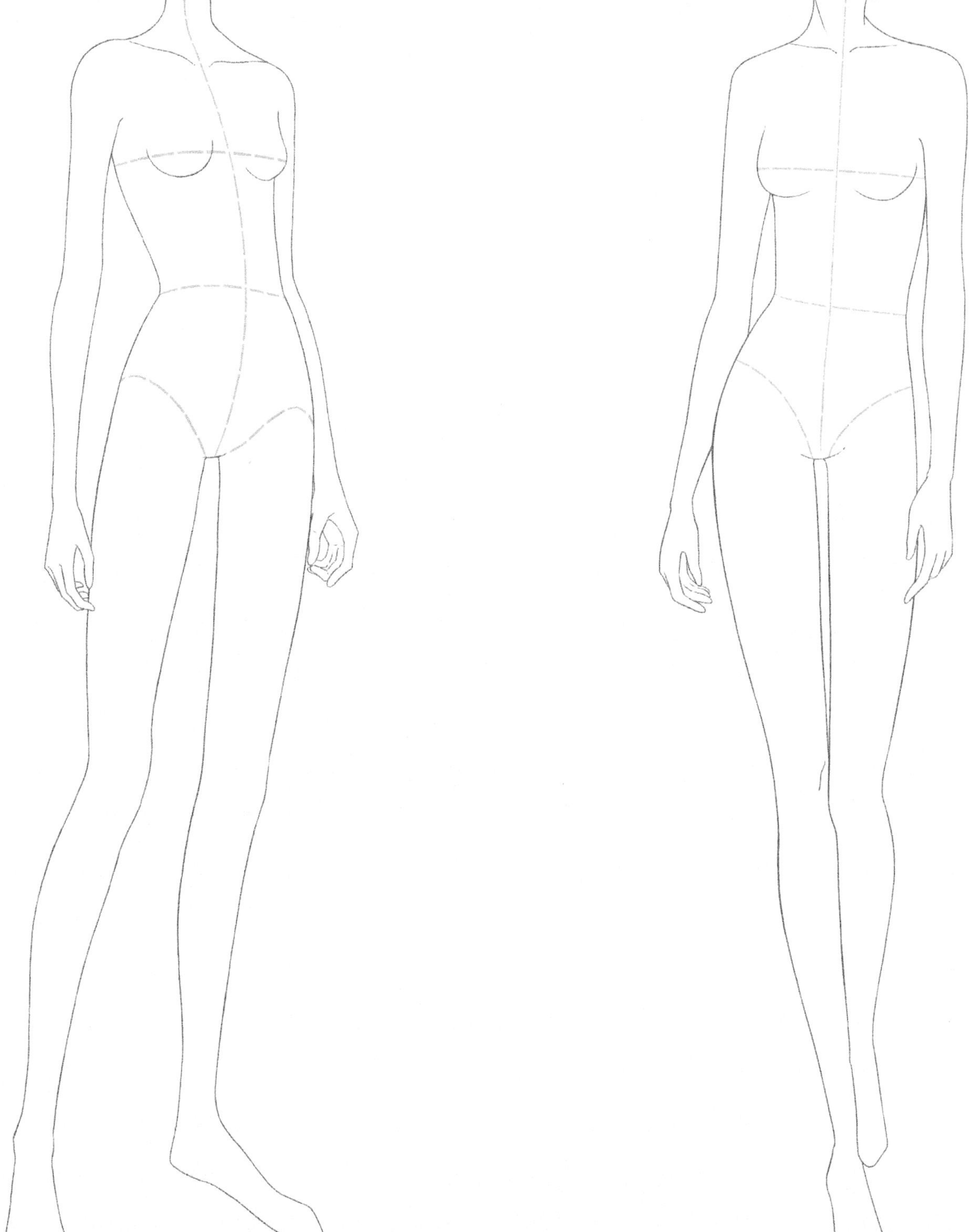

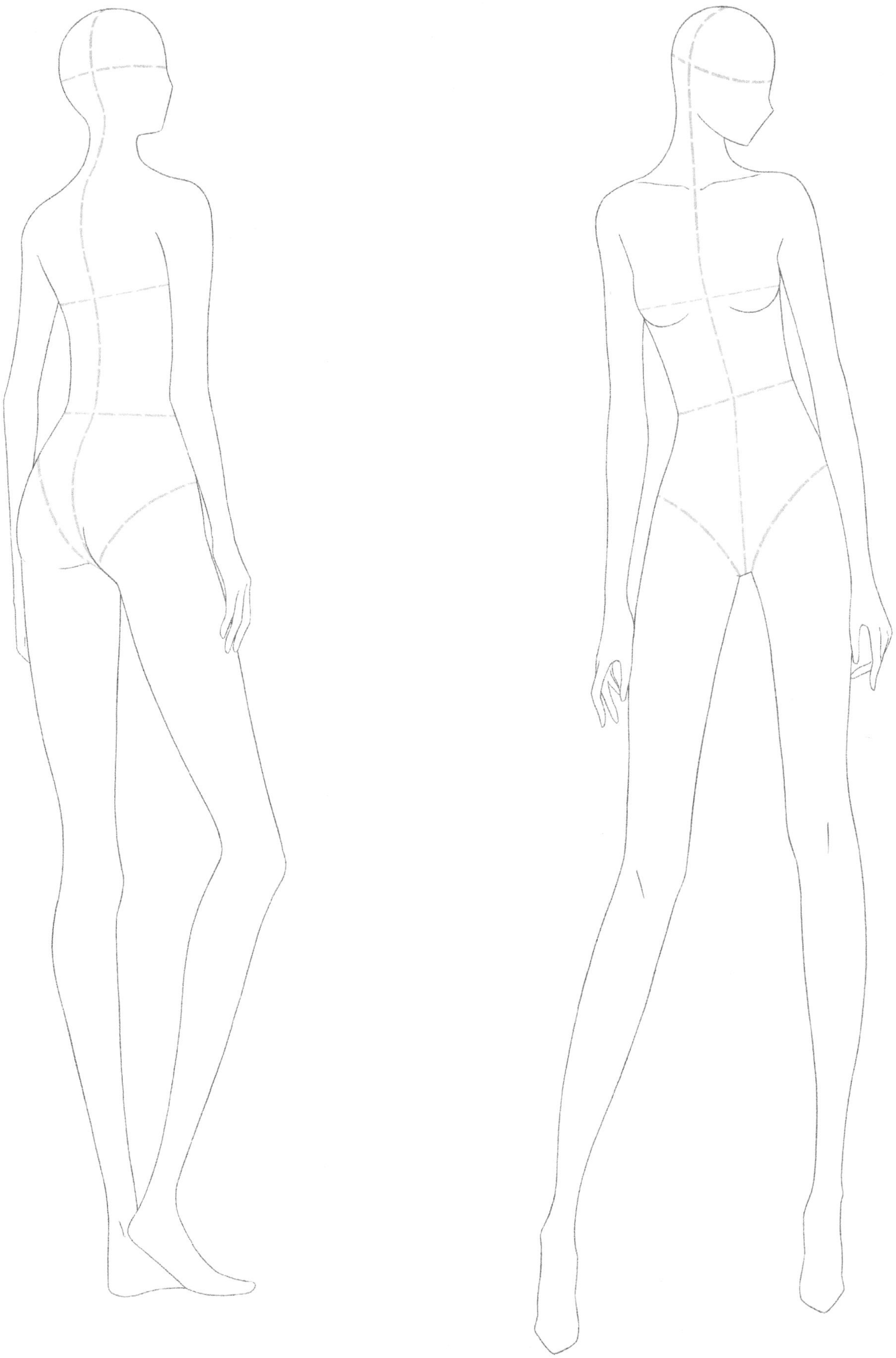

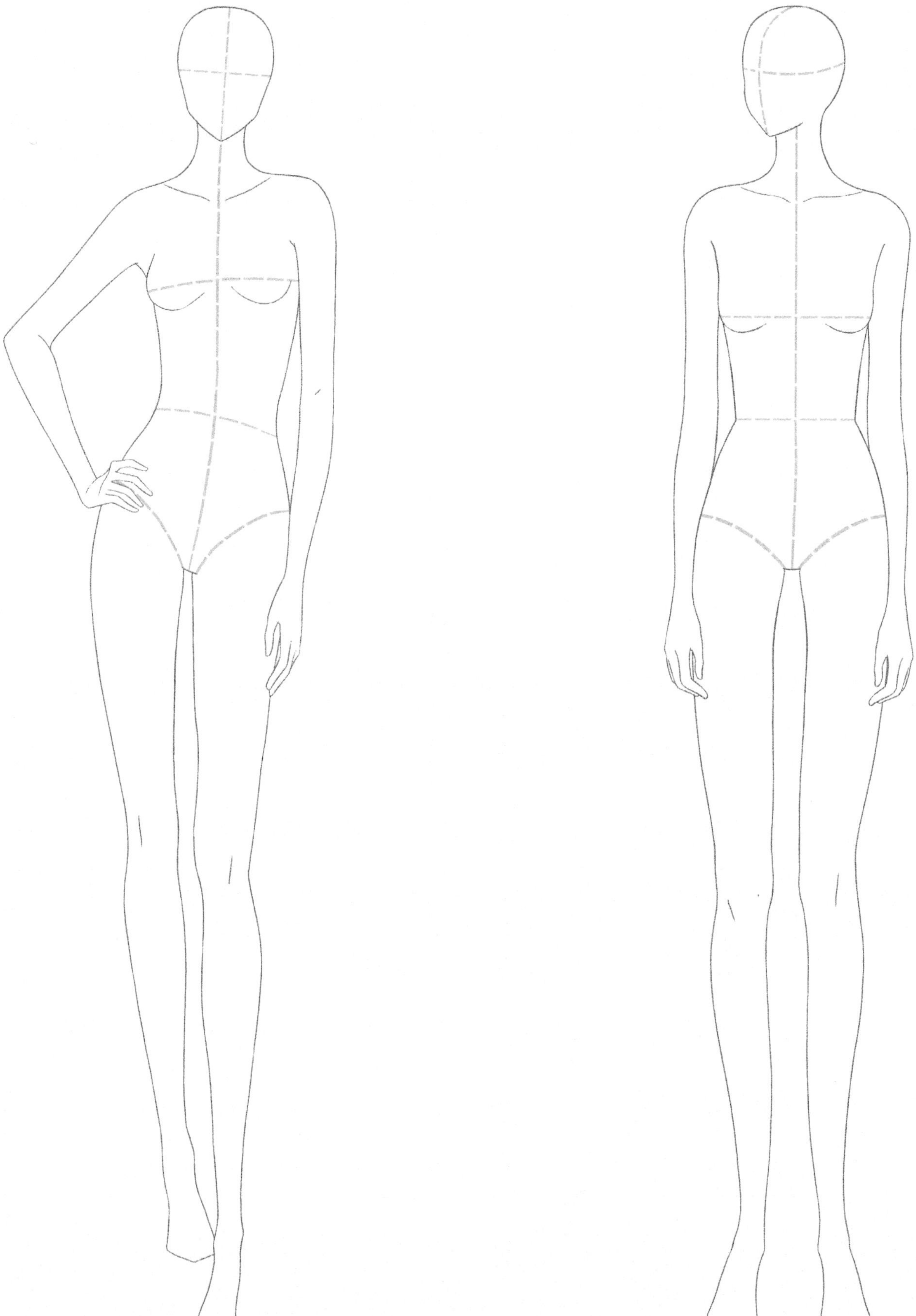

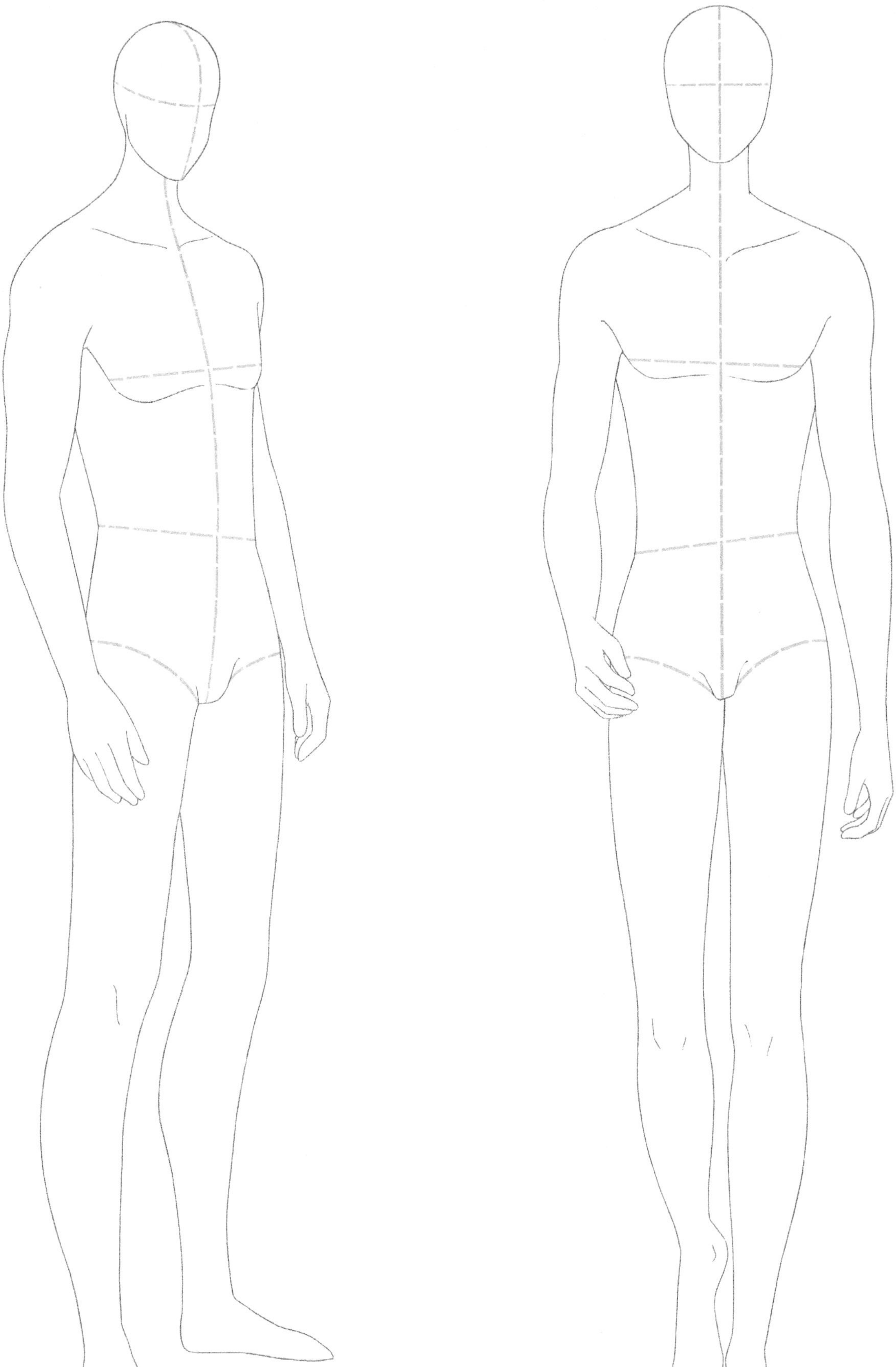

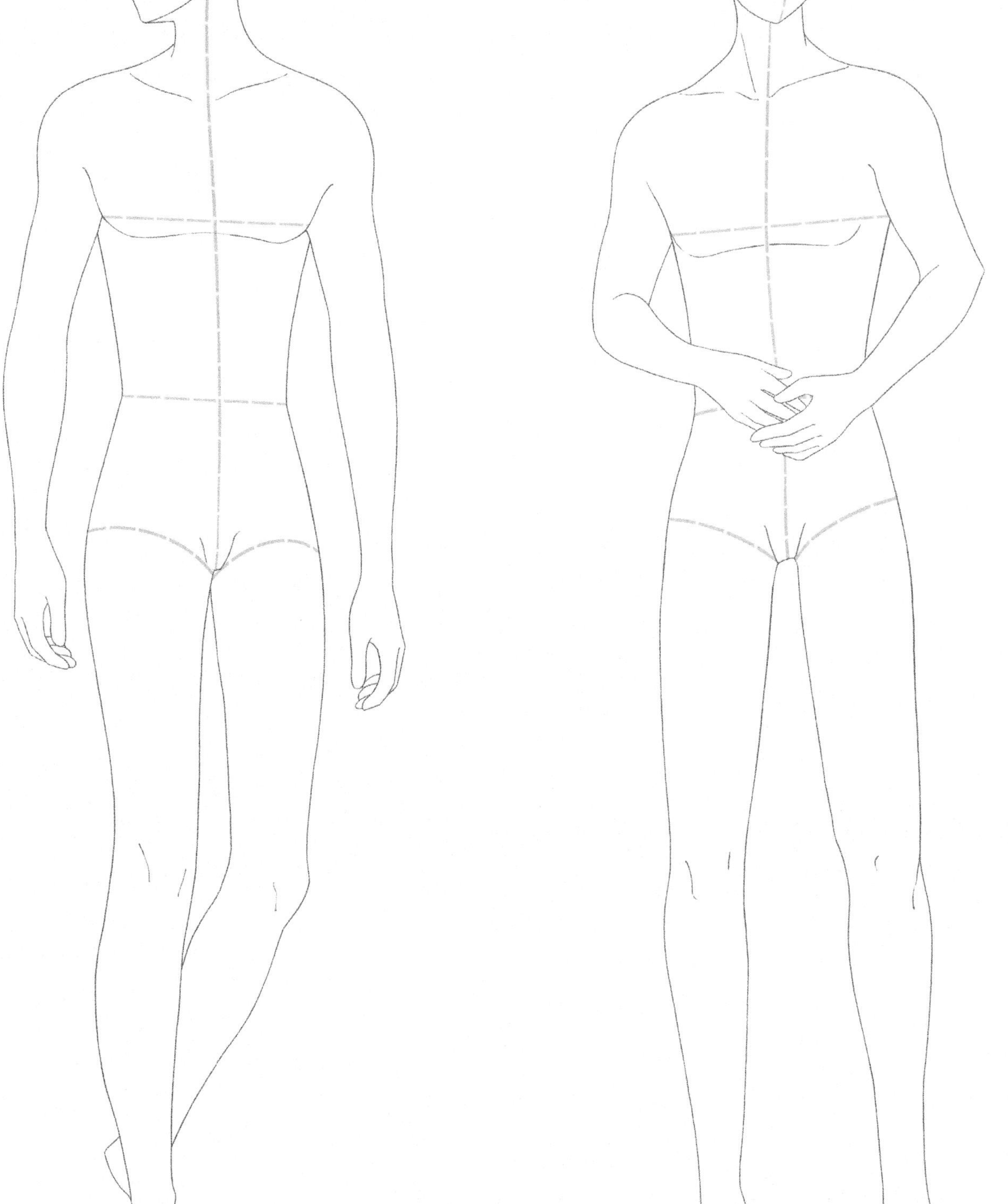

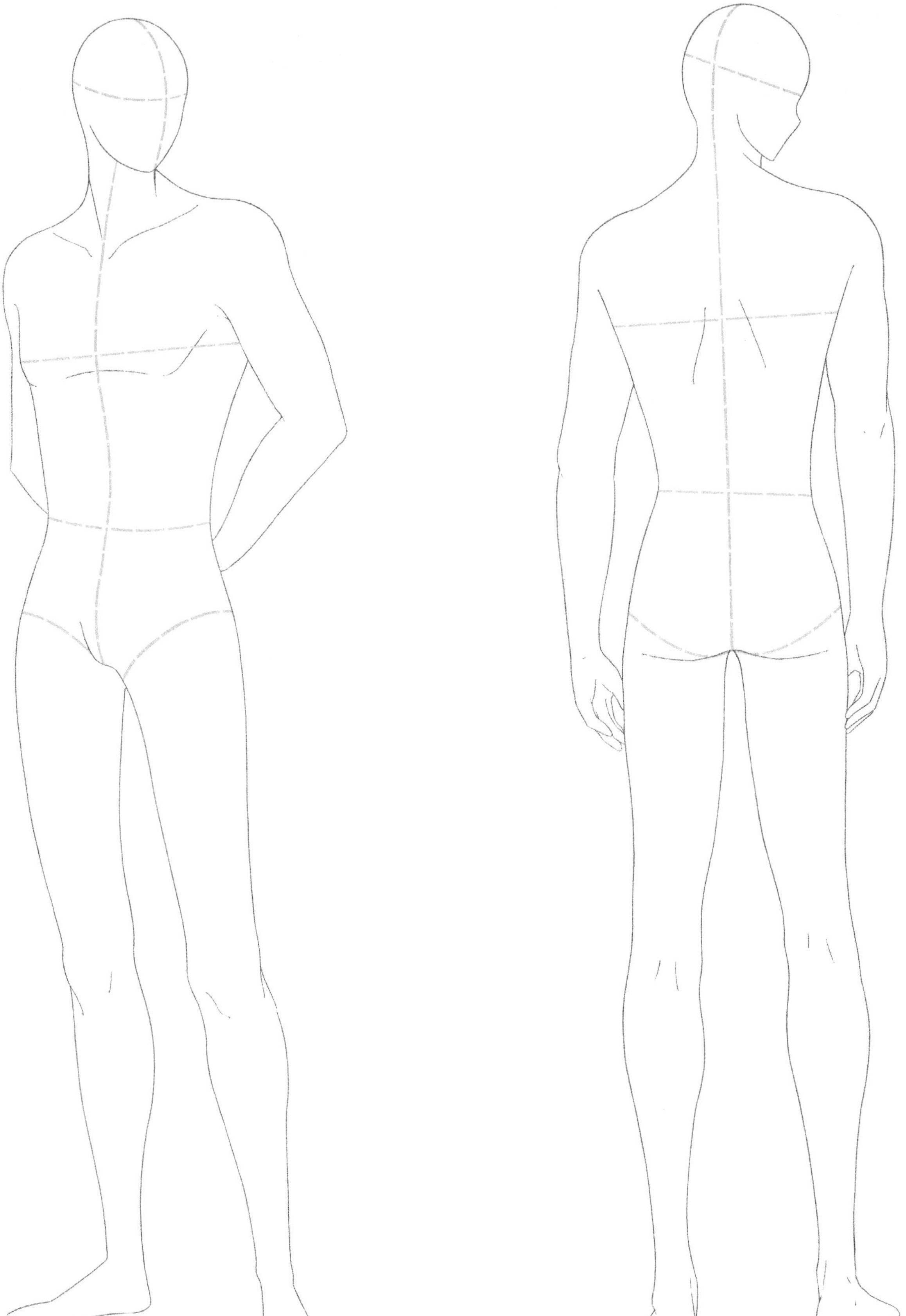

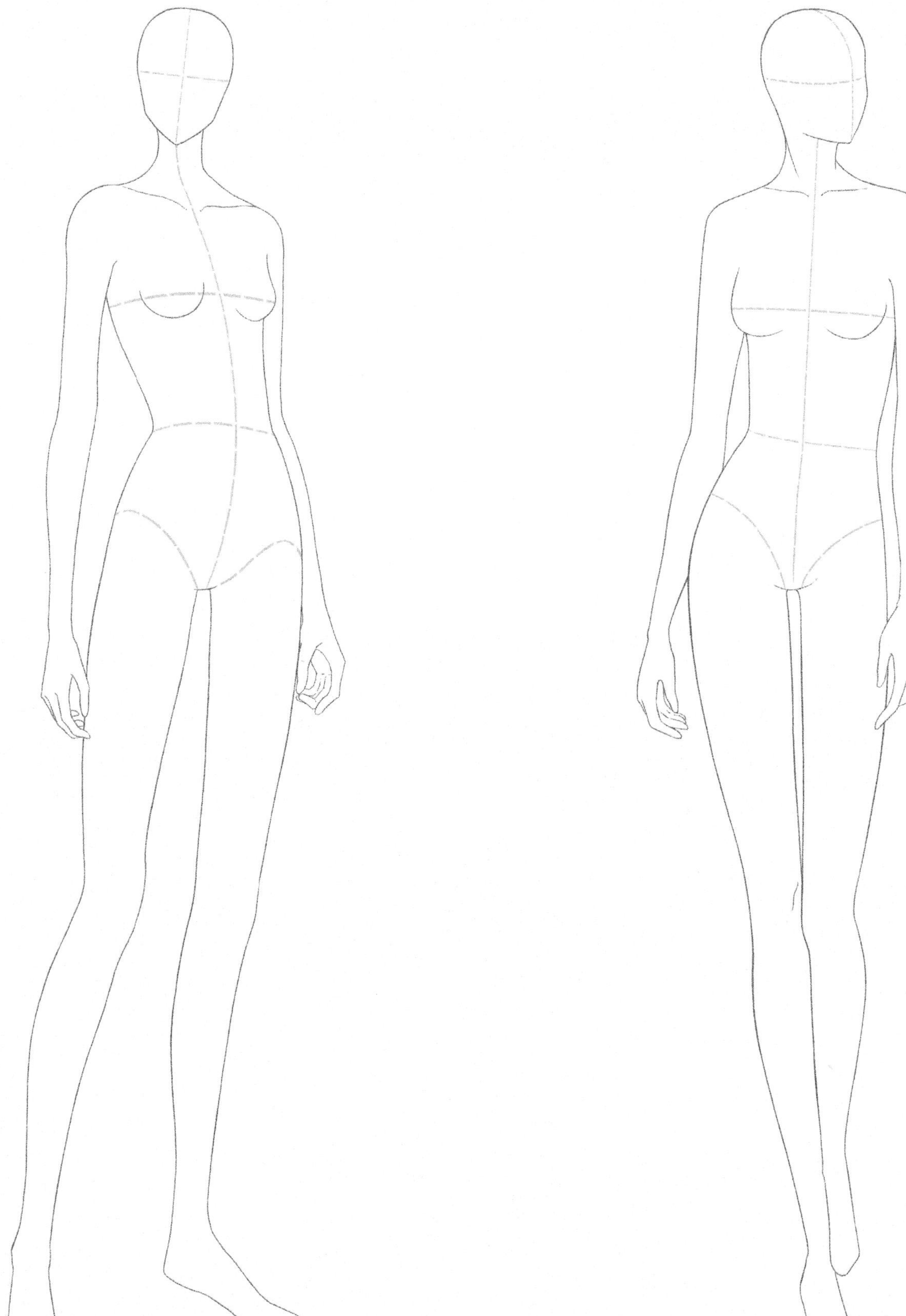

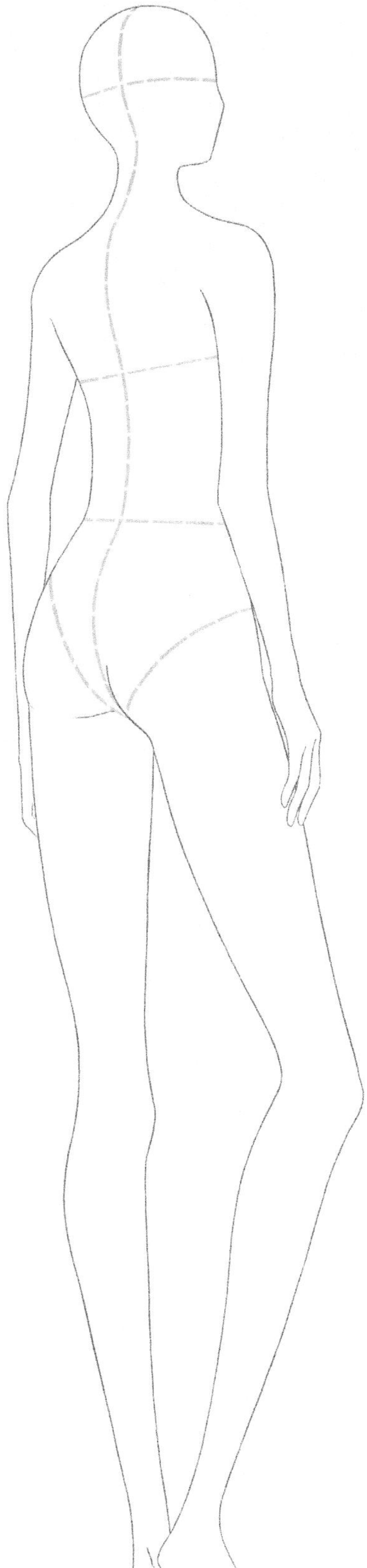

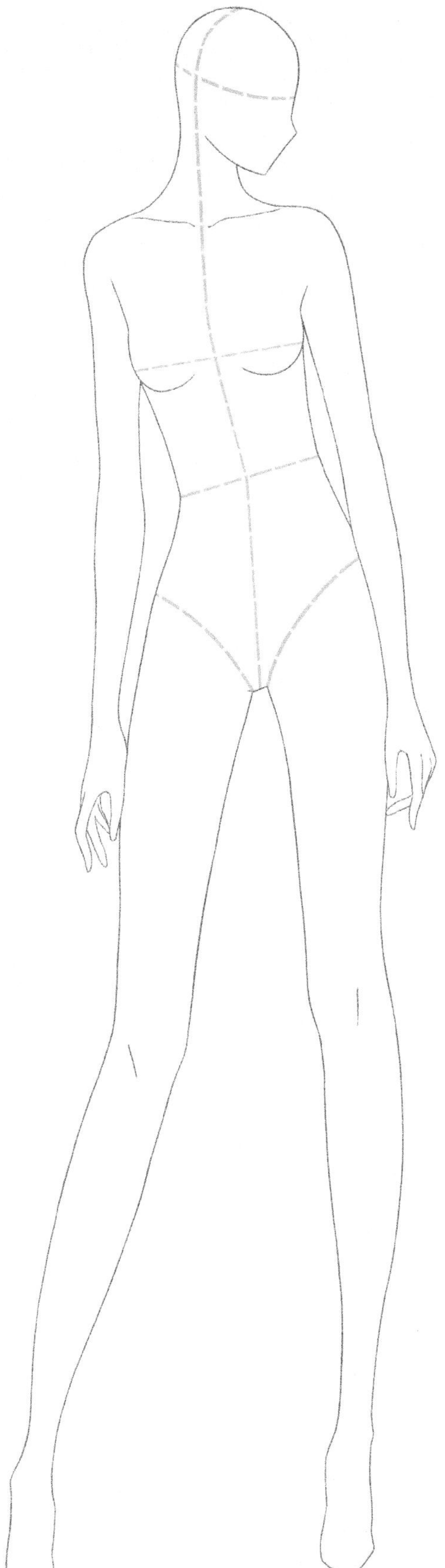

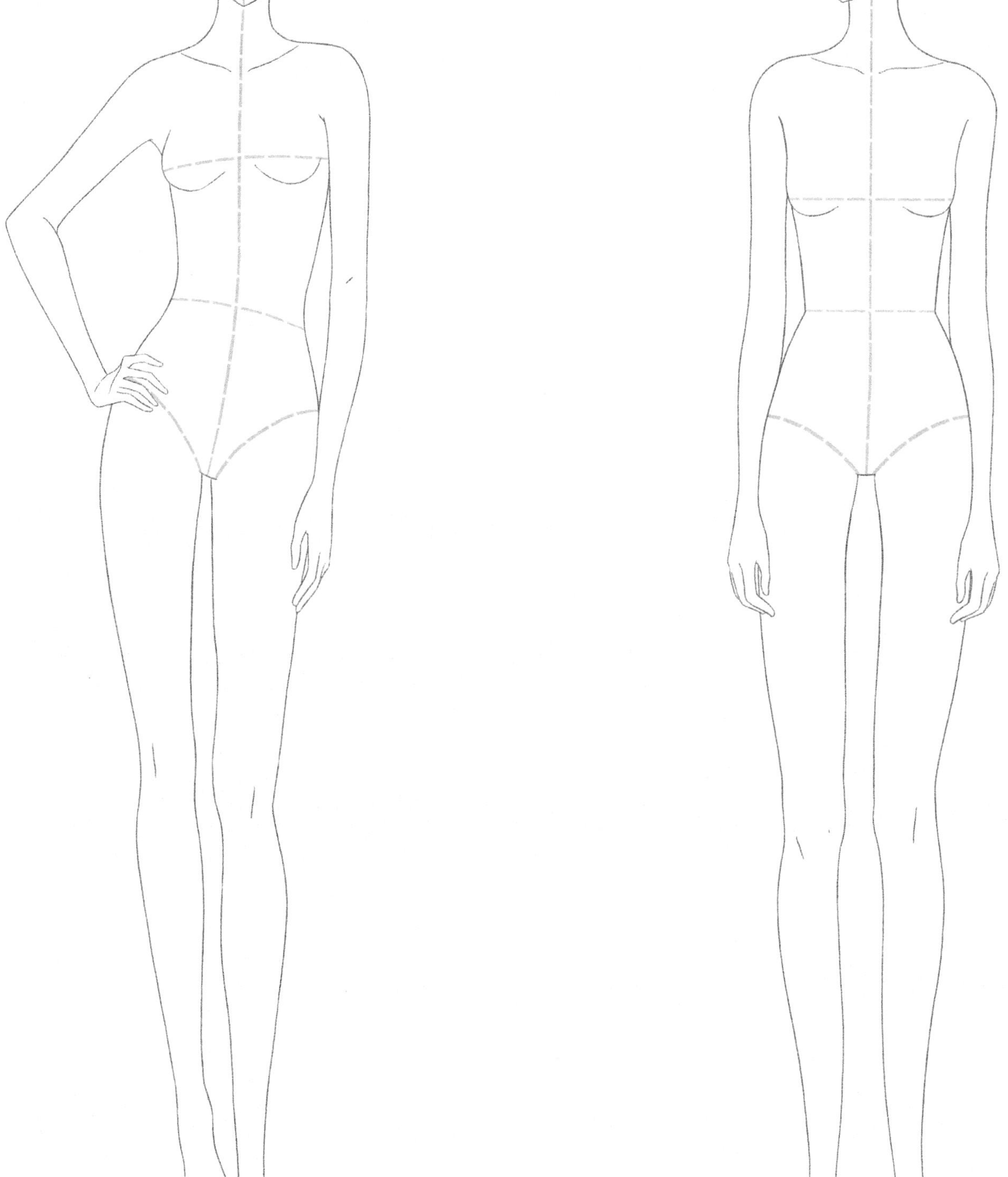

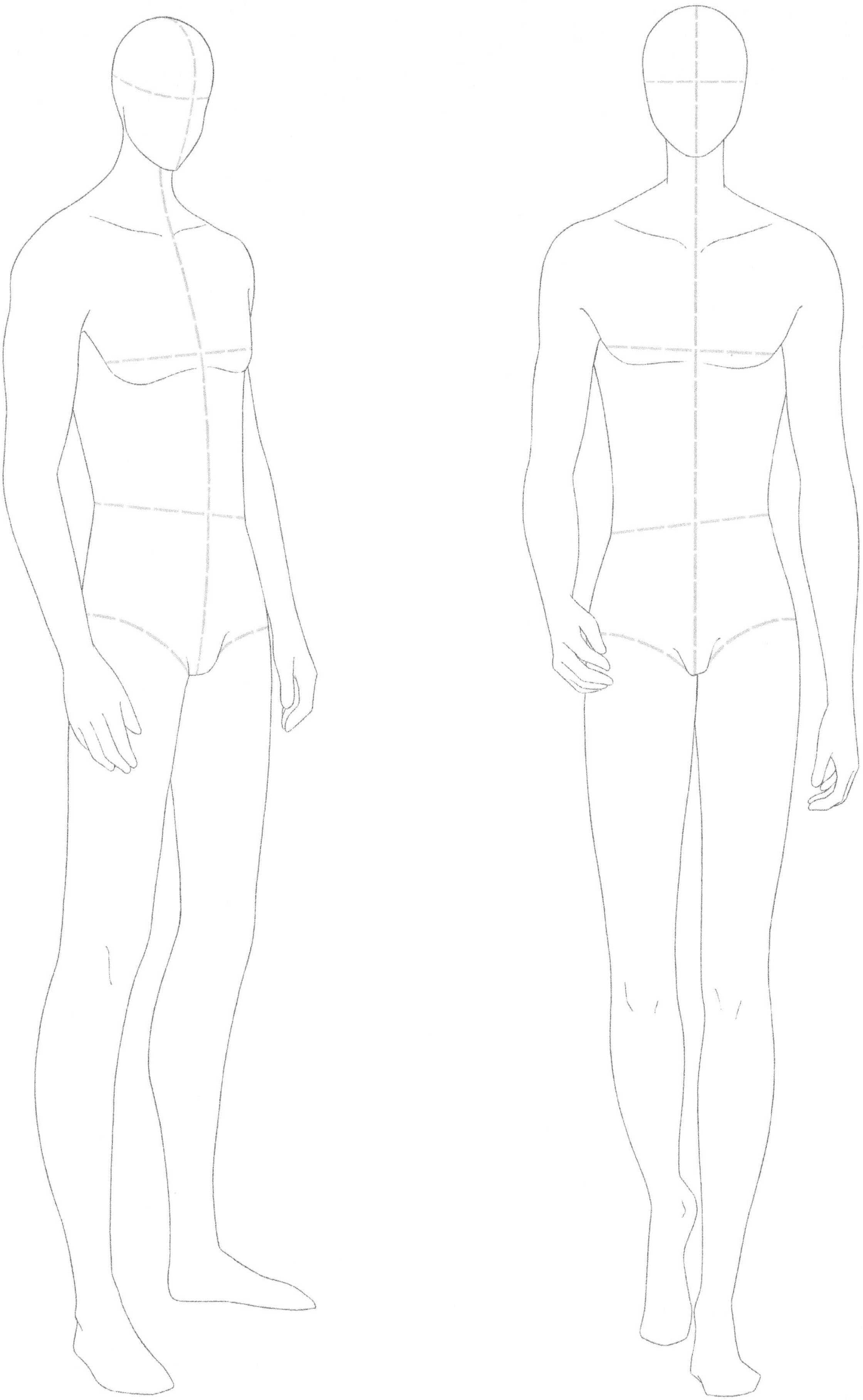

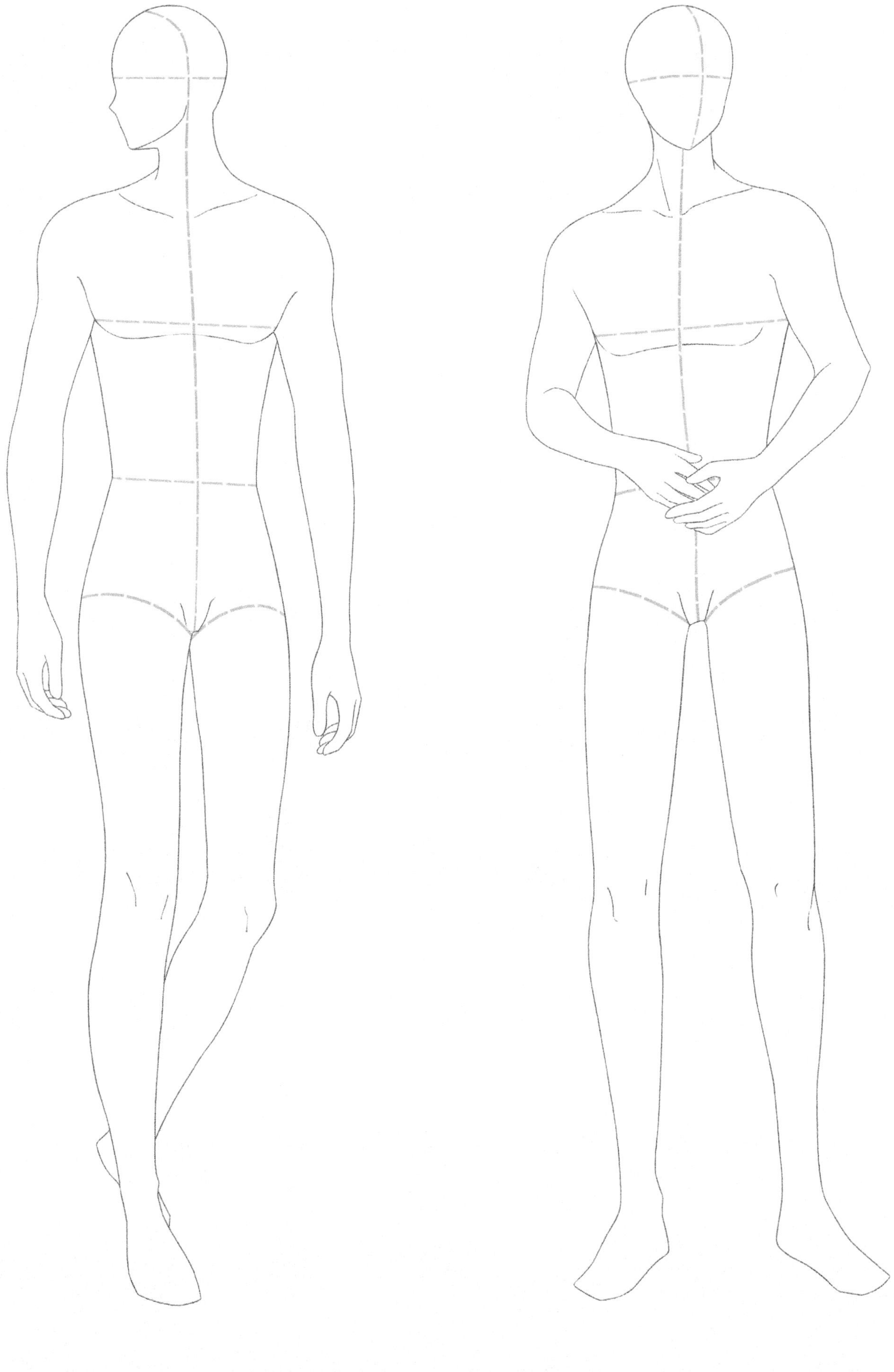

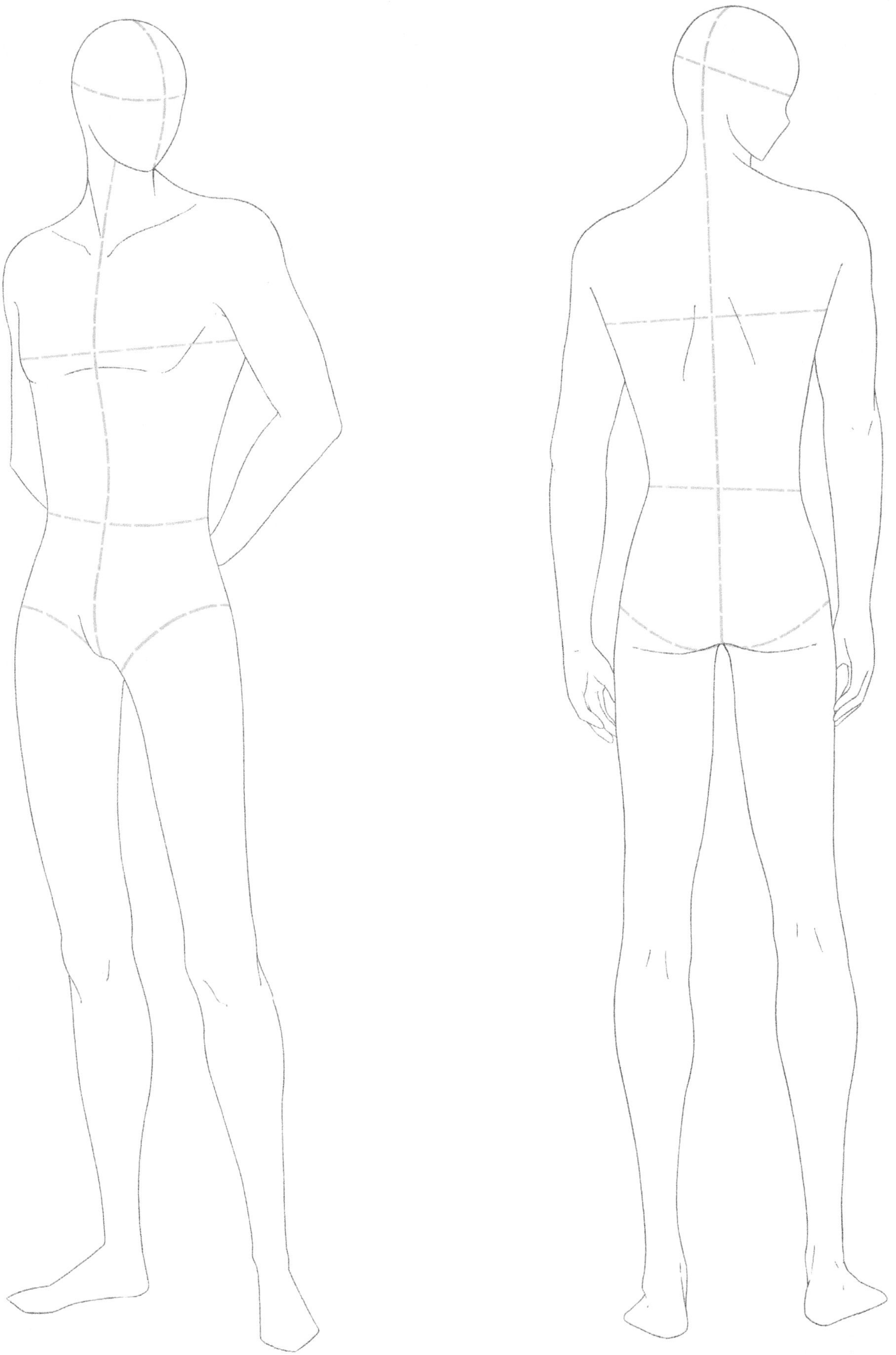

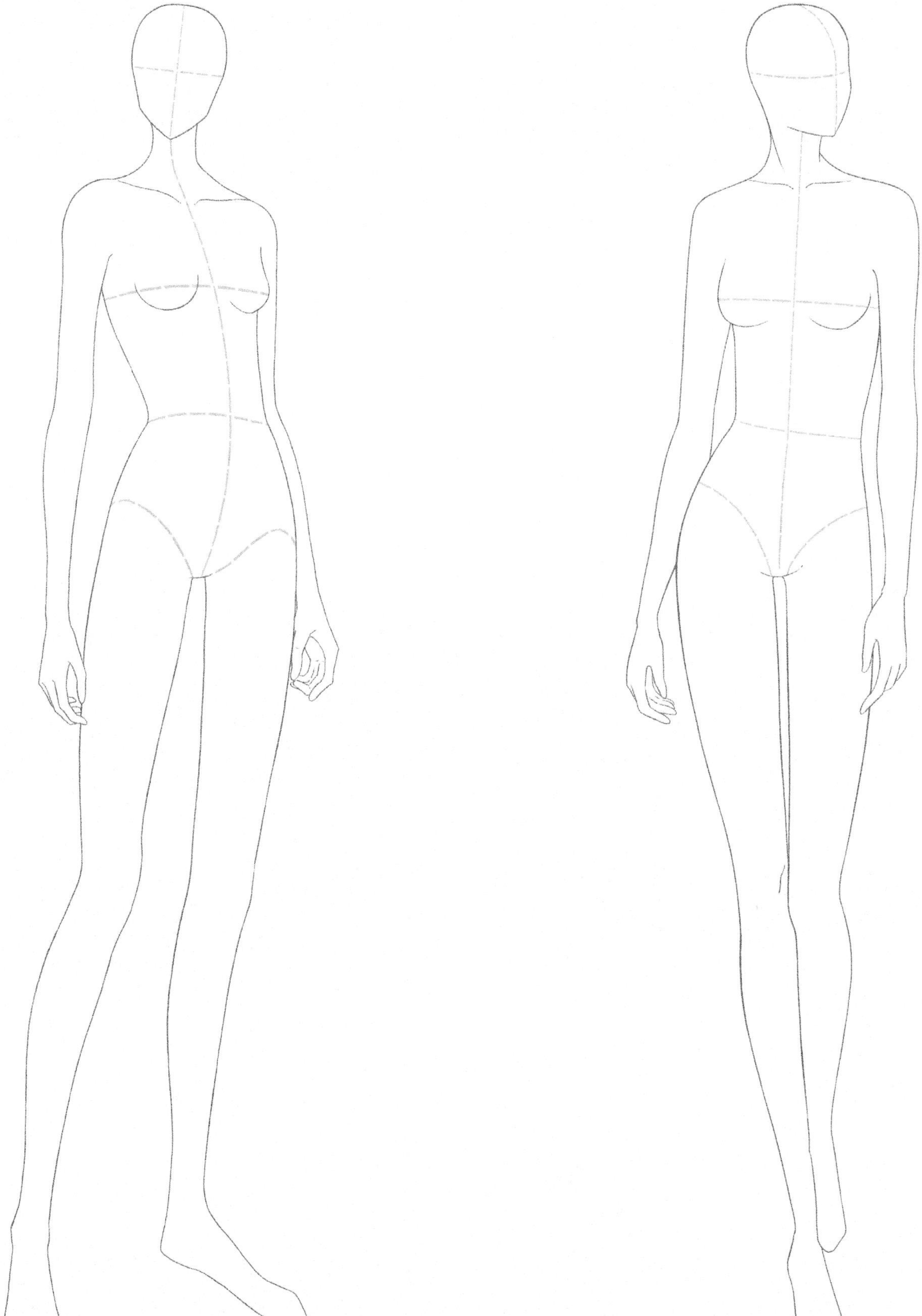

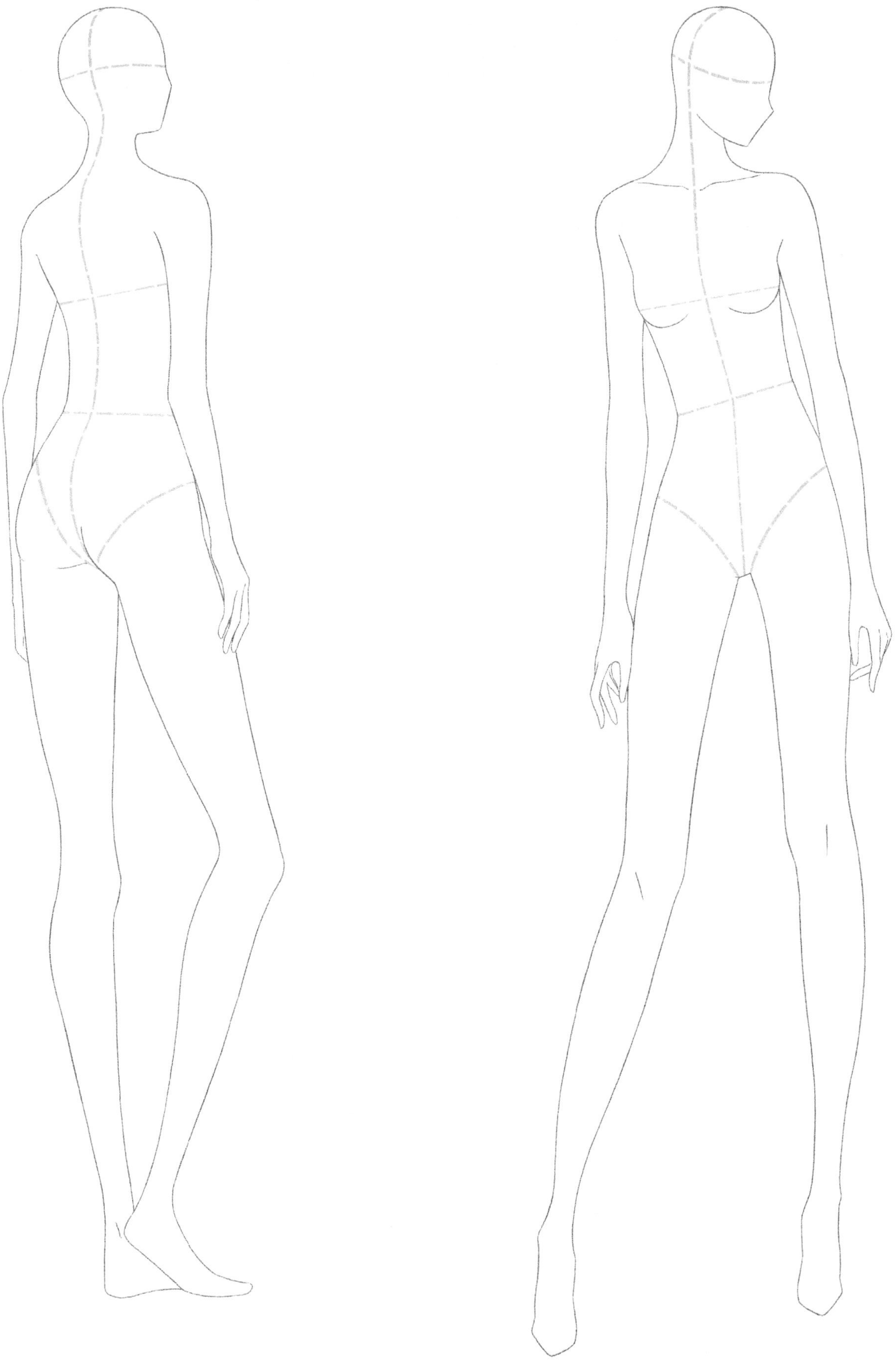

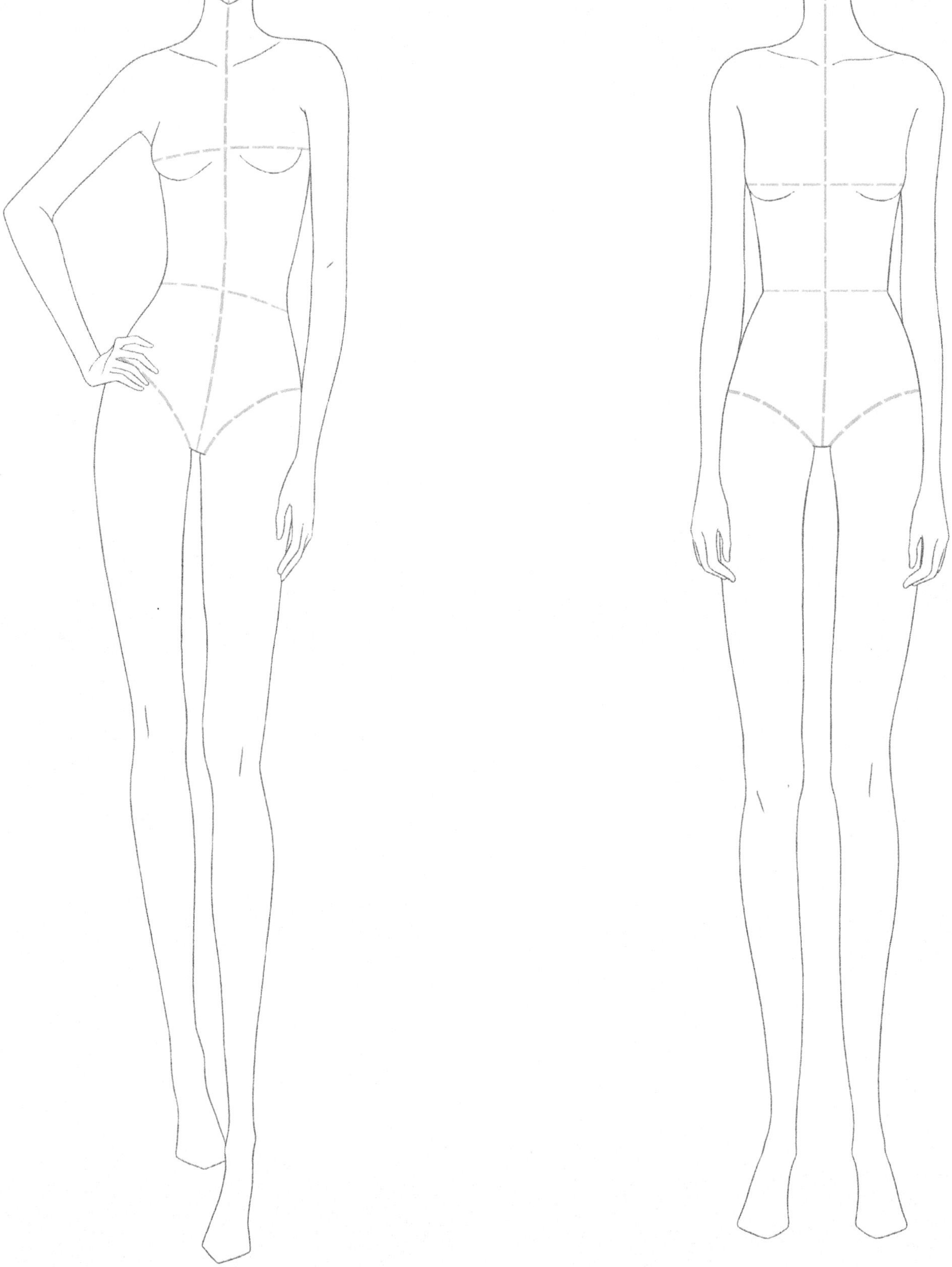

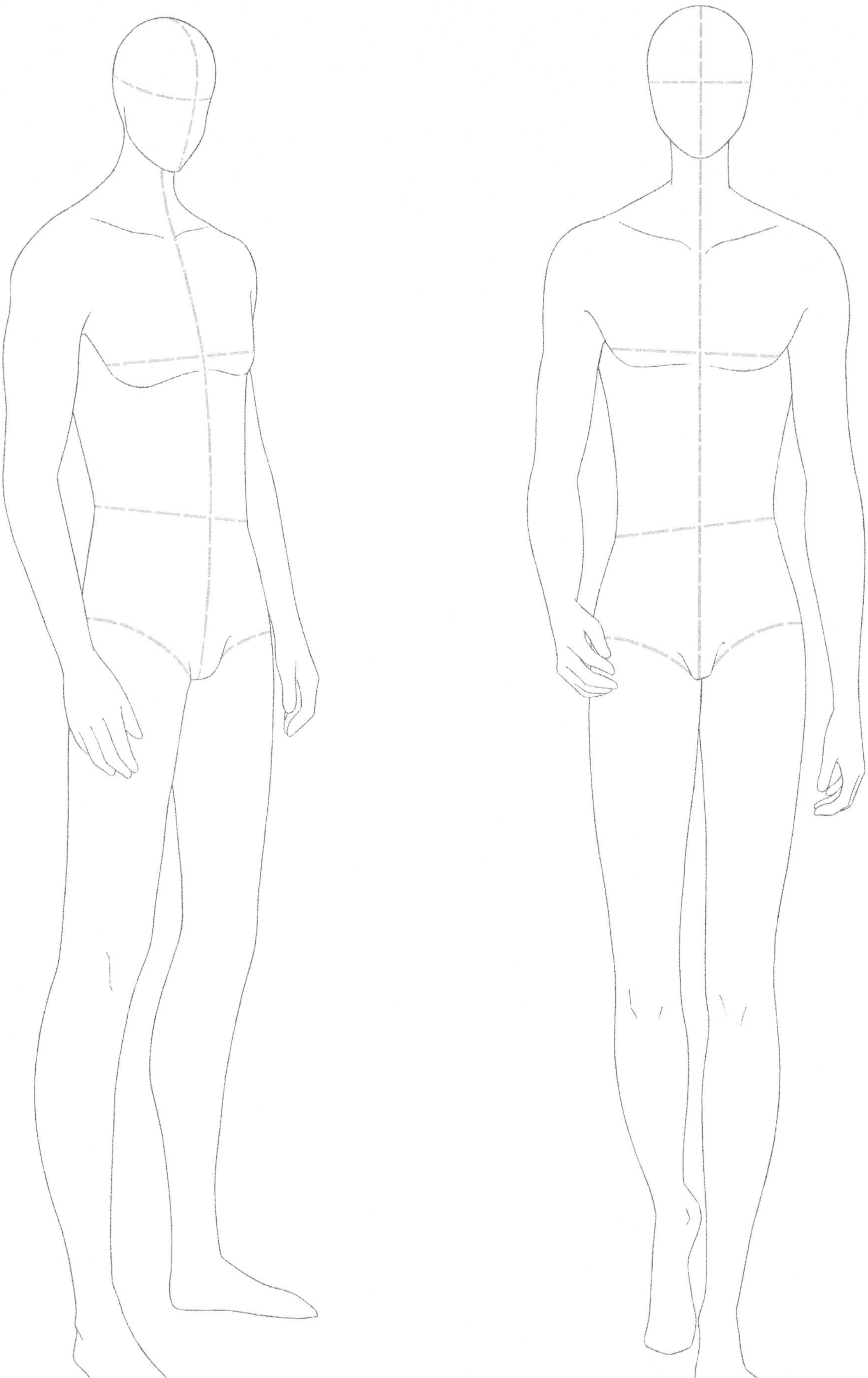

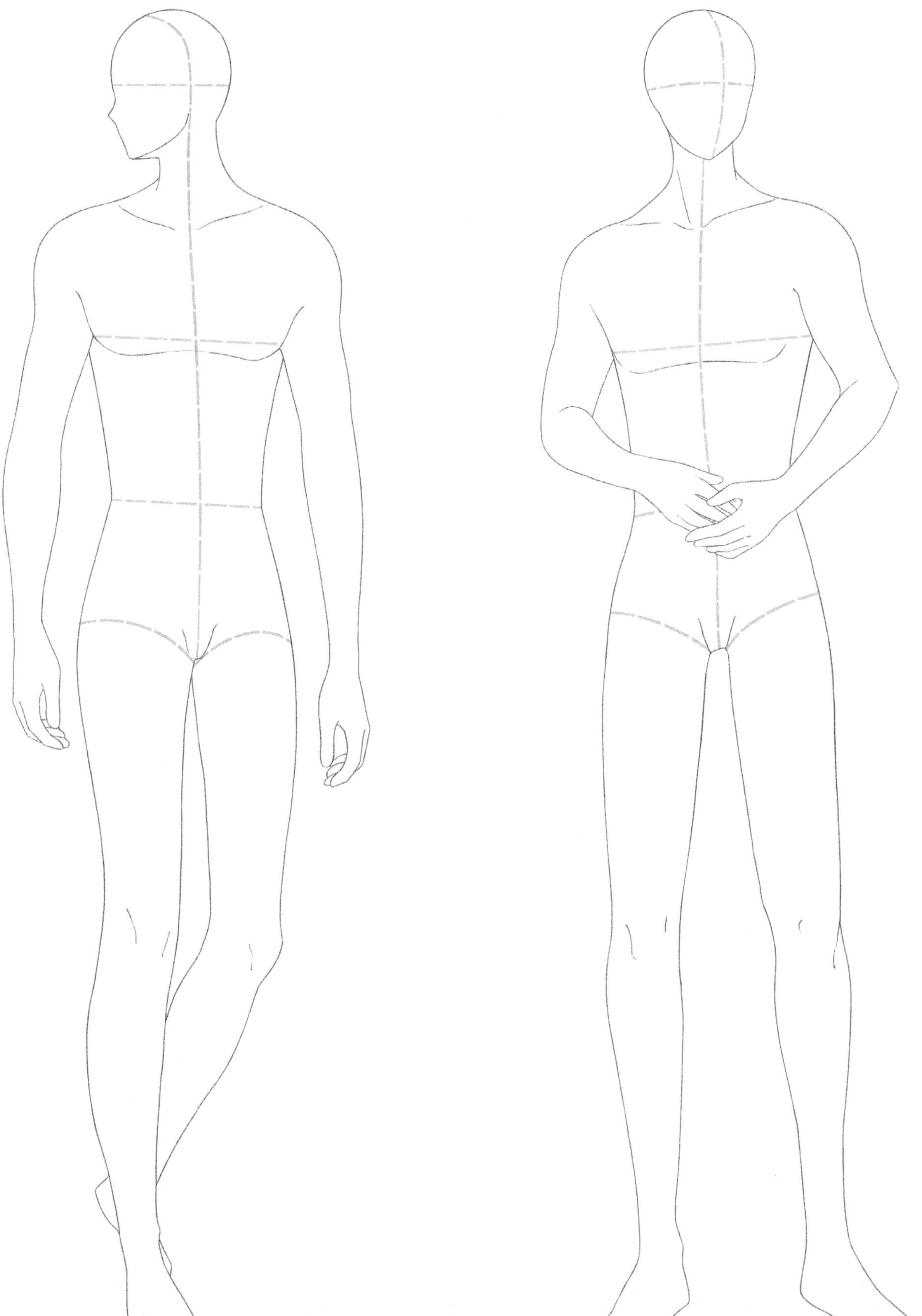

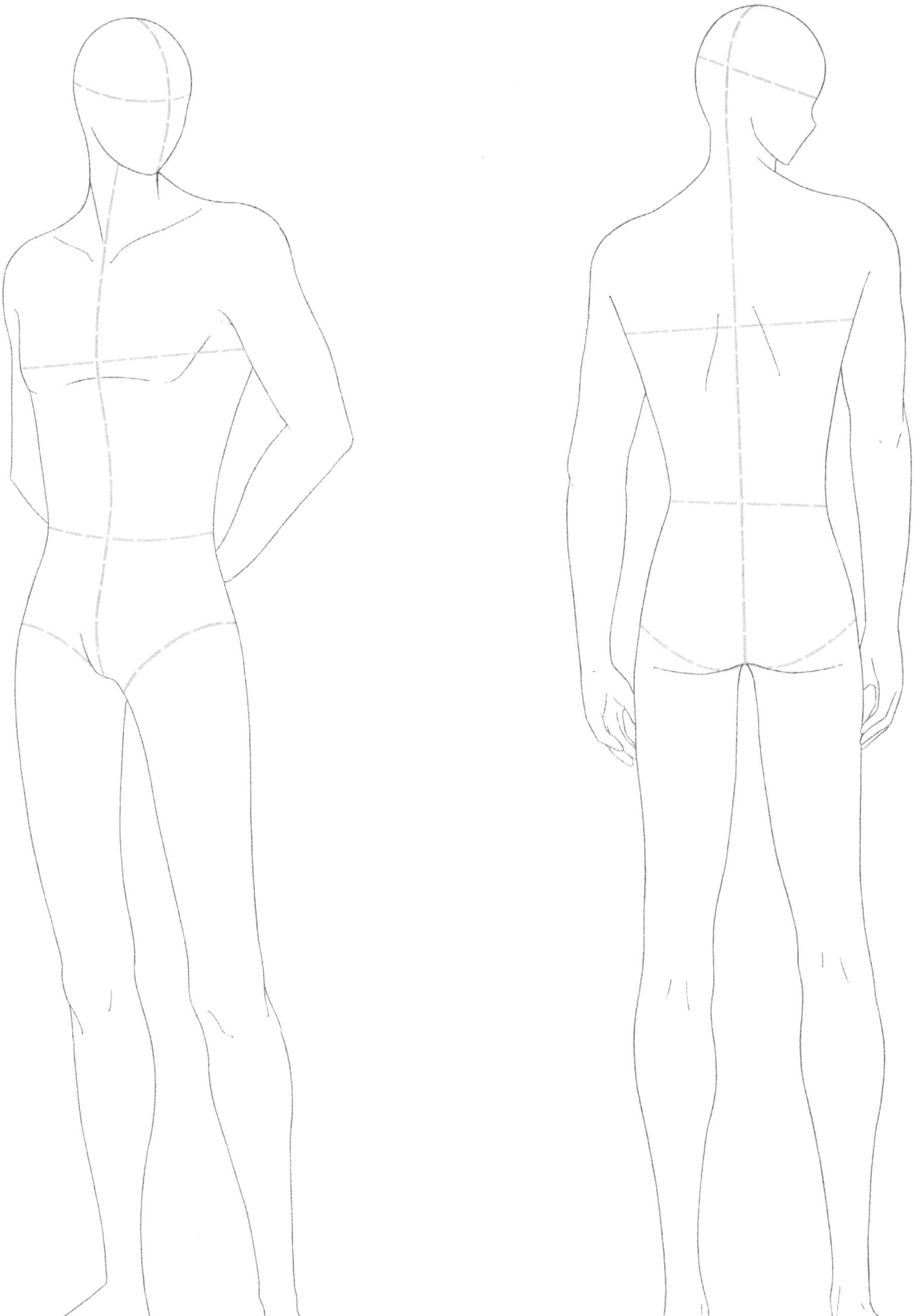

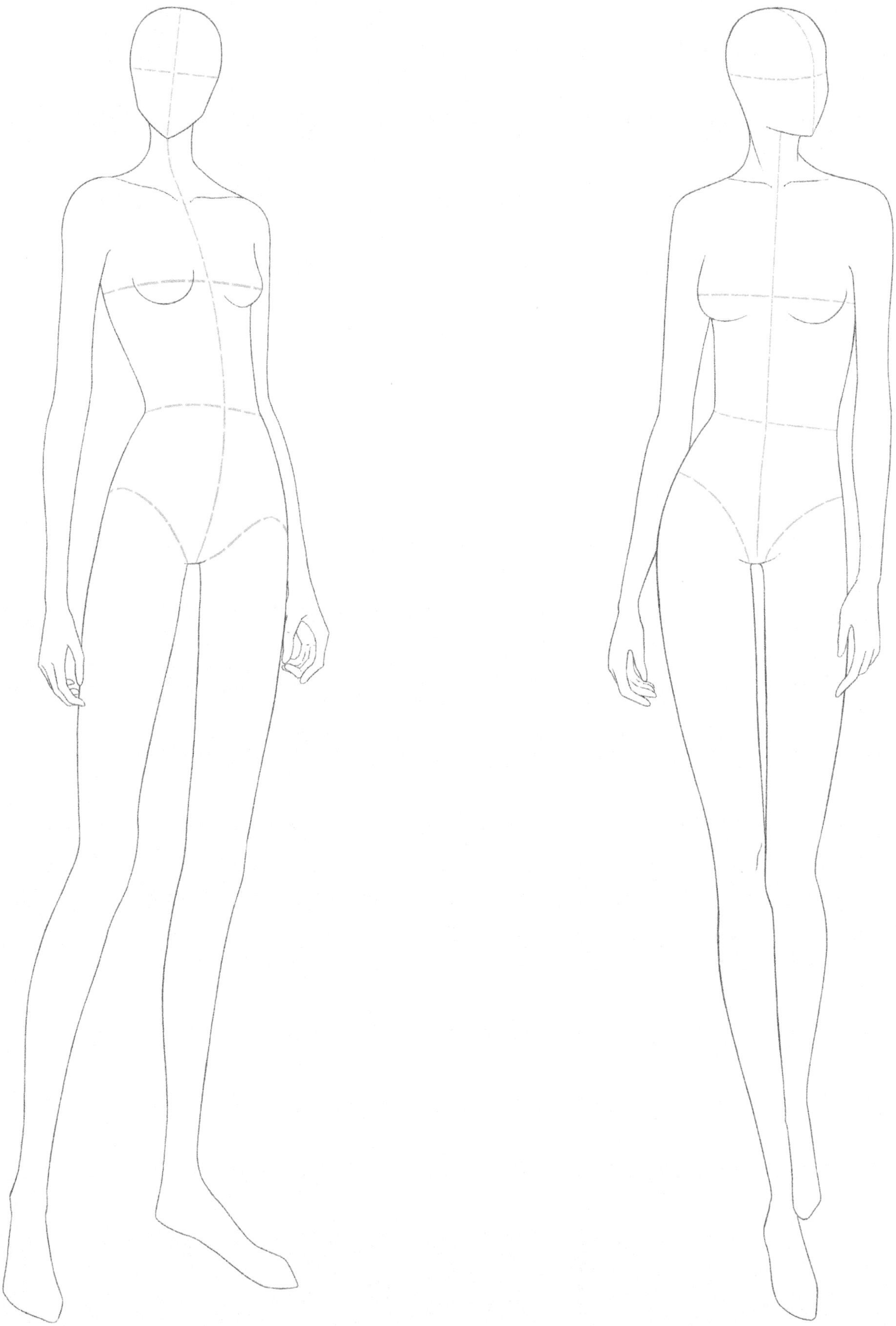

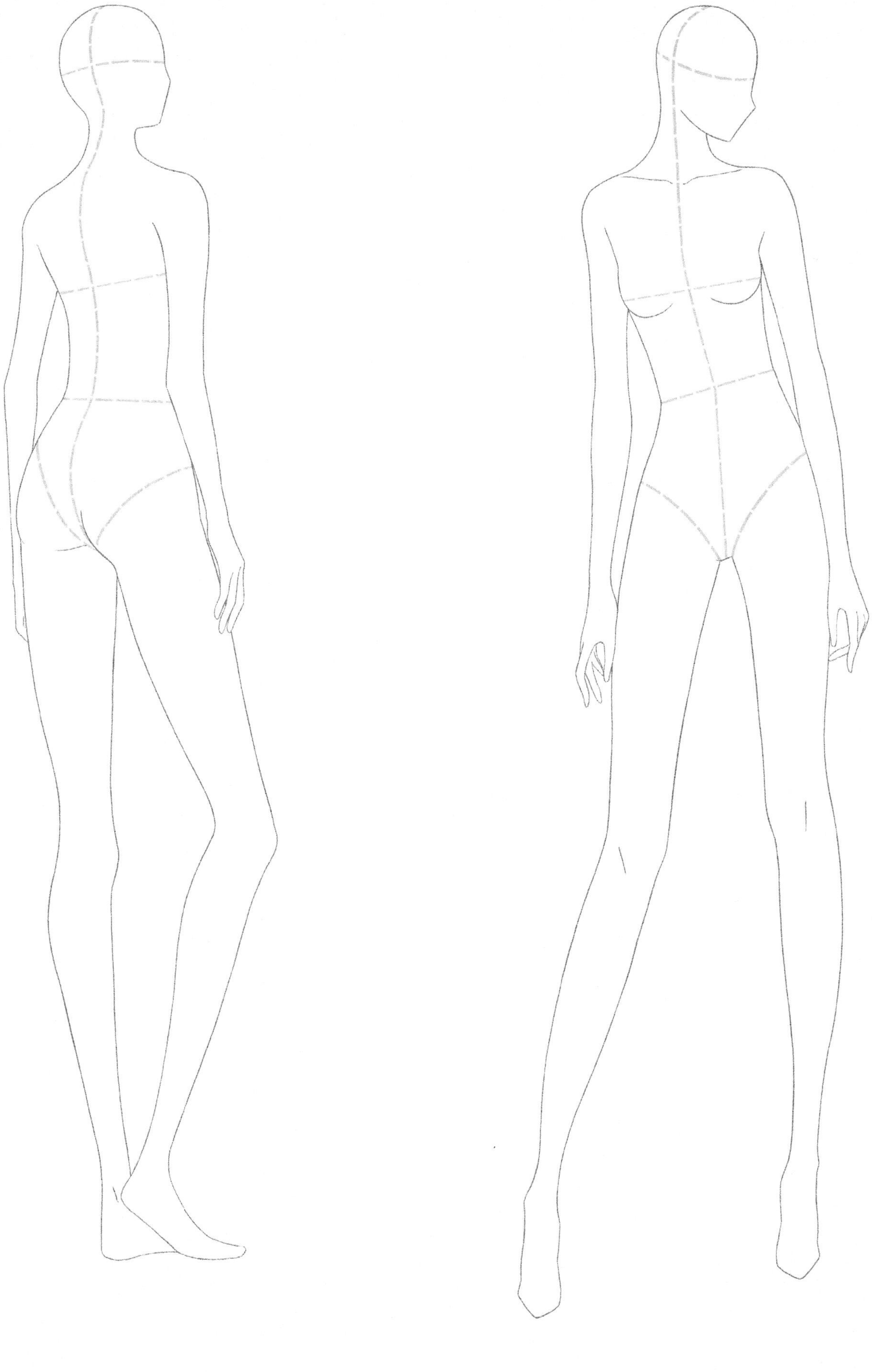

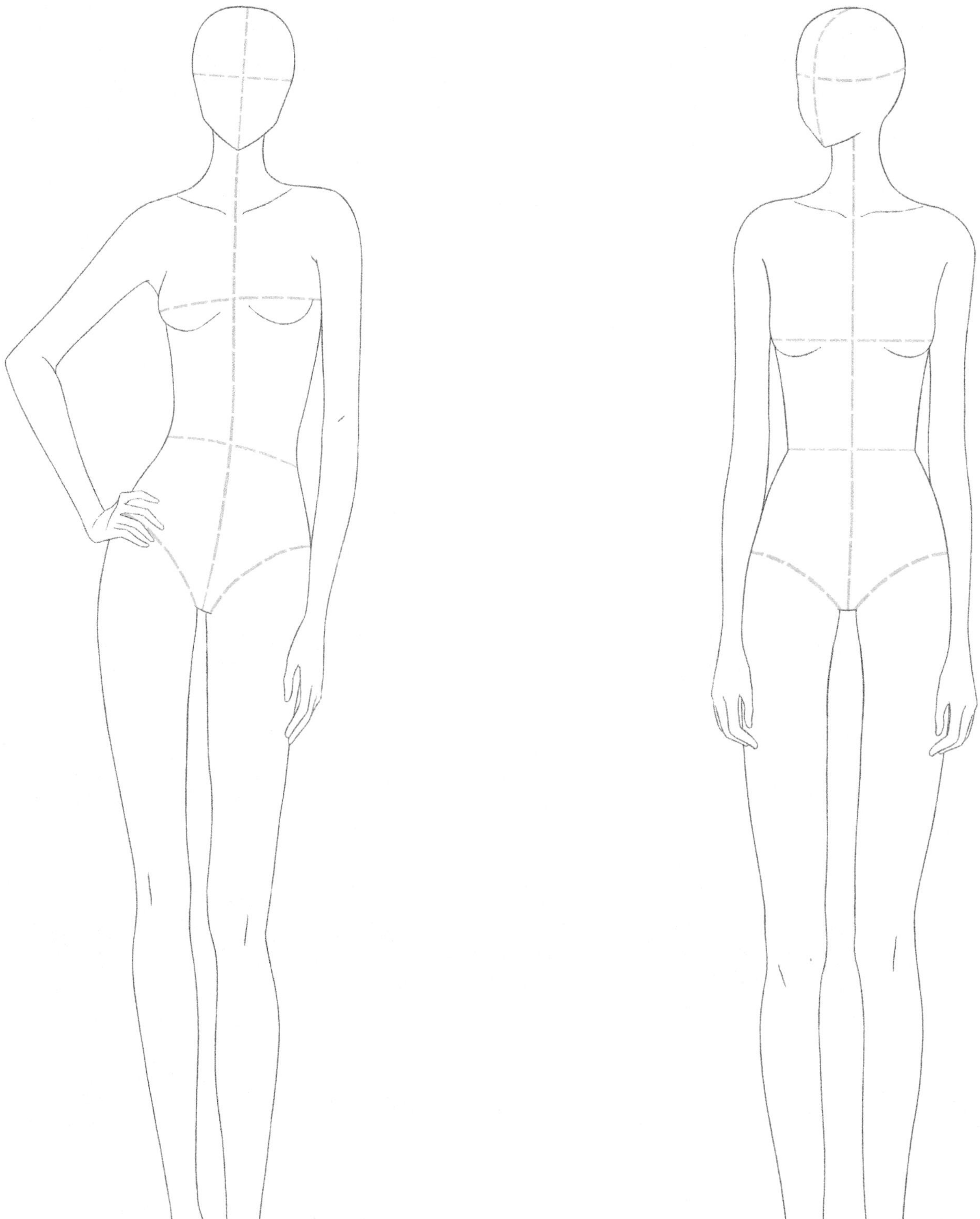

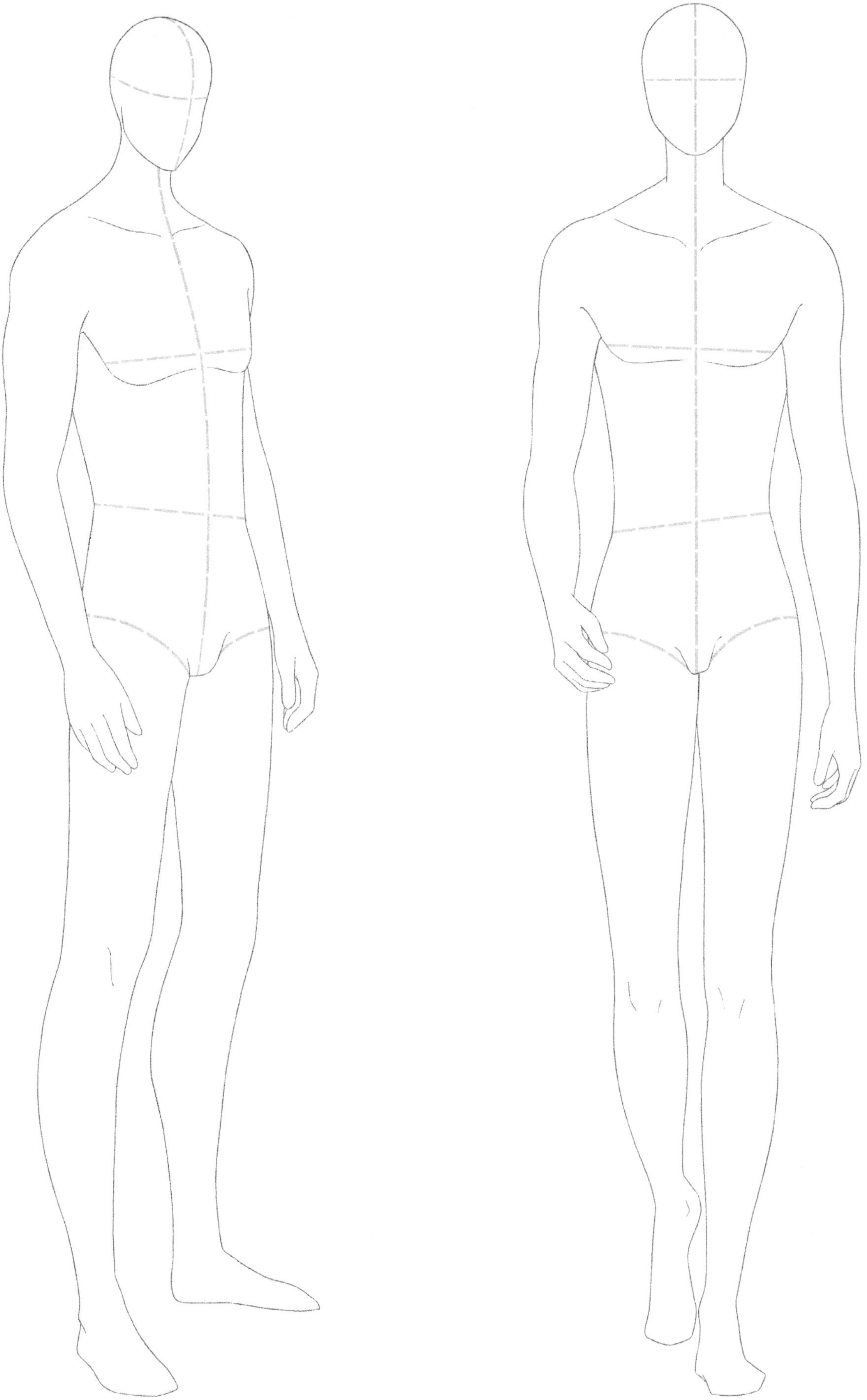

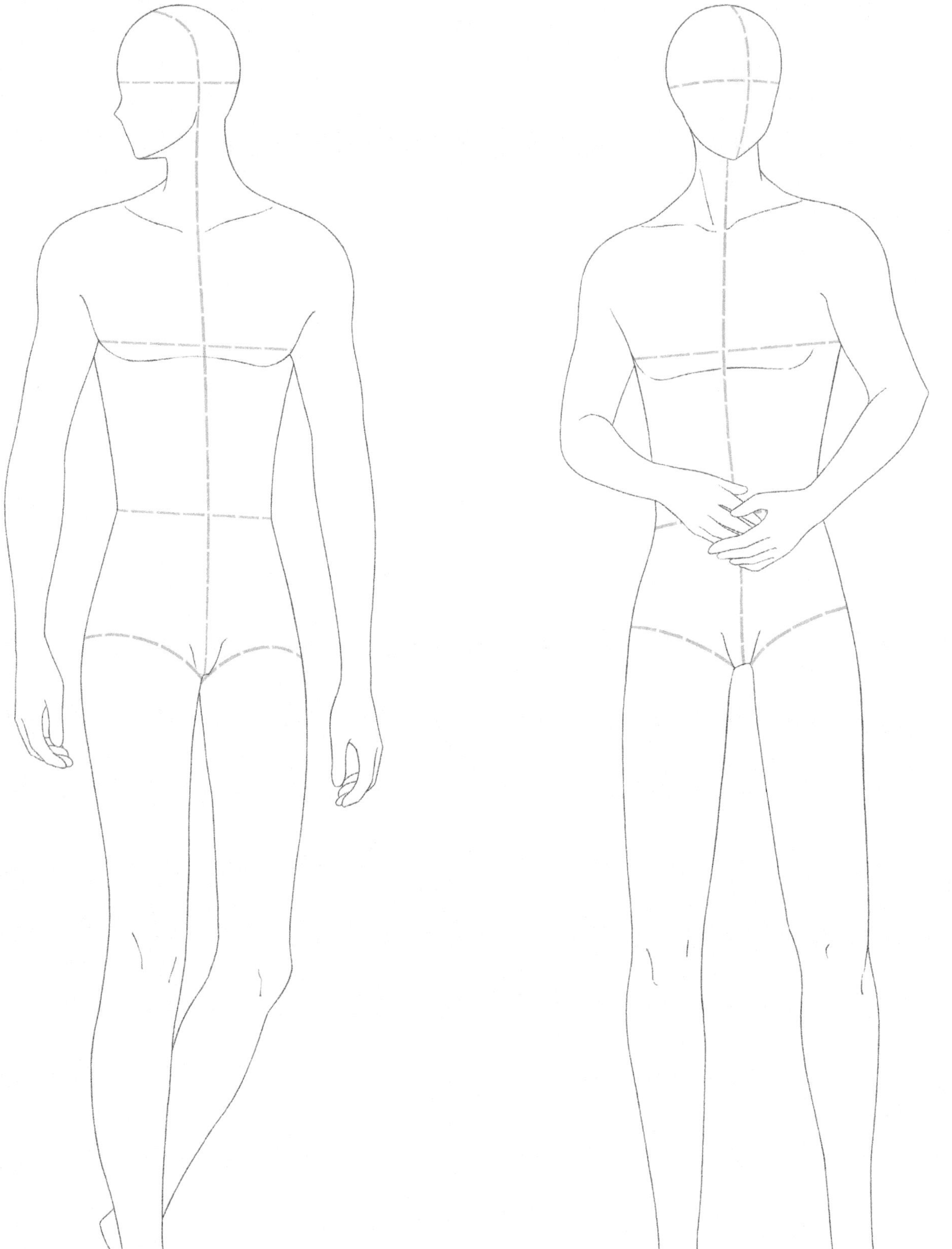

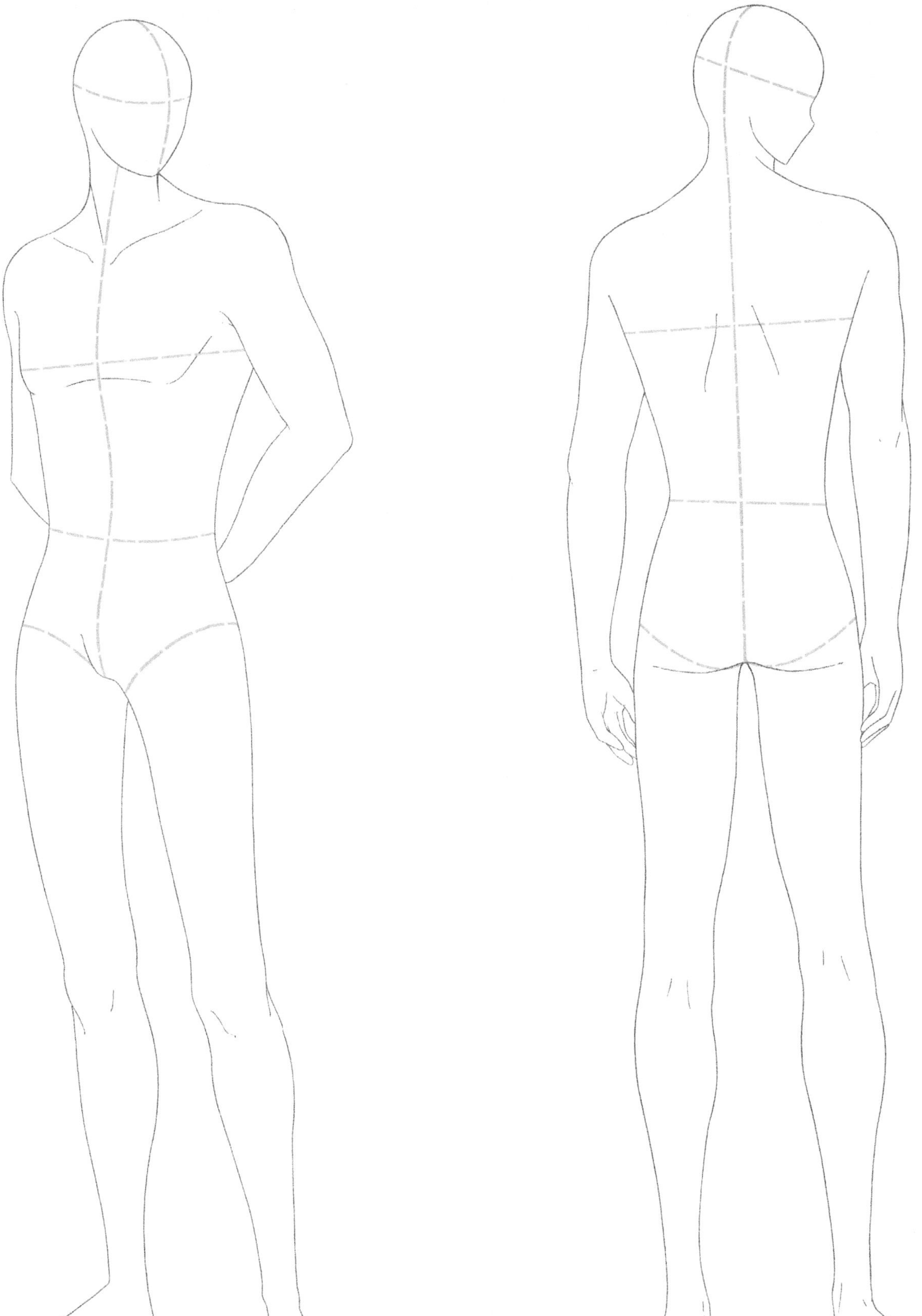

BYE BYE

STUDIO

Do you have a question or concern? Let us know.

www.byebye.studio | contact@byebye.studio

Printed in Great Britain
by Amazon

43917711R00071